Veloce *Classic Reprint* Series

BRM

A M

DICK SALMON

In collaboration with ANTHONY CARTER

CW00816282

This book is dedicated to my late wife, Mary, who tolerated my unsociable working hours with great fortitude

Other great books from Veloce –

www.veloce.co.uk

First published in November 2006 by Veloce Publishing Limited, Veloce House, Parkway Farm Business Park, Middle Farm Way, Poundbury, Dorchester DT1 3AR, England. Fax 01305 268864 / e-mail info@veloce.co.uk / web www.veloce.co.uk or www.velocebooks.com.
New paperback edition October 2017
ISBN 978-1-787112-27-8 / UPC 6-36847-01227-4

CONTENTS

FOREWORD
INTRODUCTION
ACKNOWLEDGEMENTS

Foreword by Bette Hill

Graham's seven years with BRM were some of the most exciting and successful times we had in the world of motor racing, but he had to leave as he was afraid they'd paint him over!

BRM with Tony Rudd and the talented engineers and mechanics were the most dedicated and expert team. We had our ups and downs, but a great deal of fun, too! The successes were an inspiration to all of us, making us even more determined to win. The mechanics were the most hard-working people I have come across; all-nighters never seemed to faze them and they would turn up at the circuit the next day as if they'd enjoyed a full night's sleep.

Great, great people, many of whom became our friends. I always did the timing and lap charting, which made me feel I belonged there, too.

Happy days ...

Bette Hill

Introduction

BRM was an inspired name for the team and racing cars which became an enigma of the second half of the 20th century.

Everybody had an opinion about BRM: in the 1950s it was either admired for trying or condemned for failing; there was no middle ground! By the 1960s attitudes had changed and it was a case of "Good old Sir Alfred" (Sir Alfred Owen, Chairman of Rubery Owen & Co Ltd, and owner of BRM from 1952) for holding his nerve and turning a disparate team into a winner.

It was like a dream come true when Dick Salmon approached me and asked if I would collaborate with his story (I was on the side which admired BRM, longing for it to succeed). Dick is a natural storyteller. He has set out to redress a gaping hole in the history of the sport; namely to write his own account of one who actually experienced the highs and lows of working in the heady world of Grand Prix motor racing. His story is written straight from the heart, as it really was all those years ago, and it has been my privilege to be associated with it.

Anthony Carter
Wisbech, Cambridgeshire

Acknowledgements

Technical people and motoring correspondents alike have written many books about the success and failure of BRM, but I wanted to record some of the happy, sad, amusing and frustrating moments I experienced during my time as a racing mechanic with the BRM team.

This would not have been possible without a great deal of help, and I am extremely grateful to all who assisted in getting my story into print. I would particularly like to thank Anthony and Vyvian Carter, who I was fortunate enough to meet when this project was in the doldrums. Anthony metaphorically kicked my backside and encouraged me to complete the tale, in addition to spending many hours helping with research and checking facts, whilst Vyvian spent endless hours checking and correcting my work: no mean feat!

My thanks go to Bette Hill for her contribution of the foreword; it seemed only right to me that she should be the first person I approached for this as she made such a significant contribution to the BRM story.

Sincere thanks to Jenny, widow of Dennis Perkins; Patrick Carvath; Roy Foreman; John Sismey; Jim Collins; Patricia Reeson; Don Woodward; Reg Smith; Trevor Ayliff, Andrea Thorlby; Graham Luesby; Gerry van der Weyden; the family of the late Alan Ellison; Peter Putterill, and Jim and Brenda Jones of Bourne Heritage Centre for the loan of photographs; Damien Smith of Autosport for allowing the use of certain material, and the late Mick Smith, who did the dog kennel sketch.

Thanks also to all former work colleagues for helping me recall some of the many incidents – good and bad – which occurred during those years, and to my son, Michael, for his help with my research, checking facts and assistance with photography, etc. During the research for this book, much use was made of the following publications: *BRM: The saga of British Racing Motors* by Doug Nye, *BRM* by Raymond Mays and Peter Roberts, *It Was Fun* by Tony Rudd, *Motor Racing – Reflections of a lost era* by Anthony Carter (Veloce), *Formula One: unseen archives* by Tim Hill, *Autosport* and *MotorSport* magazines: thank you all.

And, finally, thanks to Rod Grainger, Judith Brooks, Kevin Quinn and all at Veloce Publishing for agreeing to publish the book and being so helpful.

If I have forgotten anyone, I apologise: blame Father Time!

Dick Salmon
Bourne, Lincolnshire

A LINCOLNSHIRE LAD

It was a dream come true! Were my eyes deceiving me or did I really see a slender trail of smoke from Jimmy's engine? Another lap assured me that my eyes were not deceiving me; the smoke trail had become even more visible and a lap later Jimmy Clark pulled into the pits to retire his Lotus type 33 Climax V8 from the lead of the South African Grand Prix. Graham Hill was now leading in his BRM and, fifteen laps later, crossed the finishing line to become the 1962 Champion Driver of the World and BRM the winner of the Constructors Championship.

Suddenly we were top dogs: the whole world, it seemed, was talking about BRM. All these years afterwards I find it impossible to describe the emotions of elation and relief that swept through me, and those of my colleagues, in those heady days following our return to England. Messages of congratulation poured in from the most unlikely sources, and a small fenland town – which few had heard of before – was suddenly on the world map. I thought of those great drivers who had helped us on our way, many of whom had since given their lives to the sport they loved. They had paved the way to our success and now I sensed their hands stretching out to us in recognition of what we had achieved. After a decade of unwavering support, Sir Alfred Owen modestly received the acclaim he deserved and, for a few days, time seemed to stand still …

It was not to last for long: instead of attacking we were now defending our position!

I was born in May 1925 in the village of Irnham. A few miles away was Bourne, one day to evolve from a small market town in the Lincolnsire Fens to worldwide renown as the home of British Racing Motors: BRM. Irnham was then a village of only thirty-three dwellings, plus the Post Office and general store which were run by my parents. There was also The Griffin Inn, a school, St

Where it all began: the old Post Office at Irnham, a charming and historic village in South Lincolnshire.

Andrews church, and a Methodist Chapel above some stables. The village was owned by the occupant of Irnham Hall, Sheffield Industrialist Sir Frederick Benton-Jones who also owned the surrounding three thousand acres which formed the Irnham Estate. On his death he was succeeded by his elder son, Walter Benton-Jones. Sir Walter, as he became, was a fastidiously tidy man, a concept which he applied to the whole village. With the exception of my father, the blacksmith, the publican and tenant farmers, the estate employed all of the village's householders. The Chapel services were taken by a variety of Ministers from the surrounding district, one of whom was Mr Roberts, a shopkeeper from Grantham. His daughter Margaret (later to become Prime Minister Margaret Thatcher) would often accompany him.

My parents, like most of the villagers, were hard-working people, mother running the Post Office and shop in addition to bringing up four children. My father had a twelve mile postal

A typical washday scene from the 1920s, and the first signs of mischief from the young author. Funny, I don't recall a fee from Lux, though …

delivery round by bicycle, as well as being a jack-of-all-trades in the village: helping farmers and builders, digging graves, bearing at funerals and manning the polling station at elections. In addition he was one of the village Special Constables *Corby Road, Irnham, with my father just starting his 12 mile daily postal round.* during the war. Life was primitive. All drinking water had to be carried from the communal village pumps supplied from a reservoir filled by a wind pump. A lack of electricity meant paraffin lamps and candles, whilst cooking was done on coal fires or paraffin stoves. It was a very humble but nevertheless happy childhood! The 'karzi' was an outbuilding at the bottom of the garden and often, on a winter's night, a sibling or I could be heard to laughingly shout, 'Mam, the wind's blown the candle out'! For night use a chamber pot, jerry, gazunder – call it what you will – was placed under each bed, to be emptied in the morning by mother. These were quite adequate for three small boys but, as they grew and generated more liquid waste, posed a problem for mother who had to empty the vessels without spilling the contents or wetting her thumb. I am afraid her daily task was taken for granted and not until later in life did I come to realise what an unpleasant and tedious chore this must have been. Monday was the weekly washday, the first task being to light the fire for the copper. Washing would be boiled in the copper and then pummelled in the dolly tub with a set of dolly pegs, then rinsed and squeezed through the mangle to remove surplus water before being hung out to dry.

Many householders in the village – including my father – kept chickens and pigs to supplement their income. We were mostly self-sufficient with eggs and, when the hens were producing well, surplus eggs were preserved in isinglass for later use. It was normal to rear two pigs; one for home use whilst the second would be sold to a local butcher, the income paying for the feed for them both, thus ensuring that we had a free pig in effect! The local slaughterman would come to our house for the killing when due, we children watching with macabre fascination, if we were allowed, otherwise we would contrive to peep at what was going on. The day following the killing, the butcher would call to cut the carcass into joints, etc. There followed many hours of work producing the hams and bacon, with what was left made into sausages, pork pies, and bone pies. I remember my mother and I working well into the night trying to raise the pork pies. My father always insisted that the brain was his, usually served on toast. I cannot recall any member of the family challenging him for this so called 'delicacy,' certainly not me!

In the 1940s, Irnham made some progress toward acquiring twentieth century luxuries in the form of electric lighting, though not the more usual mains electricity, but via connection to the private Irnham Estate supply previously only available to Irnham Hall. An engine-driven generator charged large cells in what was known as the battery house. The engine was a most beautiful machine; a huge, single cylinder Ruston and Hornsby oil engine. When it was running it was possible to count the rhythmic strokes of the piston, almost like the tick of a grandfather clock. Each house in the village was allowed one light per room, plus one plug for an electric iron, for which the householder paid the princely sum of one halfpenny per light or plug per week, of which we had a total of nine. In the 1950s, both electricity and water were at last supplied by mains.

The only motorised vehicles in the village were those belonging to Sir Frederick; two lovely Daimler limousines and a Morris Commercial van. As the '30s progressed so mechanisation increased. I well remember the first Fordson tractor to appear and, in the late '30s, great excitement over a combine harvester. Made by the International Harvester Co, this was a far cry from the modern machine and arrived in crates to be assembled in the village. Tractor-drawn, it required a crew of three to operate and was possibly the first such machine to arrive in Lincolnshire.

I had apparently been born mischievous and, at five years of age, was persuaded to attend the Irnham Church of England Primary School. I record this because on my first day at school I absconded during morning playtime and went home to inform my mother I did not like school, so would not bother to go again!

A very early international combine harvester seen working at Irnham in the 1930s. Probably the first such machine to operate in Lincolnshire, it was towed by an international crawler tractor and operated by a crew of three.

I was, however, persuaded to return and subsequently attended the Boys Central School at Grantham, twelve miles away. This necessitated catching a bus at 7.45am, returning home at 5pm at a cost to my parents of four shillings and two pence (21p) per week in bus fares; there were no subsidies or bus passes in those days. In the 1930s, five buses ran a daily service from the village to Grantham with seven on Saturdays. Now there are none – so much for progress …

The local hero of the day was racing driver Raymond Mays who lived only eight miles away at Bourne. As children, anyone fortunate enough to own a bicycle would pretend to emulate him, often at the expense of some nasty accidents with plenty of cuts and bruises. A favourite pastime was to fasten an empty cigarette packet to the cycle frame in such a way that it would contact the spokes of the rotating wheel, thus making a noise reminiscent to us children of a car engine, though frequently at the expense of some broken spokes.

I left school in 1939 at the age of fourteen, shortly before the outbreak of World War II. I quickly got a job in a small garage at Corby Glen, two miles from Irnham, starting with a weekly wage of seven shillings and sixpence (36p) which, after a few months, I managed to get increased to ten shillings (50p) for a 44 hour week. After ten months my father told me of a vacancy in a larger garage at nearby Rippingale, which promised to be a better position. At the interview I was asked how much I was currently paid. Telling a white lie I said "Twelve shillings and sixpence," to which the proprietor, Bert Willson, replied "Well, I will pay you fifteen shillings." So it was that I accepted a 50 per cent pay increase and began my apprenticeship proper as a motor mechanic at the Windmill Garage, cycling five-and-a-half miles each weekday morning and evening, plus Saturday mornings.

In 1941 aged sixteen I joined the Home Guard, training one evening a week and on Sunday mornings. It was quite amazing how our Commanding Officer managed to get us to attack and

Raymond Mays in his Bugatti 'Cordon Rouge' seen here in a race with an aeroplane over Skegness beach in 1923.

capture a village pub somewhere in the district at noon opening time on Sundays, often arriving at the same time as the Fire Brigade. In 1943 I was summoned to attend the Armed Services medical board at Grantham with a view to conscription into one of the three services or, in some cases, directed to work in the coal mines as what was commonly known as a Bevin Boy, so called after Ernest Bevin, the Minister of Labour, who came up with the idea. As quite a few of my mates were already serving, I was disappointed to fail my medical on the grounds that my feet were 'faulty,' though in what respect I had no idea as they seemed alright to me. I counted them and there were two and I was able to walk … how dare they fail me!

One year later the British Isles were in danger from Hitler and the situation was desperate. I was sent for at last, Spike Milligan being unable to cope on his own! I was recalled to Grantham for a second medical examination and, lo and behold, my feet were miraculously cured; now there's a funny thing … I was conscripted into the army in June 1944 and instructed to report to Newcastle-upon-Tyne to do my basic training.

The accommodation there was in spider blocks, so called because a series of wooden huts formed the outline of a spider. The camp was situated in Sandy Lane opposite the racecourse at Gosforth Park. One incident there made me realise I was in the army; relaxing one evening, a new recruit had fallen asleep on his bed with a lighted cigarette between his fingers. The duty sergeant spotted this and made us watch until the cigarette had burned down to the unfortunate man's fingers, forbidding anyone to wake him, whilst at the same time emphasising that a tragedy could have occurred had it fallen from the man's fingers

A proud young recruit to the Royal Engineers Regiment in 1944.

and set light to the wooden building. A valid point. The man did wake up with a start and was deemed to have learned his lesson without further punishment.

Basic training completed, I was posted to the Royal Engineers at Ayr in Scotland, a transport training depot, for secondary training; our accommodation being the grandstands on the Ayr racecourse. I thoroughly enjoyed my time there. No matter how efficient a driver one was, driver training in lorries followed by driving tests were still applicable. If possible I would try to manipulate my position in the ranks to go out with Corporal Mathews as my instructor. Out in the Scottish countryside the crafty corporal would say "It's time we had a cup of tea," whereupon he would instruct his pupil to stop, always conveniently in front of houses. He would get out of the lorry, raise the bonnet, scratch his head feigning a problem and invariably some kind lady would come out and offer us a cup of tea, quite often with cakes as an added luxury. Amazingly, after devouring the refreshments, the vehicle would start immediately! When attending a church parade in Ayr, it made me feel quite proud to be addressed by the Colonel as 'Gentlemen of the Royal Engineers and men of other Regiments.' During my training period, the monotony was broken somewhat when the unit was moved to Gibraltar Barracks at Aldershot, travelling down in convoy.

I was eventually moved to Wellington Barracks in Halifax, there to await an overseas posting. Not knowing where we would be going and, even more daunting, wondering if we would be coming back, generated a devil-may-care attitude amongst us with discipline often disregarded to a certain extent. On one occasion I recall walking diagonally across the parade ground where I met an officer and we were the only two people on the square. I knew if I saluted him a big cheer would come from the surrounding barrack rooms and so I failed to do so. Stopped and asked why I had failed to salute an officer I said, "I'm sorry, sir. I didn't see you." What a pathetic excuse! Luckily, I think he saw the funny side of it and left me with a ticking off. I had the consolation of not hearing the cheer from the barrack room.

Our days were spent in various tasks, one of which was building a Bailey bridge over an old quarry, and then dismantling it the following day. The war on the Russian front was at its most fierce and the senior officers were not impressed when graffiti appeared on the guardroom wall: *Russia bleeds while Britain bullshits*. The culprit was never found. Early in December I was given fourteen days' embarkation leave, thereafter all leave was cancelled. On Christmas Eve one of our colleagues was determined to visit his home in Wolverhampton. We agreed to cover for him during his absence on Christmas Day by answering his name on morning roll call, on condition he returned on Boxing Day. He agreed to do so but failed to keep his promise. After a week of this subterfuge we assumed he had deserted and stopped answering for him. However, he arrived back the next day, by now marked absent, was charged for being absent without leave (AWOL) and spent a few days in the detention centre at Selby.

Finally, we got our instructions to proceed to the Quarter Master's stores to be issued with tropical kit which included a sola topi, or pith helmet. We had no idea where we were going but at least we knew it would not be the Arctic … but then again, why not? after all, this was the British Army! Eventually, we were mobilised and marched to Halifax station. It was a very moving experience with old ladies lining the streets to see us off, some in tears, some running out and kissing us and giving us sweets and fruit. Eventually, we arrived at Gourock on the River Clyde to board the SS Volundam, a Dutch ship that had returned to England after transporting evacuated children to America, so was therefore stocked with lots of American goodies. Still not knowing our destination, we eventually left the Clyde to form a convoy somewhere off Ireland.

It was now January and we encountered some very rough seas in the Atlantic Ocean, with the crowded sleeping quarters below decks smelling vile through seasickness. Still not aware of our destination we eventually recognised the Rock of Gibraltar; a very welcome sight. The calmer waters of the Mediterranean were greeted with sighs of relief and watching the porpoises following the ship became a fascinating pastime. Three weeks after leaving the Clyde we arrived at Port Said in Egypt. Once docked, bumboats plying for trade swarmed around the ship. Members of the ship's crew bombarded them with potatoes, whereupon the small boats retreated, only to return later laden with pebbles and armed with catapults to pay us back!

After spending a few days in the transit camp at Port Said our movement orders came through. We travelled by road to El Kantara alongside the Suez Canal, followed by a 250 mile journey by train to Haifa in Palestine. During this overnight train journey we were advised by the accompanying Military Police to sleep on our rifles as theft was rife. I took heed of this advice, but a few ignored it only to find the following morning that they had been relieved of their weapons. Next came a 500 mile journey across the Syrian Desert to Baghdad via Al Mafraq, travelling in an articulated American Mack bus run by Nairn Bros Transport. (For those readers raising an eyebrow at this Scottish name appearing in such a remote region, I gather that the two Nairn brothers, Norman and Gerald, spotted a business opportunity by setting up a taxi service between Damascus and Baghdad as long ago as 1917. This eventually led to the brothers exploiting the developing oil industry ten years later by moving American-made rigs and equipment to locations in this inaccessible region. Full marks for enterprise!)

We were fascinated by the occasional appearance of a camel train, a Bedouin camp or a fleeing gazelle – the only living things to be seen. These created a biblical-looking scene and we marvelled at how they survived in such isolation. Much of the travelling was done at night to avoid the intense heat, the drivers navigating by the stars. Refreshment stops were made at Rutbah Wells and Habanya. After a few days in the transit camp at Baghdad we discovered that our destination was to be Shu'aiba in Southern Iraq. From Baghdad to Shu'aiba, we travelled in rather decrepit railway carriages with wooden shutters in lieu of glass in the windows which let in lots of dust and sand. Even so, it was a fascinating train journey with Arabs selling eggs and bread at all stations en route, and children running alongside the train shouting "Buckshees sahib" meaning "Any freebies, sir?" The first three days at Shu'aiba were spent in yet another transit

camp where the usual practice prevailed: all new arrivals spent their first night on guard. I was delegated to patrol the perimeter fence. All was quiet when, in the still of the night, suddenly from out of the darkness beyond the perimeter fence came the bray of a donkey followed a moment later by a loud bang as a dent in a 40 gallon oil drum was released as it contracted in the cool night air. I must have leapt all of a foot into the air: welcome to Iraq!

I was to spend the next three-and-a-half years at Shu'aiba, with the exception of a four week period of home leave in the spring of 1946, and what a fascinating and historic part of the world it was. Shu'aiba was a military garrison situated ten miles west of Basra, comprising both army and RAF units. This area of Middle East Command was designated Paiforce (Persia and Iraq Forces), identified by a pink elephant as our insignia. *The Oxford Dictionary* description of a pink elephant is hallucinations caused by alcohol and this was occasionally correct. I was posted to 338 Royal Engineers Works Section, a small unit that came under the command of 30 Company, Royal Engineers. It was a unit in which rank and discipline were secondary to friendliness, and whose main objective was to maintain and secure the network of oil pipelines. The task would entail journeys far out into the desert to places like Amara, Al Nasarya and Samawa, so necessitating overnight stops at distant outposts. The area was generally very poor and one particular local occupation was salt panning by the Arab women, all dressed in their black burqas. This was achieved by low lying areas of ground being excavated to a shallow depth and allowed to flood with water from the tidal rivers. These areas would then dry out in the hot sun as the tide receded, leaving a deposit of salt. I imagine the trade had been improved by the arrival of the British forces in Iraq, as a regular intake of salt was deemed necessary. Indeed, in the more disciplined camps salt parades were held where officers would witness their charges swallowing a salt tablet, a most unpleasant experience.

This posting enabled me to see many interesting and historic sights. I was privileged to visit the Hanging Gardens of Babylon, the ziggurat at Ur (reputedly the birthplace of Abraham), Kuwait city and Southern Iran. We would often watch the giant Short Sunderland flying boats land and take off on the Shatt al Arab

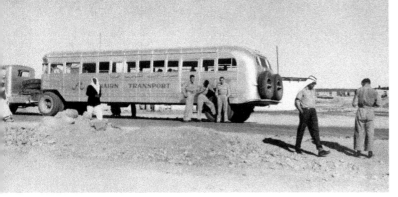

On the road to Iraq. Taking a break somewhere between Damascus and Baghdad.

A Mack articulated bus operated by Nairn Brothers, a company which began as a taxi service between Damascus and Baghdad.

waterway, a stretch of water where the Tigris and Euphrates rivers meet. One of our favourite weekend recreations would be to pack picnic lunches and drinks in iceboxes and take a motorboat owned by our RSM out on to the Shatt al Arab. Once out in the river, a slab of gun cotton explosive would be fitted with a length of fuse, lit and dropped overboard, the fuse still able to burn in the water. We would then speed off to get clear of the explosion. Stunned fish were then collected to replace the food in the iceboxes, giving our mess a supply of fresh fish that included small sharks and catfish. Accommodation in the camp was a collection of bungalow-type buildings. On more than one occasion a colleague and I, always ready for a prank, would carry a heavily sleeping comrade out on his bed and deposit him about 100 yards from the building, which gave him quite a surprise when he woke up!

My home leave date arrived and so I departed on the long haul back to Port Said, this time not to sail direct to England but via Malta to Toulon where much of the French fleet still lay after being scuttled in 1942 to evade capture by the Germans. From there I travelled by train to Calais for the crossing to Dover and home, returning by the same route at the end of an enjoyable leave. Whilst travelling I had noticed that the NAAFI supplies in Israel and Egypt were far superior to those we were accustomed to in Iraq, and wrote to my Member of Parliament pointing this out. I received a polite reply from my MP, but a rather less polite one from the Secretary of State for War! As I had not divulged to anyone what I had done I was rather surprised when my Commanding Officer remarked that I was "the chap that had written to his MP": doubtless he had been advised of my 'misdemeanour' by some 'jobsworth' seeking to improve his future. Needless to say, nothing changed.

In October 1947 I was nearing my release date and started to consider my options. I could stay in Iraq or Iran and work in the oilfields where numerous jobs were on offer, or I could return to England and civilian life. After some deliberation I chose the latter, eventually sailing into Liverpool via Malta on the SS Samaria. Whilst in the harbour at Valetta I was fascinated to see an elderly man in a small boat urinate in a tin, empty the contents over the side of his boat and rinse the tin out. Why he could not pee straight into the sea was a mystery but may have had something to do with harbour etiquette!

A moment of fun whilst serving in Paiforce, the name given to British forces serving in Persia and Iraq during WWII.

Disembarked at Liverpool I took the train to York, there to be relieved of my ill-fitting battle dress in exchange for an even more ill-fitting blue suit and a trilby hat. That was it; my career as a soldier was at an end, never having fired a shot.

However, I had to return to uniform briefly for a two week refresher course known as 'Z' training. I was summoned to Ripon in Yorkshire and what a farcical and, dare I say, enjoyable fortnight it proved to be. Established in the camp, the gaggle of part-time soldiers was asked if anyone could drive a Bren Gun Carrier? Amazingly, almost everyone could. The novelty of driving such vehicles certainly appealed and nearly every man raised an arm, even though quite a number of them had probably not even seen a Bren Gun Carrier, never mind driven one. No training would be complete without rifle firing practice, and so off we went high into the Yorkshire Dales to a purpose-built range. It so happened that sheep were grazing peacefully between the firing point and the butts and, though they were well below the firing line, it was fairly obvious what would happen, and sure enough it did – two dead sheep. The culprit or culprits were never found but, I can honestly hold my hand up and say it wasn't me.

One dark night on all-night manoeuvres out on the moors we had eaten our evening meal and were preparing to move on. Assisting the cook to stow his equipment, one man who

Contemplating the future, perhaps, little guessing what excitement lay ahead ...

had rallied to the call emptied a large pan of what he assumed in the darkness was washing-up water. Proudly informing the cook of what he had done, as if he deserved a medal for effort, he was surprised by the irate cook's reaction: "You stupid bloody fool, you have just thrown away the liver for tomorrow's breakfast." After a hasty salvage operation we had liver and grass for breakfast next morning!

Eventually I returned to civvy street again to find my demob trilby missing. I suspect my mother had destroyed it, not wanting her son in the house looking like Al Capone. The big question to be faced was "What now?" The initial euphoria of returning to civilian life quickly evaporated. Back at home I found that Irnham seemed even smaller than I remembered; I had been away for nearly three-and-a-half years, mostly overseas, and now I was seeking wider horizons. Opportunities for a young man in the Fens were few and mostly revolved around agriculture. Ploughing the fields on a winter's day, white mist hanging low over a dead flat landscape with just the wheeling seagulls for company and an old potato sack slung across my shoulders for protection, had limited appeal. Returning to Mr Willson's garage at Rippingale no longer interested me so, as an interim measure, I took a job

Raymond Mays demonstrating the V16 BRM to the national press on the disused airfield at Folkingham on a bitterly cold December day in 1949.

as a farm mechanic and subsequently as a lorry driver, neither of which was really what I had in mind.

By this time a popular topic of conversation was BRM, local pre-war racing hero Raymond Mays taking up again from where he had left off at the outbreak of war. This ignited a flame of ambition in my mind: what better way to use my qualifications and fulfil my ambitions than in the sport of motor racing? The sound of racing cars being tested on the nearby old Folkingham airfield could often be heard. This proved a great attraction and my pals and I would visit the airfield in the hope we would be lucky enough to see the cars in action. These excursions further increased my desire to be involved with this exciting sport, maybe even to become a racing mechanic …

The British Motor Racing Research Trust was the brainchild of Raymond Mays and his old friend and engineer Peter Berthon. The two men had been associated pre-war in the production and racing of the ERA racing car, and in 1939 decided to launch an appeal to British industry to support them in building a national racing car. Because of the Second World War this project was delayed until 1946, when Raymond Mays successfully canvassed many prominent members of British industry to enlist their support. The two principal industrialists who agreed to help were Oliver Lucas of Joseph Lucas Ltd, and Alfred Owen, Chairman of Rubery Owen & Co Ltd, of Darlaston; both gave a positive reaction. Upon hearing Raymond Mays' objectives, Alfred Owen was quoted by Raymond Mays as saying "This is important because it is impossible to know where pioneering work like this will lead us. Do you realise it is hardly an exaggeration to say we owe the existence of this country to Lady Houston? When the government would not build machines to fly for the Schneider Trophy, she came forward and put the money down. The research that went into building the Supermarine seaplane which won the Trophy outright led to the development of the Rolls-Royce Merlin engine and the Spitfire fighter. Without those engines and those machines, which were then the finest fighters in the world, it is doubtful whether we would have won

Eastgate House Bourne, where Raymond Mays was born and spent his lifetime.

Raymond Mays with his great friend and rival Prince Bira of Siam.

A 1935 Gordon Ashby cartoon of Raymond Mays in his Bourne-built ERA.

The Raymond Mays Special. A small number of these cars were produced in 1937 by the Standard Motor Company of Coventry.

the Battle of Britain. So the building of a powerful new car may have important consequences."

After the initial meetings of supporters of the project, held during November 1946, it had been decided to form a committee which would then work out a plan to form the Trust. The Trust was to be comprised of a consortium of British industrialists who would contribute to an attempt to build a Grand Prix racing car that could compete in the Formula 1 World Championship series, to be introduced in 1950, and ultimately take on the world. The Trust was duly formed under the chairmanship of Alfred Owen. The car was to be called the BRM, the initials of British Racing Motors. Three years from the date of those first meetings, on 15th December 1949, the first BRM racing car was unveiled to the press and ran at Folkingham Airfield. Prior to the launch, Raymond Mays had proved his undoubted skills as a salesman, having spent countless hours enlisting the help of no fewer than 236 companies to support the venture.

Finance and materials were to be supplied by the various industrialists. The office accommodation, design office, machine shop, engine build and test bed were based in Bourne in South

Lincolnshire at the former Maltings in Spalding Road, right next to the house of Raymond Mays. Here, before the war, ERA (English Racing Automobiles Ltd) racing cars had been built and successfully raced by Raymond Mays and other famous drivers, including Richard Seaman and Prince Birabongse of Siam. In 1939 Richard Seaman joined the German Mercedes-Benz works team, a quite unpopular and controversial move with war between Great Britain and Germany imminent.

To further supplement the BRM facilities, premises were acquired at a disused wartime airfield at Folkingham, nine miles north of Bourne. During the war Folkingham was occupied by the 9th AF Troop Carrier Group which transported the 325 Glider Infantry Regiment to Holland. The gliders earned the nickname 'Flying Coffins' and only 200 of the 238 which left England

Raymond showed a great interest in local amateur dramatics; here he is appearing in the Bourne Operatic Society production of The Quaker Girl.

reached their destination. Located at Folkingham was the racing car final build workshop, a second engine shop, a sheet metal and panel beating shop, and a transport garage. One runway and part of the perimeter track were used to form a circuit for testing the racing cars. The buildings – with the exception of the transport shed – were enclosed in a fenced compound which also contained the old control tower and a four-berth caravan. Initially, the caravan was the home of Chief Engineer Peter Berthon and his wife Lorna, while the tower housed a flat for Jock Milne, the resident caretaker. These accommodation arrangements were later reversed.

The immediate objective of the project was to challenge the dominant Italian Alfa Romeo 158s. The inaugural World Championship, comprising six races in Europe plus the Indinapolis 500, had been won in 1950 by Italian driver Guiseppe Farina (one of the famous three Fs: Farina, Fagioli and Fangio which formed the team that year) in one of these cars. At this time the only

A copy of the Lincolnshire Constabulary warrant card issued to Raymond Mays during the Second World War, when he served the local Bourne community as a Special Constable.

real challenger to the Alfa Romeo was the rapidly improving works Ferrari driven by Italian Alberto Ascari.

The format for the Driver's World Championship was 8 points for a win and 6 points for second place, followed by 4, 3, 2 and 1 points for third, fourth, fifth and sixth places respectively, plus one point for the driver recording the fastest lap during the race. The 500 mile Indy race was virtually a non-event as the European circuit drivers did not normally take part in the Indy race.

My good friend Maurice Dove had joined BRM during the summer of 1951 to work on transport maintenance. The management decided he needed an assistant and so Maurice quickly conveyed the information to me, with encouragement to apply for the job – not that I needed much persuasion! I applied and was given an appointment to be interviewed by Company Secretary Jim Sandercombe at the Bourne offices. One of the questions asked was had I done military service? Knowing I had served in the Royal Engineers seemed to be a plus point and he said he would let me know. Had I, like him, been in the Royal Corps of Signals I would probably have been taken on there and then.

COUNTY OF LINCOLNSHIRE   269.

This Warrant Card was issued to

Mr.   R. Mays

of   5 Eastgate, Bourne

on   1/ 21 1939, who has been sworn in as a

Special Constable for this County.

Chief Constable of Lincolnshire

P.T.O.

The Six Bells Inn, Bourne, a popular hostelry and regular haunt of BRM personnel for socialising, quality lunches and accommodation.

Late in November 1951 I received the positive reply of which I had been dreaming: I was to start work with Maurice Dove at Folkingham Airfield in early December under the supervision of chief racing mechanic Gordon Newman. Gordon was a tall, moustached man who hailed from Kent. An unmarried loner with no family ties, he was an excellent mechanic and practical engineer. He was also good company and a regular visitor to the Bourne hostelries. The fact that I was only employed to assist in the maintenance of the company transport mattered not one jot, I had got my foot in the door!

Also starting his chequered career with the company in 1951, as assistant to chief engineer Peter Berthon, was one Tony Rudd who had joined BRM from Rolls Royce. He had arrived in an old box-type, fabric-bodied Austin 7 of 1926 vintage and had quickly been nicknamed 'Moleskin Harry' due to the tatty moleskin coat he wore.

Folkingham Airfield was to become a significant part of my life and still holds many memories for me. For example, prior to my National Service I had been indirectly involved in its construction. Hundreds of lorries had been employed transporting sand and gravel to the site, many of which were in a deplorable state of repair and had become regular customers for petrol and mechanical repairs at the Windmill Garage at Rippingale, where I was employed at the time. Although Britain was at war the inevitable fiddles took place, one such being as follows. There were two approach roads to the airfield, one through Folkingham village and the other through the neighbouring village of Aslackby. All lorries loaded with gravel entered the airfield via Folkingham and deposited their load, but in some cases the more dishonest drivers would drive straight through the airfield and exit through Aslackby gate without discharging their loads. They would then proceed to the Folkingham entrance again and re-enter with the same load. Was this the start of buy one, get one free?

It was also here that I had taken my first flight. Construction of the airfield completed, it was now an operational American Air Force station, the base for Dakota C47 aircraft and Horsa gliders which would eventually take part in the Arnhem landings. One Sunday summer evening before I began my military service, a friend and I (wearing our Home Guard uniforms), watched from the perimeter fence the American airmen going about their duties. Being inquisitive and adventurous young men, we often cycled to the airfield, hoping to be invited to go for a flight; we had heard of people who had been lucky in this way and hoped it would happen to us. One day our wish came true; one of the American aircrew came across to us, probably to ask if we had any sisters. After a pleasant conversation he invited us onto the airfield and asked if we would like to go for a trip in a Dakota. Would we! A smartly uniformed RAF officer accompanied us on our flight, looking down his nose at us in our ill-fitting Home Guard attire. No doubt such an invitation would not have been forthcoming in the Royal Air Force. Our epic flight, one of three aircraft, lasted for two hours. It was very noisy and uncomfortable sitting on the floor, but a wonderful experience, albeit a bit nervy when the flight changed formation. As we came in to land, little did I realise then that in future years I would spend many happy and tired hours on that very same airfield.

After the introductions and familiarisation to begin my career with BRM, it was down to work and taking every opportunity possible to admire and familiarise myself with the racing cars. The transport consisted of a Commer workshop vehicle, three Austin Lodestar transporters fitted with 6 cylinder Austin Princess engines, a Dodge lorry, various cars and vans, a tractor and a Norton motorcycle and sidecar. By now it was the middle of December 1951 and things were winding down for Christmas and, whilst I was enthusiastic, everybody else was more interested in the festive season than me. It helped that I had been blessed with a good sense of humour and a penchant for mischief, and I wondered what it would be like here, especially as I was the 'new boy.' I was seeing evidence of plenty of fun in the form of satirical remarks and mischievous pranks, and was very excited at the thought of getting involved.

On Christmas Eve lunchtime drinks were suggested and so we all adjourned to The Six Bells in Bourne, the hostelry where some members of the BRM staff lodged. A group of us went there daily in the back of the Dodge lorry for the excellent lunches provided by landlady Mrs Allen. Today was to be slightly different. Many of the other members of the Bourne staff arrived to celebrate the festive season and, having lunched, we joined them in the bar. Things were going along swimmingly with people chatting and reminiscing when Aubrey Woods, an engineering draughtsman sometimes referred to as 'Strawberry,' decided neckties were too long. He produced a pair of scissors from his pocket and started to reduce the length of ties to about three inches from the knot. I suspect this was a traditional exercise, as most people raised no objection. To the amusement of Peter Berthon and others, the lower part of the ties were later pinned to the notice board in the Bourne works where they remained for several weeks.

I felt confident I was going to enjoy my new job. The sense of humour I loved was here, everyone appeared jocular and friendly, and I was looking forward to 1952 with a feeling of great anticipation. In fact, future years at BRM would bring me more than I could ever have dreamed of …

A FOOT IN THE DOOR

With the festive season over, the excitement of starting a new job in earnest – albeit in January on a bleak and windswept airfield in Lincolnshire, with temperatures hovering around zero – was intense.

The first task for Maurice and I was to manufacture new ramps for the dual purpose of loading cars into the transporters and to serve as mechanical lifts to raise cars to a comfortable working height, both at Folkingham and away at the circuits. The ramps were to be made from U-section aluminium channel, with folding legs attached under both ends, and a central pivot point located on a trestle which would enable cars to be raised by a see-saw method. Cars would be pushed up the ramps to the point of balance, the lower ends of the ramp could then be raised and the legs lowered and secured, allowing mechanics to work above and below the cars in relative comfort and safety. It was an excellent concept designed by Gordon Newman, though not quite so excellent for us working with cold metal in January's freezing weather conditions. Had any brass monkeys been around at this time, I guess they would almost certainly have been geldings!

On the evening of 1st February, 1952, Chief Engineer Peter Berthon – almost always referred to as PB – was returning from Grantham in thick freezing fog when he overturned his Standard Vanguard near Ropsley, a village on his route to Folkingham. The car remained upside down all night; it is reputed that PB walked into the village to summon help and, on this dark and foggy night, walked into the village duck pond. The following morning Maurice and I were sent to recover the stricken vehicle but were unable to start the engine. Assuming a flat battery, we towed it back to Folkingham where, on inspection, with the exception of mud and grass, surface damage appeared minimal. However, the engine would not rotate. Rather surprised, PB and Tony Rudd were scratching their heads over why the engine was seized. I suggested that whilst the car had been lying on

its roof overnight the sump oil had drained into the combustion chambers, causing an hydraulic effect. This proved to be the case and I received my first Brownie points.

On 6th February, the death of King George VI was announced and the country went into mourning. Sombre music was played on all radio stations and an air of gloom enveloped us.

Work, however, had to proceed and, about this time, Harry Mundy, an engineer who was fond of playing practical jokes, realised that due to the task in hand, engine fitter Dave Turner was going to be about an hour late going for lunch to his home in Bourne. Harry went to Dave's house where he had previously been a lodger and mischievously told Mrs Turner that Dave had gone out for the day, and to avoid wasting his lunch had invited Harry to go and enjoy it on his behalf. Mrs Turner fell for it, Harry obliged, ate the meal and departed. When Dave got home a little later he was less than pleased to say the least, to discover his lunch had been devoured! Dave, like Harry, was good at playing jokes, but did not like them being played on him, so took a dim view of Harry for a while.

Raymond Mays would frequently visit Folkingham to test drive the cars. A very superstitious man who almost always dressed in blue, he would only get into a racing car from the left-hand side. At fifty-plus he was still a very competent driver, a pleasant man to talk to and well respected in Bourne, despite a doubtful sexual reputation of being 'one of them,' as homosexuality was referred to colloquially.

Each racing car was usually allocated a crew of two: a chief mechanic to each car and an assistant, a role I was soon to fulfil. In addition, there were mechanics specialising in engine and gearbox build and maintenance. All came under the supervision of Tony Rudd, in turn responsible to Peter Berthon. Tony also operated the engine test house with Willie Southcott. All shop floor workers were initially paid an hourly rate but, when the management noted the extensive working hours necessary to keep cars raceworthy, this was quickly changed to a weekly wage, regardless of hours worked. Little doubt who got the better of that deal …

Two V16-engined racing cars were being prepared to leave

The compact V16 engine fitted in the Mark 1 BRM chassis, showing the supercharged induction system and cooling system between the cylinder heads.

One of the 16 Hepolite pistons as fitted in the 1½-litre V16 BRM engine. It's pictured alongside a modern golf ball for size comparison.

He usually arrived by light aircraft complete with pilot. On his arrival on one occasion he told us navigating had proved difficult owing to poor visibility. The pilot had seized the opportunity to use a break in the cloud and had gone down low, spotting a signpost pointing to the village of Bottesford in Leicestershire. From this he had established his position and arrived safely at Folkingham.

Nearing the end of February I was approached by Gordon Newman who wanted to know if I held a current passport. Answering in the negative, I was asked if I could get one urgently and be available to go to Italy. I could hardly believe my ears; needless to say I was off to see the Reverend Goodrich, the local vicar, to ask if he would sign a passport application form, which he was pleased to do. Then I was off to the Peterborough Passport Office pretty quick. To say I was delighted was an understatement. Had Maurice and his girlfriend Myrtle not decided to arrange their wedding at this time I doubt whether I would have been chosen as I am sure Maurice would have been selected for the trip. So thanks, Maurice, or was Myrtle responsible?

The day of our departure for Monza arrived and Gordon Newman, Willie Southcott and I were to crew one of the Austin Lodestars, with Arthur Ambrose, Tony Rudd and Cyril Bryden in the Commer workshop wagon. A delay in the delivery of components meant Dave Turner and Stan Hope were to leave three days later in the third vehicle, together with the second car fitted with the disc brakes. Willie was a Devonian, an ex-merchant navy man who had survived four wartime shipwrecks. He was an expert at engine carburation and tuning. Cyril (who later became my brother-in-law) was an ex-flight engineer in the RAF with eighteen Lancaster bombing raids over Germany to his credit. One of the

for a variety of tests at the Monza circuit in Italy on 8th March, to include one car which had been fitted with Girling disc brakes. I believe this was the first racing car to have a disc braking system and, if testing was successful, it was then to race in the Grand Prix of Valentino at Turin on 6th April that year. Folkingham was a hive of activity, both in the racing shop and the transport department as the day of departure neared.

Racing driver Ken Wharton, the British Hill Climb Champion, had been signed to drive and was a frequent visitor to Folkingham.

The beautifully engineered Girling disc brake system with six-pot caliper as fitted to early BRM V16 cars. It was probably the first disc brake system to be fitted to a racing car, and the forerunner of the systems we know today.

One of the Ferodo brake pads as fitted in the Girling callipers of the V16 BRM. Each calliper had six pads, making a total of 24 per car. It's pictured with a 2006 fifty pence coin for size comparison.

stories Cyril told us of his experiences was that during one particular raid it was his job to throw 'window' out from the flight deck, 'window' being thin strips of metal foil which would float in the air with the intention of obstructing radar detection. When daylight broke, however, he found he was ankle deep in foil, most of it having blown back in! He was now a skilled machinist who would operate the lathe in the mobile workshop.

Dave Turner, a local man, was an engine build fitter who had worked on munitions during the war. Prior to joining BRM he had been employed building the prototype Kendal car at Grantham, a project initiated by Dennis Kendal the Independent Member of Parliament for Grantham, which it was hoped would be the British answer to Adolf Hitler's 'people's car' – the Volkswagen Beetle. Sadly, only about six of these Kendal cars were built. Arthur Ambrose was a jack-of-all-trades, well thought of by PB and often ribbed for being a 'crawler,' a description he appeared to take as a compliment.

Stan Hope, a powerfully built Coventry man, was a skilled panel beater by trade and an expert at metal fabrication. With his very delicate hands, he could well have been a surgeon. Frequently, asked to fabricate a part from a drawing, he would study it and remark: "You can't do that old son, it's physically impossible," then go away and produce the part in question. He was a genuine wizard; well educated, he was comfortable using both eloquent speech and the more brusque language of the shop floor, according to the company he was addressing. Often he would quote a piece from Shakespeare, having performed

in amateur dramatics earlier in life. A single man, Stan was often referred to as Widow Twanky.

We actually left Bourne on 12th March to catch the night ferry at Dover. Approaching Dunkirk it was natural to imagine what the scene would have been like on those beaches in 1940, when British troops were evacuated to safety from the approaching German army. This particular route was the less favourable of the Channel crossings, but would be a familiar one to us for several years to come. Apparently Raymond Mays, almost invariably referred to as RM, was a friend of the owner of the Townsend ferry that plied that route and so had probably got a special rate!

Bourne to Monza was a three day journey, our first stop being Reims where we almost lost Tony Rudd when he stepped off the pavement into the path of a cyclist. Tony escaped unscathed but the same could not be said for the cyclist, unfortunately, who required first aid treatment for cuts and bruises. A suitable hotel found, I shared a room with Cyril who asked if I knew which room Willie was in. Picking a number at random I replied: "Room seven." "Are you sure?" he asked. "Fairly sure," I said. He entered the room without knocking only to be confronted by a young lady in a state of undress. He made a quick exit with a wide grin on his face! The moral is always to lock one's hotel door. He eventually found Willie …

The excitement of travelling with the racing team had caused me to disregard the subject of remuneration, and it was only after we arrived in France that I learned that we received normal pay plus ten shillings (50p) per day personal allowance with accommodation and meals provided.

The Albergo Ristorante 'Marchesi' at Villasanta, Monza. The hotel became a firm favourite with BRM personnel and also a rather different type of clientele …

France was still recovering from the war, with bomb-damaged houses and buildings very much in evidence and roads which appeared not to have been repaired for years. Driving a loaded transporter at speeds of around 60mph (96kph) on such roads was like a mountain goat leaping from crag to crag. Due to snow on the alpine mountain passes it was necessary to go via Monte Carlo, which seemed to delight everyone! I enjoyed travelling through France then, and have done so every time since. The locals could be difficult at times but the varying scenery was pleasant, and here I was getting paid to travel through the French countryside, sampling the food and wine. Life was good!

I was now living in the world of racing car and transport vehicle modifications and improvements, and on one occasion Gordon Newman – whose thoughts were rarely far from the female figure – saw what he decided was a suitable opportunity to make a modification of a different kind. An uneven road surface was indicated by a sign displaying two upward symmetrical curves; with some black paint from the mobile workshop

French uneven road surface sign with Gordon Newman's modification.

the inevitable nipples were added to one of these signs.

Late the following evening we arrived in Monte Carlo for our second overnight stop. We had earlier taken dinner at a restaurant near Frejus where, if choosing trout from the menu, customers could select a live fish from the glass tank in the foyer. I have doubts that you actually got the one you chose but, Gordon Newman being the purse keeper, took a dim view when a number of us ordered expensive trout, impressing upon us we must choose a less costly dish or forfeit the wine, to keep within his budget.

Unfortunately, time did not permit us to explore Monaco so, suitably rested and refreshed, we left the Principality the following morning and admired the beautiful scenery along the Mediterranean coast, much of it very suntanned and skimpily clad!

We made our way to the Italian frontier at Ventimiglia. Here, we almost lost our precious cargo, causing a major panic. The frontier post was situated on a steep gradient, the racing car secured on the front of the transporter by leather straps. Willie made to move our vehicle forward and, in doing so, released the clutch too quickly with the result that the vehicle moved with a jerk. The racing car did not follow at quite the same speed, the straps stretched and the tail panel of the car forced open the transporter rear door, leaving the car hanging perilously out of the back. Sanity was eventually restored but, needless to say, a modification to car security was to be a major priority on our return to England, whilst an unspecified temporary modification to the tail of the car had already been carried out by Willie.

A lunch stop was made at a seafront restaurant in San Remo, where the popular choice was steak. Cyril admired his with a look of eager anticipation and, remarking on the size, measured it with a six-inch rule, a piece of equipment most mechanics carried in their pockets, if only with which to stir their tea! On tasting the steak he found it had been overloaded with garlic, a seasoning he did not appreciate and so it was not really enjoyed, though helped down with copious glasses of Chianti.

We eventually arrived at our accommodation, the Albergo Ristorante Marchesi at Villasanta, near Monza, situated opposite the gates of the Royal Monza Park. We were to be housed here during our stay, with the primitive workshops conveniently situated at the rear of the hotel enabling us to work on the cars. It was only a matter of crossing the road and travelling through the park to reach the world famous racing circuit. We were told that the workshops had been used for the detention of prisoners during the war and executions had taken place there; there were certainly what appeared to be bullet marks still evident on the walls. I also learned we were quite near the place where the body of Italian dictator Benito Mussolini had been hung on display following his assassination by Italian Partisans in 1945.

The hostelry was clean with good food, but it soon became apparent this was no ordinary hotel. Prosperous looking couples, many of the ladies very beautiful, frequently arrived in luxury cars. Signor Valentino, the proprietor, would summon his right-hand man with words something like "Ettori, Macchina," upon which the little fellow would rush out to greet the clients. Sometimes they would take a meal before retiring to their bedrooms, there to be left in peace for varying periods of time to pursue their carnal activities. One can imagine that if Victor Meldrew of the television sitcom *One Foot in the Grave* had been a member of the BRM team, he would have exclaimed "I don't believe it, we're staying at a bloody knocking shop"! Many times we were to witness couples leaving, eyes sparkling, while we mechanics looked on with envy. Some customers would call early in the mornings, obviously on their way to work. Now, that really was breakfast in bed!

Our arrival was greeted by a local Italian character, whose primary aim was to collect any waste oil not required. He had become a BRM acquaintance during a previous team visit and

had been nicknamed 'Oilio.' He proved a useful contact in helping to locate any services or commodities we might require, and we saw and heard more of him later.

Villasanta was a typical old Italian town situated on the main road from Milan to Brescia, which passed immediately in front of the hotel. In 1952 every other person seemed to own a motor scooter, resulting in incessant morning traffic noise. Sunday mornings were the exception when the droning of the scooters was replaced by the rather tinny-sounding church bells. Often a cycle race took place, causing great excitement in the town. Our evenings were usually spent having a beer at one of the nearby bars, where local customers made us welcome and we did our best to converse with each other, the many misunderstandings causing much amusement. Their favourite subject was football and the Italians would invariably mention Stanley Mathews, the only English footballer of whom they seemed to have heard. We also had the use of the Italian equivalent of an English bowling green, the difference being it was just an earthen surface and the game played a cross between bowls and petanque.

Raymond Mays arrived at Monza in a brand new, dark blue Bentley, of which he was obviously very proud. A day or so after his arrival he was extremely distressed when it was noticed that the paint on the scuttle of the car was beginning to bubble up. It was later discovered that a garage hand back at the Raymond Mays garage premises in Bourne had mistakenly replenished the windscreen washer reservoir with battery acid instead of distilled water.

Stirling Moss had been engaged for the early testing, later to be relieved by Ken Wharton. Test days came and went, management appearing fairly satisfied with the results. Monza was a very fast circuit and to see the BRMs going down the long straight at full speed was most exciting, particularly for me, a

Stirling Moss in the V16 BRM during testing at the Monza circuit in March 1952.

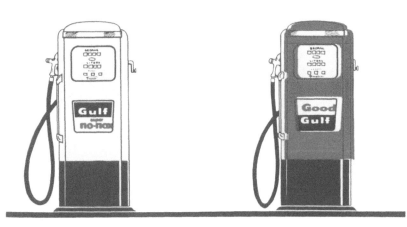

newcomer to the racing team. One day Stan Hope stood alone in a pit – which were reminiscent of cattle market pens – looking rather forlorn, so I decided to auction him off as a pedigree bull, much to the amusement of the rest of the team. Even the bull managed a smile! On one occasion Stirling hit a hare whilst travelling at speed, resulting in considerable damage to the front of the car, which meant we now had a car whose rear end had been modified by Willie and front end by Stirling.

Working one day on the cars as lunchtime approached, PB suggested it was time to go and eat. Willie replied "Yes, we'll just finish nailing this old thing together." PB looked at Willie with disgust and replied seriously "That, Willie, is an expression I do not care for."

A few days before testing was complete Cyril left by train for home in order to perform his duties as best man at Maurice's and Myrtle's wedding, leaving Tony Rudd with the remaining six personnel to take the cars to Turin, or so we thought and hoped. However, news came through from Bourne that Juan Manual Fangio and Froilan Gonzales, the Argentinian drivers, were arriving in England to test drive the BRMs with a view to signing contracts to drive. We were to return both cars to Bourne, a devastating blow to a team of men who had worked so hard to try and ensure that our performance at Turin would be successful. Peter Berthon and Tony Rudd tried in vain to get this instruction

reversed to allow us to take part in the Grand Prix at Turin as planned, but to no avail. Eventually we were told a telegram had been received direct from Alfred Owen with strict instructions to return to England at once. It was a dejected body of men that made their way home to read on arrival a rather critical article in *Autosport* dated 11th April, 1952. Editor Gregor Grant, a staunch BRM supporter, was provoked to write about the management reneging on our entry in Turin, which I quote in full as follows under the title "The Truth About Turin":

"When the two BRMs were sent to Monza for testing, the sponsors gave out that there was a possibility of an entry for the GP of Valentino at Turin on 6th April, if tests proved satisfactory, and if sufficient first-class opposition was present to justify such a step. Naturally, the race organisers publicized the possibility of BRM participation, and it was entirely due to this that Enzo Ferrari was persuaded to prepare a team of 4½-litre GP cars. The prospect of a BRM-Ferrari duel excited continental motor racing circles, and organisers of Europe's main races looked to the Turin race to give them some sort of lead as to whether it would be worthwhile staging pukka Formula 1 events during 1952. It was freely stated that if BRM could provide evidence of offering anything like a serious challenge to Ferrari, then it was likely that several races now in the melting pot for Formula 2, would possibly be organized on a full-scale Formula 1 footing.

"Naturally, the sequence of events keyed up the BRM mechanics as nothing has ever done before. Weary men were transformed into a group full of enthusiasm. Nothing was spared to make the two cars as raceworthy as possible. Stirling Moss did the preliminary testing, and during his absence on the Lyons-Charbonniers Rally, Ken Wharton took over.

"Technical Director Peter Berthon expressed himself more than satisfied with the results obtained at Monza, and many minor modifications were carried out to both cars, one of which had experimental Girling disc-type hydraulic brakes. Girling technicians Redmayne and Davis obtained valuable data on braking, whilst 'Dunlop' Barlow was there to carefully check tyre behaviour at the high speeds possible on the Monza circuit.

"Wharton returned to England, and Moss took over testing

Juan Manuel Fangio signs to drive for BRM. Raymond Mays and the Argentinian ambassador share the microphone, watched by Fangio seated on the back of the car. Near left is Peter Berthon and other guests and BRM staff.

once more. It was a tonic to see how the BRM mechanics, under team manager Tony Rudd, worked on both cars. These were Dave Turner, Willy Southcott, Gordon Newman, Arthur Ambrose, Stan Hope and Dick Salmon – all determined that the cars in their care should be 100 per cent.

"The disc brake car had shown signs of a slight falling off in oil pressure, but this was rectified and the BRM sang round Monza with the joyous note of a real thoroughbred. On a wet track, Moss circulated at 2min 08sec with plenty of revs in hand. The brakes were truly phenomenal and it was small wonder that 'PB' and his men were confident that the car would not disgrace itself at Turin. However, things were happening back in England. News was received from Argentina that Fangio, accompanied by Gonzales, was flying to England and would arrive on 5th April to try out the cars. The BRM organization immediately ordered the return of both the Monza cars, and steadfastly refused to consider even the possibility that either of the machines could put up a showing at Turin. Priority was given to the Argentinians and Stirling Moss was informed that there would be no Turin drive for him.

"The disappointment of both Moss and the BRM contingent was almost heartbreaking to see. A statement was published in the Italian papers that no entry would be forthcoming at Turin because the cars were not ready. This was most unfair on men who had sweated blood to make the cars ready.

"A last minute effort was made to convince the sponsors that entry of one car at Turin, even on the basis of giving it a test under full racing conditions, would prove more than beneficial to the future of the marque, if not to the entire framework of the existing Formula 1. However, Bourne insisted that the possibility of another fiasco could not be contemplated, and cars must be available back in England for the Argentinian drivers to try out.

"So ended yet another chapter in the sorry history of the 16-cylinder cars. The decision admittedly was difficult, but to those on the spot it was evident that the whole motor racing community on the continent had its eyes on Turin. The presence of a green car, and the sound of that wonderfully defiant exhaust

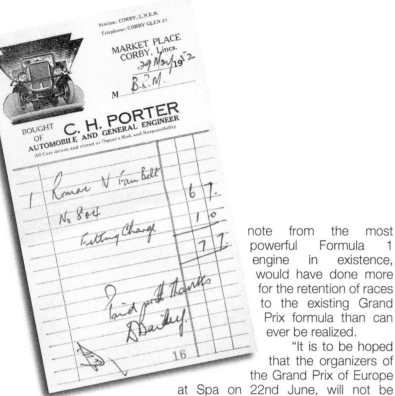

note from the most powerful Formula 1 engine in existence, would have done more for the retention of races to the existing Grand Prix formula than can ever be realized.

"It is to be hoped that the organizers of the Grand Prix of Europe at Spa on 22nd June, will not be unduly influenced by the events at Turin, otherwise, convinced that the race will be a foregone conclusion for Ferrari, they might switch over to Formula 2 – even although it has been announced that the race will be for Formula 1 machines."

BRM's failure to turn up at Turin was the final nail in the coffin. Gregor Grant's worst fears were realised and the Belgian Grand Prix – along with the entire World Championship Formula 1 season – was run to Formula 2 regulations and continued through to the start of the 2.5 litre-formula of 1954. The BRM V16, on which a fortune had been lavished, was at last proving its worth after four years in the making but was suddenly rendered obsolete by the stroke of a pen.

Fortunately, we were thrown a lifeline: organisers still keen to see these magnificent cars in action. Short Formula Libre races were arranged, almost entirely in the United Kingdom, and splendid battles were to take place against Tony Vandervell's Thin Wall Special and even the odd works Ferrari. However, we were in a minor league, out of Formula 1.

The cessation of hostilities in Europe had left the British Isles with many disused wartime airfields, a number of which were now being utilised to accommodate the growing sport of motor racing, and of which Silverstone would become the most famous; the former Wellington Bomber base of 17 Operational Training Unit located in central England eventually became the principal motor racing circuit in Britain. It was here on 8th April, 1952 – a very wet Tuesday – that Fangio and Gonzales first drove the BRM, Fangio in particular demonstrating what a master he was in the rain. Both drivers subsequently signed to drive, returning to Folkingham for a press conference and photo session the following day.

The first race which catered for our (suddenly) obsolete cars was to be the Albi Grand Prix in Southern France on 1st June with two cars entered. Both drivers were large men, Gonzales (nicknamed the Pampas Bull), the larger, and the cockpits of both cars required modification to accommodate their respective frames. More test drives were undertaken and the cars prepared for the race. After the Ventimiglia incident, the method of securing cars in the transporters had been modified by the use of the winch mechanism and chocks, eliminating the flexibility previously experienced with leather straps.

I was thrilled at being chosen to be part of the team going to Albi. It was an important event for BRM and I felt I was rapidly earning my spurs towards becoming a regular member of the racing crew for these continental encounters. For this race Maurice Dove also joined the team and so, together with Cyril, we shared a vehicle and made a jolly trio as we had all been friends in pre-BRM days. On Sunday 25th May we began our journey to Dover. Shortly after leaving Dunkirk we ran into a severe thunderstorm, one flash of lightning momentarily cutting out the transporter engine with rain and hail quickly flooding the highway. We eventually reached our destination on the Tuesday evening. Albi is a pleasant cathedral town situated in Southern France on the river Tarn in the region of Languedoc-Roussillon. It was the birthplace of the French artist Toulouse-Lautrec and a place much approved of by Raymond Mays, who had enjoyed some success there in pre-war races with the ERA. The result of RM's popularity resulted in fantastic hospitality, everyone greeting us like long-lost favourite cousins!

The racing cars were garaged in a local car dealer's workshops, which would be at our disposal during our stay. We then discovered we had arrived a day earlier than expected and the hotel could not accommodate us until the following evening. Frantic enquiries were made on our behalf and beds found in a variety of private houses for one night. Maurice and I were taken

Raymond Mays and Juan Fangio talk to fellow Argentinian driver Roberto Mieres during the Albi Grand Prix meeting.

Mechanics make adjustments to Fangio's BRM in the pits at Albi, prior to the Albi Grand Prix, watched by Raymond Mays, Fangio (with foot on wheel), and Froilan Gonzales wearing a white hat.

for a hairy ride on motorcycle pillions to humble digs in a very rural setting about two miles out of town, where we were shown our host's wine making facilities and I sampled Benedictine for the first time. We moved into the hotel the following day and found things to be pretty basic, en-suite facilities being comparatively unknown in 1952, Maurice and I shared a room and quickly found the communal bathroom was conveniently situated next to us. On entering the bathroom it became apparent that either Heath Robinson or his mate had installed the boiler and plumbing. Maurice decided to investigate how to light the thing and have a bath whilst I took the opportunity to rest my weary bones and have a lie down. I quickly dozed off but was soon awakened by an almighty bang and vibrating walls. It seems Maurice had managed to light the boiler … He soon returned to the bedroom looking pale, muttering "Christ, I don't know what happened then."

Despite our busy schedule we made time to visit some local hostelries. One mechanic, who shall be nameless, succumbed to the power of the grape. On seeing a nearby handcart the decision was taken to borrow it and load the unfortunate chap onto it for his return journey to the hotel. The owner of the handcart must have been a light sleeper and took a dim view of our intention, however. From high up in the adjacent flats someone shouted

in what I can only assume was foul language. Mindful of the fact we had signed an agreement before our departure to be of good behaviour (as we were ambassadors of Britain), like good boys and not wanting to sour public relations we left the cart and manhandled the poor soul back to the hotel. Next day at the garage we started to prepare for practice, our invalid not feeling at all well. So, good mates that we were, we covered for him and allowed him to rest in the cab of the workshop wagon, using the age-old excuse to our superiors: "It must have been something he ate"! The vehicle had its own generator to operate the lathe and other equipment unless we had access to a mains electricity supply. In this instance the connection to the mains suffered an earth problem and our mate in the cab was not only feeling unwell but was getting electric shocks as well if he touched anything conducive! I suspect these probably did him good and assisted his recovery.

Facilities in the garage were basic to say the least. French toilets of that period consisted of a hole in the floor with platforms on each side for one's feet, quickly referred to as Harley Davidsons by Cyril after the vintage motorcycle footrests. The toilet was malodorous, remedied by copious amounts of Jeyes Fluid. It made it more usable for visitors although, much to our amusement, the local workforce seemed to prefer the natural stench and appeared reluctant to use the disinfectant.

The weather was extremely hot and working conditions generally unpleasant, and we could have done without the problems experienced. Tony Rudd noticed the cylinder head securing studs were breaking during warm-up, causing coolant leaks. This would soon wreck the cylinder heads completely and was a serious problem. The likely cause was that the studs were manufactured from the wrong type of steel, either incorrectly specified in the design or, more likely, wrongly supplied from the stores. All steel held in the Bourne stores was colour-coded, and the suspicion was that the person who issued material from the metal store had marked it with the wrong colour, either by mistake or deliberately. As the storeman concerned appeared to be a somewhat disgruntled individual with a large chip on his shoulder, it was probably the latter option. Whatever the reason, as far as I am aware, guilt was never proved.

Makeshift repairs were made to enable the cars to practice. Working in such stifling heat made us desperately thirsty and, on top of that, new overalls had been provided which resembled army battledress material. They were horrendous, grey in colour and can only be likened to the sacks one saw containing corn. Whoever had been responsible for the purchase of them obviously had no experience of manual work.

Following practice, Cyril gave me the nod and said "Come on, let's go for a drink." A nearby bar was found and we each ordered a bottle of beer. What we were drinking I know not but it went down very well, and so we had another. At the time the beer did not seem particularly strong but, bearing in mind we had taken little food, it must have been stronger than we realised. When the hot sun hit us it was unreal and I recall Cyril saying "I feel pissed." It was a statement to which I had to agree and replied "So do I." We struggled through the rest of the day though, needless to say, kept a low profile for a while.

New cylinder head studs were manufactured at Bourne and flown out by charter plane accompanied by Material Controller, Clarrie Brinkley, almost always referred to as 'Brink' until, after his epic flight, he was also dubbed 'Bleriot.' Due to the heat the cars had been running far too hot. All spare hands became makeshift panel beaters, including Fangio and Gonzales, to cut additional louvres in the bodywork and increase airflow over the engine. An all-night session was worked to fit the replacement studs and tempers became frayed. PB and RM were holding a conversation nearby with some visitors and generally getting in the way. It was becoming apparent that Cyril, who was working in a grimy and smelly pit below the car, was becoming annoyed with the distraction. At last he could stand it no longer and exploded, saying "Why don't you lot do something useful or get out of the bloody way?" though probably with a more colourful choice of words. Either way it had the desired effect; PB replied "Yes Cyril," and moved away. Only Cyril could have got away with that!

Race day arrived and Fangio went to test his car on the main road out of Albi. RM became quite concerned when he failed to return after a few minutes and, being prone to panic, said "Get in the Bentley. We must go and look for him. Something must have happened." The two of us accompanied him to make a search. Now RM was no slouch behind a steering wheel and travelling out of Albi I noticed the Bentley speedometer was hovering around 90mph (145kph) when we met Fangio coming towards us on a slight bend and doing God knows what, but the closing speed must have been pretty high. Quite a hairy moment!

Both cars started on the front row of the grid. Fangio made an electrifying start and quickly built up a considerable lead. Gonzalez made a poor start and initially trailed the rest of the field. However, he was really motoring and quickly set a new lap record so that the cars were running first and second by the end of lap three. Alas, it was too good to last and Gonzalez came into the pits at the end of six laps to retire, steam billowing from under the bonnet. The engine had overheated due to cylinder head failure. Then, at half distance, Fangio also came in to retire with a broken cylinder head stud, allowing coolant to escape. Again our drivers had demonstrated the speed of the Bourne cars, only to be defeated by poor reliability in races we should have won.

Our next race (the International Ulster Trophy) was less than seven days away at Dundrod in Northern Ireland with Fangio and Stirling Moss as our nominated drivers. After the French race little

th. R.A.C. BRITISH GRAND PRIX 1952
MECHANIC
B.R.D.C. — DAILY EXPRESS

Juan Fangio congratulates French driver Louis Rosier on his victory in the Albi Grand Prix in his privately-entered blue Ferrari.

time was lost in packing cars and spares to go to the airport. To enable the team to fulfil this engagement a Bristol freighter aircraft of Silver City Airways had been chartered to fly the race cars from Toulouse to Belfast. Arthur Ambrose, Stan Hope and Maurice Dove were to drive the transport vehicles back to Bourne and later join us in Belfast. Travelling to the airport in a Renault Dauphine taxi I soon fell asleep, to be awakened by a panicking driver trying to explain that the car was on fire. He was right and I made a quick exit and fortunately was given a lift by a following car. I never discovered what happened to the Renault.

After touching down to refuel at Hurn airport in Hampshire we arrived at Nutt's Corner airport, Belfast, to be immediately confronted with more work and to find that someone with a weird sense of humour had booked us into a temperance hotel; not the best thing to do with BRM staff! More long hours followed with cars being dismantled to await the arrival of Stan and other Bourne personnel. Stan had left his toolbox with us in France, requesting we transport it to Northern Ireland. Asking for his toolbox on arrival we told him a pre-arranged story; that it was last seen at the side of the runway at Toulouse. He looked at us in disbelief. Stan was very proud of his toolbox, which contained some very valuable and specialist tools. After five minutes or so, and a make-believe argument about who had been responsible, we considered he had suffered enough and his box was produced, much to his relief.

The two cars were eventually prepared. However, hopes were not high as racing along narrow country roads was not the ideal circuit for the BRMs. Stirling did not relish the task at all and Fangio was non-committal. On the morning of the race a minor panic ensued when one of the cars was found to be losing coolant. With no time for a proper repair, in went a tin of Coleman's mustard and fingers were crossed. (Mustard was recognised as a good, old-fashioned remedy for minor water leaks.) Alas, that was not to be the last panic of the day. As the race plugs were being fitted to Stirling's car, one broke, leaving the thread in the plughole – the only time in my long career I can recall such a freak failure. It was eventually removed by tapping a file tang into the broken plug, much to everyone's relief.

Sadly, again both cars failed to finish. Practice times had not been good, the cars languishing down on the grid with Fangio twelfth ahead of Moss in thirteenth position. The start of the race was wretched, both BRMs left on the grid with stalled engines, Stirling's clutch having failed. We mechanics ran out onto the track to give the two cars a push-start and Fangio managed to get up to third position before retiring with fuel starvation, controversially attributed to dirty fuel supplied by the petrol company. Stirling Moss was never happy with the car and struggled round, eventually retiring with an overheating engine. One memorable moment in the race was when Fangio spun approaching the hairpin bend, ending up facing in the wrong direction. Stirling famously reported "As I approached the hairpin, I came upon

Fangio facing the wrong way, but travelling towards the bend in reverse at almost the same speed as I was travelling forward." Fangio continued to the hairpin to rejoin the race travelling in the right direction!

Arthur Ambrose, our jack-of-all-trades, frequently disappeared. We soon discovered he was visiting a bar to sample the Guinness, of which he was very fond. Post-race we accepted an invitation to visit a working men's club and one of the members began to sing. He was no Matt Munro and when we were inclined to laugh at his rendering of Irish songs it did not endear us to our hosts. All ended happily, however.

Fangio was not so lucky. He left Dundrod to fly to Italy where he was to drive for Maserati in a Formula 2 race at Monza. Due to bad weather his flight from Belfast ended at Paris from where he was obliged to drive all the way across the Alps arriving at Monza only half-an-hour before the race started. He was involved in a serious accident early in the race due to fatigue, breaking a bone in his neck which kept him out of racing for the rest of the season.

Back at Folkingham, Maurice and I were alternating between maintaining transport and the racing cars. We were both spending more time working on the cars, sometimes officially, on other occasions due to our own initiative. Stirling resigned from BRM after Dundrod, never happy with the handling of the V16, which meant that Gonzales and Ken Wharton would drive in the next event at Silverstone on 19th July.

Once again I was seconded to the racing team much to my delight. Preparations for the race were remarkably uneventful by BRM standards; our race headquarters were at Adcock's Garage at Brackley with late nights and early mornings the norm. Other mechanics also stayed in Brackley, accommodated in private houses or bed and breakfast establishments, whilst Raymond Mays would retreat to the Welcome Hotel at Stratford-upon-Avon. In practice our two drivers, Gonzales and Wharton, qualified first and third respectively sharing the front row with two Ferraris.

The race under way, Gonzalez again drove like a man possessed, lying four seconds behind the flying Pierro Taruffi in his Ferrari but unaware he was actually twenty-six seconds ahead of him as Taruffi had been penalised thirty seconds for jumping the start. Whether or not he was trying too hard we will never know but, on the eighth lap, Gonzalez crashed at Stowe Corner and eventually limped back to the pits with a leaking radiator. As the number one driver, he asked for Wharton to be called in and took over his car, only to retire two laps from the finish in third place with gearbox failure. Why Gonzalez had not been signalled that Taruffi had been penalised is something I never understood and suspect the 'Pampus Bull' was simply trying too hard. Could it have been another example of where a BRM *should* have won the race ...?

Our next venue on 2nd August was another wartime airfield circuit at Boreham, Essex, a former base of the United States Air force and once armed with Martin B-26 Marauder and later Douglas C-47 Skytrain aircraft. Two cars were entered for the *Daily Mail* International Trophy for Gonzales and Wharton. The accommodation allocated to us for this meeting left a lot to be desired as we were all installed in one large dormitory-like room with camp beds: army days all over again. Complaints were made and we were relocated to the completely contrasting comfort of the Crown Hotel at Writtle, where even steak was available for breakfast, providing the resident dog allowed you into the restaurant!

5th R·A·C BRITISH
GRAND PRIX
SILVERSTONE
SATURDAY JULY 19th 1952
ORGANISED BY THE
B·R·D·C
SPONSORED BY THE
DAILY EXPRESS
OFFICIAL PROGRAMME 2/-

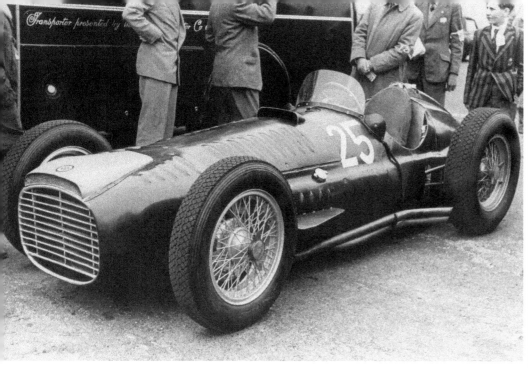

The MkI V16 BRM of Froilan Gonzales in the paddock at Boreham, Essex.

Froilan Gonzales looking quite composed before the International Trophy race at Boreham, a mood that changed markedly during the race ...

On race day I was asked by an onlooker why a third Austin Lodestar had arrived and had we sent for a third car? Assuring the enquirer that we had only two, he argued he had just counted three transporters, and investigations proved him correct. A new employee, hired to replace either Maurice or myself in the transport department, had decided to drive down in the third Austin to watch the race and had also tried to sell some tyres to finance the trip. The would-be purchaser of the tyres rang Jim Sandercombe to ask if the sale was all above board. Needless to say it was not and that man's career with BRM was cut short.

Alas, race success was to elude us once again. After practice Gonzales had expressed satisfaction with the car and said we were not to change anything. Unfortunately, PB knew better and decided to give the car a final tweak, instructing different carburettor needles be fitted – much to the annoyance of the driver. The general opinion was he was so enraged that he drove with such temper he overdid it and crashed. The final indignity of the meeting came when, as we were exiting the gate, a policeman removed his helmet and held it waist high as if paying respects at a funeral. We had no answer to that!

It was increasingly apparent that the V16 engine was becoming something of an enigma with its numerous problems, the most frequent of which were cracked cylinder liners, melting pistons and porous engine castings. A piston failure invariably made it necessary to remove the engine for repair, unless it was the foremost piston, which could be changed with great difficulty by removing the supercharger; that, in itself, a lengthy task. The gearbox was ultra reliable, as was chassis and running gear. Roadholding generated varying opinions. I believe Stirling Moss once described it as the worst handling car he had driven, Ken Wharton appeared non-committal (probably just grateful for the drive), whilst Fangio and Gonzales just seemed to take its idiosyncrasies for granted (language difficulties may have contributed to this attitude!) Countless hours were spent changing plugs. A softer plug would be used for warming up, then changed to a harder version for track work. After a few test drive laps PB would frequently want to examine the plugs for fuel mixture assessment: removing and replacing sixteen plugs was a time-consuming task ...

Mike Hawthorn came to Folkingham to test drive a BRM in early August, with a view to driving at Turnberry on the west coast of Scotland on the 23rd of that month. He had also been invited to test drive Tony Vandervell's Thin Wall Special and, unfortunately for us, this is what he chose to do. Working until the early hours of one morning during this period, for some reason that escapes me, Maurice and I were offered the loan of the works Norton motorcycle and sidecar to travel home. Asked if either of us had driven one previously, Maurice rather flippantly

"Don't panic." Mechanics work feverishly to plug a water leak on Reg Parnell's BRM on the starting grid at Turnberry. A sporting Mike Hawthorn watches and assures the BRM people he will not start the race in his Thin Wall Special until their car is repaired.

replied in the affirmative; a complete falsehood. Off we went, however, with Maurice driving and, as the sidecar was simply a box with fold-down lid, I was riding pillion. Now anyone who has driven a motorcycle combination will know that it is vastly different to riding solo, something at which we were both experienced. The first right-hand bend was no problem, Maurice coaxing the contraption round. The first left-hand bend was different, however, since the thing refused to obey Maurice's instructions, resulting in our landing in a hedge. After extricating the machine and ourselves unharmed, we laughingly went on our way, only for these off-road excursions to become the 'norm.' I was quite surprised to see Maurice, who lived five miles beyond me, arrive to collect me the following morning!

Turnberry airfield was originally opened in 1917 and used for aerial gunnery training. After temporary closure it reopened in 1942 and was operational throughout the war, largely for training purposes. It was another very bumpy airfield circuit close to the famous golf course and hotel. As the Turnberry race was only a national event, Gonzales was ineligible to drive, so Reg Parnell was engaged to partner Ken Wharton. The BRM team stayed at a delightful small, family-run hotel at nearby Maybole. The proprietor was a total abstainer when we arrived, but this shortcoming had been resolved by the time we left! His son, Hamish, was a keen salmon fisherman and so fresh salmon was a popular choice on the menu; poached, I believe. Hamish also played the piano and was consistently playing tunes requested by a Pimm's-drinking Raymond Mays: I think he quite fancied him!

On the start line on race day (*The Scottish Express* National Trophy) it would have been so unlike BRM not to have had a panic session, and so we did. One of the hoses on the cylinder head water rail was found to be leaking on the Parnell car. Both cars had qualified on the front row of the grid with Mike Hawthorn on pole position in the Thin Wall Special. When Mike, good sportsman that he was, realised the problem, he immediately got out of his car and told we mechanics to take our time, he would not start until the leak had been fixed. Ready at last and then, sod's law, Mike could not find a gear and was left on the line, eventually starting last only to retire after a few laps. Reg went on

to win the race, a victory at last, albeit a minor one. After a hot bath and a meal allegedly paid for by RM, we were invited to a late-night party at the Turnberry Hotel, where fully clothed people were seen being thrown into the swimming pool, with, of course, Mike Hawthorn very much involved.

At this time, following the resignation of some of its members, including Tony Vandervell, the BRM Trust decided to offer the organisation for sale as a going concern. A very uncertain time ensued for all members of staff: who would buy the Trust? Alfred Owen was rumoured to be interested, along with various others, one of whom was a speedway rider. Offers were made to buy various parts of the organisation. All employees hoped that Alfred Owen would become the new owner; he was reputedly the only member of the original consortium to show an interest in purchasing and, with the support of the Owen Organisation facilities behind us, success seemed more achievable and continued employment more certain.

With the BRM problem solved, sod's law strikes Mike's Thin Wall Special: he cannot engage a gear and is left at the start.

The season continued despite the uncertainty of the ownership situation, with three cars entered in two races at the September Goodwood meeting, the Woodcote Cup and the Goodwood Trophy. Our accommodation at The Nags Head in Chichester became a favourite hotel for BRM mechanics and we were always made very welcome. On this occasion when enjoying a social evening, we were paid a visit by a police sergeant, enquiring who was responsible for parking the Commer workshop vehicle. Almost everyone laughingly pointed to Arthur. There is nothing like good mates! He was left with no option but to step forward, pleading guilty. It was pointed out to him that it was illegally parked and he was politely asked to move it, the sergeant pointing out that Arthur was lucky he was on duty and not a keen young constable. Arthur, a lovable sycophant, could apply a bit of flannel when required and invited the sergeant to have a drink. Being in uniform the officer declined and, as he departed, said to Arthur, who had a wonderful head of hair "Let me give you another bit of advice. Look after that head of hair; see what happened to mine." He lifted his helmet to reveal a completely bald head.

Reg Parnell wins the National Trophy race at Turnberry on the west coast of Scotland.

Starting racing cars in a built-up area was always a problem, and the garage we then used at Chichester was a good example of this. Situated fairly centrally in the town, and next door to Shippam's meat processing factory, firing up the cars and revving them did not endear us to Mr Shippam's staff one iota, especially as they apparently spent much of their time doing business on the telephone.

Race day came, and to say we were elated to have three cars sharing the front row of the grid with the Thin Wall Special was an understatement. The noise of three V16 engines raring to go was an unbelievable sound, and certainly not appreciated by drivers on row two of the grid. Although a minor race compared with a Grand Prix, Goodwood was always a very popular venue, often attended by Royalty and film and television personalities. In particular, HRH the Duke of Kent could often be seen at motor racing events, so we were hoping to put on a good show. Fantastic things followed because Froilan Gonzales won both races for us. Could this be true? BRM had won its last three races and, even better, in the Goodwood Trophy the cars finished first, second and third. The Nag's Head was lively that night and mechanic Arthur Hill was up late the next morning and had beer for breakfast. The hair of the dog!

There was one more race to conclude the 1952 season, this time north again to Charterhall, an airfield circuit on the Scottish borders. Like Turnberry it was a training station, this time for night fighter pilots. It had the unfortunate local nickname of 'Slaughterhall,' due to the high number of casualties sustained during training. Two cars were entered here to be driven by Reg Parnell and Ken Wharton, our principal rival again the Thin Wall Special. Tony Rudd, Maurice and I travelled in one of the Austin Lodestars. After stopping for lunch in Grantham we headed north with Tony driving. Going down a long straight about three miles out of Grantham and travelling at speed, a car was approaching overtaking a lorry. Now, although the oncoming car was at fault, I would have eased slightly to let him complete his manoeuvre, but not Tony. It was becoming increasingly apparent that unless someone took evasive action there would be an almighty accident. Fortunately for all concerned the car driver preferred

the ditch and hedge to the front of the Austin. Tony did stop then and we went back to see if the car driver was okay. He was and said he had not realised we were approaching so fast. We helped to get him back on the road and went on our way, while I imagine he probably went to Marks and Sparks in Grantham to buy some new underwear!

Our garage for the Charterhall race was to be at the premises of Jock McBain at Chirnside, who ran the racing team Border Reivers which would see a number of aspiring racing drivers pass through its doors, Jim Clark the most famous of all. We were accommodated at the Allanton Arms, a wonderful little pub in the village of the same name. The sale of BRM had still not been completed; at least that is what we mere underlings were given to understand. On hearing this I told RM that if I won the football pools I would consider buying the Trust. "How would you like to work for me?" I asked, "I would love to, my lad" was his reply. Concluding the season by winning the race was not on the cards as Ken Wharton was beaten into second place by – dare I say it? – a Bourne-built, pre-war ERA driven by Bob Gerard. Ah well, you can't win them all …

The final excursion of the year was to accompany Gordon Newman to Sutton Coldfield, hometown of Alfred Owen. We took a BRM to display in a garage showroom to raise money in aid of the *Birmingham Mail* Christmas Tree Fund of which Mr Owen was a sponsor. We had been booked into a dingy little bed and breakfast where the beds were noticeably damp. Gordon's remedy was several barley wines to keep out the cold, and who could argue with that? The event did attract quite a lot of visitors, one of whom was Alfred Owen's sister, Jean, who was to be so much a part of the BRM story in the future.

So, my first season of active motor racing had come to a close, a season I had thoroughly enjoyed and during which I had become almost a full-time member of the racing team. I had started the year working for British Racing Motors, but was to conclude it in the employ of Rubery Owen, Dept 31. On 1st November we became part of the giant Owen Organisation; a move, I have little doubt, which allowed BRM to survive.

Bringing home the bacon

Rubery Owen was a conglomerate of companies with factories in the United Kingdom, South Africa and India, and was reputed to be the largest family-owned business in Britain. With the head office based in the Midlands town of Darlaston, the various plants manufactured such diverse products as nuts and bolts, domestic equipment, agricultural machinery, components for the motor industry, office equipment and machine tools and the like. In 1951 the business became known as the Owen Organisation with the slogan "A Linked Family Business of more than Fifty Companies."

Department 31, the Engine Development Division at Bourne, now came under that umbrella with the objective of building race-winning cars. In addition, development of high performance engines, transmissions and other commercial products – including technical know-how – was to be vigorously pursued and marketed. One such commercial project was the Ford Zephyr cylinder head conversion, marketed as the Raymond Mays Zephyr Conversion, which significantly increased the performance of that car, one of which was successfully raced by Ken Wharton. A second commercial project was the production and testing of Bowser high pressure pumps.

I was now beginning to consider myself a full-time member of the racing team, daily becoming better acquainted with its workings. We each provided our own tools. Many spanners and other tools had to be individually modified to suit a particular purpose, like, for example, removing and refitting the supercharger on the V16 engine. The engine as fitted in the chassis meant that conventional spanners were unsuitable, some nuts being almost inaccessible. The same applied to fitting exhaust manifolds, secured by no fewer than sixty-four nuts! One thing I had learned of, albeit not personally, was Peter Berthon's dislike of adjustable spanners; anyone caught with such a tool was quickly advised to dispose of it – or else.

PB was treated with great respect by all mechanics, and was generally pleasant, but could be very sarcastic in his comments of disapproval. His relationship with wife Lorna did not appear to be on solid ground. Lorna was disliked intensely by Raymond Mays' mother, and her last exit from Eastgate House, the Mays family home, had reputedly involved her belongings being deposited on the front lawn, thrown there from the bedroom window by Mrs Mays. Lorna made frequent visits to London and often, when away, Peter Berthon's secretarial requirements appeared to increase with his lady secretary replacing Lorna at Folkingham. Jock Milne, the caretaker on the airfield site was a Scot with a large chip on his shoulder and a man who, one imagined, could quite easily have obtained a degree in foul language. He treated everyone with the same respect, which was practically none, and was as equally rude to PB and his wife as he was to us. Being in such a remote location probably allowed him to get away with it, or did he simply hold some secret knowledge which could have been embarrassing if revealed? However, treated with the necessary respect he could be very helpful and seemed a fairly contented man, living alone with his dog and cats.

By now all bodywork panels, fuel, oil and water tanks were being made at Folkingham; in the past George Gray and Co of Portsmouth had produced these items. Now, under the supervision of Stan Hope, sheet metal workers from the Owen Organisation's subsidiary company, Motor Panels of Coventry, had been seconded to Folkingham, among them Alan Ellison, Don 'Danny' Woodward, and Bill Wilcox, all of whom eventually settled in the Bourne district, plus additional craftsmen as required. The facility for building bodies in-house was of tremendous benefit. It was fascinating to see these skilled men at work, persuading sheets of aluminium and steel into the various panel shapes required. The lengths of sheet aluminium were then fused together without the use of welding rods, leaving a neat herringbone pattern as if done by a sewing machine.

Alan Ellison had arrived with a Ford van which he used on occasions to transport the workers to Bourne for lunch. The van had been extended at the rear which resulted in a considerable overhang. Occasionally and mischievously, at a given signal, all of the passengers in the back would move to the rear, making the van tail-heavy and resulting in a very annoyed Alan having difficulty steering with front wheels almost off the ground!

In addition, more staff had been taken on at Folkingham, including Jack Heward, progress chaser and transport manager, plus Dennis Perkins, Reg Smith, Ken Williamson and John Speight as mechanics. Jack Heward was a prolific smoker of both pipe and cigarettes, often referred to as 'Puffing Billy,' his inhalations sounding like the village blacksmith's bellows and his exhalations exuding smoke like an ancient Sentinel steam wagon. If he was wanted and could not be found it was sometimes possible to just stand quietly and listen for the direction from whence his cough came. Often his pipe was left lying around and, on one occasion, Maurice and I – known as the terrible twins – found the pipe fully loaded with tobacco. Gently teasing out the contents, we put a small piece of oily rag in the bottom and replaced the tobacco. Unfortunately, we did not witness it being re-ignited, but they could probably hear him coughing nine miles away at Bourne.

Dennis Perkins, a pleasant and fun-loving idividual from the Kidderminster area, was a man of small stature, who eventually became the gearbox specialist. He regularly wore a pair of cowboy-type boots, which resulted in him being known as the 'Sheriff,' a nickname given him by Tony Rudd, I believe, one he seemed to enjoy which stayed with him throughout his BRM career and beyond, even used internationally. Ken Williamson, for no apparent reason, acquired the nickname 'Flojo.' He eventually left and, I believe, went on to do the 'knowledge' in order to became a London cabbie. Nicknames were the norm during that period, more so than today, I feel. For some reason, Willie had given Gordon Newman a fictional knighthood, and had dubbed him Sir Humphrey Bagwash, after which he was almost always referred to by one and all as Bagwash or Baggie.

Flojo became the victim of a Bagwash practical joke when he was told of a party to be held at Stamford, ten miles away. Unfortunately, the others could not take him, but if he cared to go on the last bus to Stamford they would give him a lift back. The big drawback to that arrangement was that there was not, and never was going to be, a party, and a very disgruntled Flojo had to pay for a taxi back to Bourne after his wild-goose chase.

John Speight (no connection to the one of *Steptoe & Son* fame) was dubbed Sergeant Bilko due to his likeness to the film character of that name. Reg Smith arrived from the Midlands, the proud owner of a vintage Sunbeam car named Primrose, which gives an indication of its colour. A further addition during the winter was the acquisition of a secondhand Greenline Leyland bus to ferry workers from Bourne to Folkingham, a big improvement on travelling in the back of the Dodge lorry. Reg Smith also served as the driver of the bus which was parked overnight near the BRM works. One cold morning when warming it up, Reg became aware of someone already aboard saying "Here, let me get off, mate." A knight of the road had sought refuge from the cold and spent the night sleeping on the rear seat.

Although the year at Folkingham had started quietly, things were vastly different at Bourne where much research and development work was being carried out on the V16 engine. Even though the cars would not be eligible for Formula 1 events, they would continue to be entered for Formule Libre races where possible. Also, preliminary design work was being undertaken on a new 2.5-litre engine to meet the criteria of the incoming Formula One regulations for 1954, together with a chassis to accept the new engine. The first of the Formule Libre races were to be the Chichester Cup and the Glover Trophy at the Goodwood Easter meeting on 6th April.

In the meantime a number of modifications, repairs and improvements were carried out on the V16 chassis and on transport vehicles, equipment and buildings, prior to engines and gearboxes being delivered from Bourne. Life was never dull! Wherever possible all building and machinery maintenance was done in-house, whilst at the same time Jock would invariably request help with some task, which was seldom refused as he made the tea!

Mischief and practical jokes were rife amongst staff at Folkingham during the 'quiet' period. Something not advisable was to advertise when visiting the primitive toilet, an Elsan chemical bucket in a rusty corrugated iron-clad hut. Many people would be doing what comes naturally when a passerby, realising it was occupied, would throw a brick on the roof, which not only startled

the occupant, but also dislodged a shower of rust particles onto the unsuspecting victim. Glancing towards the same roof one day I was astonished to see what I thought looked like a sheep's head and further investigations proved my assumption correct. Arthur Ambrose, a keen fisherman, had obtained the head from the local butcher and put it on the roof to attract flies, the purpose being to breed maggots for bait, a frequent and rather smelly occurrence. Hacksaw blades were often removed and refitted the wrong way round, much to the annoyance of the operator. It was not unusual for a man to arrive home for his wife to discover her spouse's lunchbox contained a quite useless item, for example, a large old padlock minus its key. I think most people took one home at some time, the most frequent recipient being metal fabricator Arthur (Snip) Chambers. The surprising fact was that it was invariably returned!

The engine shop at Folkingham was a flimsy-looking, wooden-framed building on a concrete base. An infestation of rats had made their home beneath the concrete and were rapidly multiplying, with numerous holes evident around the building. Bagwash decided he would become the anti-vermin officer and rid us of the problem. He blanked off some of the holes and poured some time-expired racing fuel, a mixture of methanol and benzene, in the remainder. He then tied a fuel-soaked rag to a long pole, set light to the rag and applied it to one of the fuel-filled holes. An enormous explosion followed. The occupants of the engine shop were unaware of this exercise and left the

building after feeling the concrete floor shake beneath their feet, and probably wondering what it measured on the Richter scale. As for the rats, they were no longer evident. (I might add that none of these frivolous pranks interfered with the main objective of motor racing.)

During this period I enjoyed the occasional cigarette. RM was a heavy smoker who enjoyed Players, and had been described as "a cigarette smoker who only bought matches," often asking anyone who did smoke, including myself, "Have you got a cigarette, my lad?" his request invariably meeting with success. It was getting quite expensive and also annoying to see him discard them half-smoked, but it was very difficult to refuse him. So, like Baldrick of *Blackadder* fame, I had a cunning plan. The next time he approached me and asked for a cigarette I said, "Yes, certainly," offering him a cheaper Woodbine, which had the desired effect. He said "Oh my God, I couldn't smoke those" and so tried elsewhere.

Towards the end of March the two cars due to race at Goodwood were rebuilt and on Good Friday, 3rd April we travelled down to the Sussex circuit, making our traditional call for refreshment at the pub in the delightful little village of Singleton at the foot of the Goodwood Downs. From Singleton village the narrow road took us over the South Downs past the famous horse racing track and on to Goodwood House, home of the Duke of Richmond and Gordon, before finally reaching the old airfield motor racing circuit. Story has it that, before the days of modern communications, the bookies at the horse racing track would send tic-tac messages down to a man at the telephone box in Singleton, from where information would be relayed to London.

The motor racing circuit was another redundant wartime airfield built, I believe, as an emergency satellite landing field for RAF Tangmere. Saturday practice saw Ken Wharton gain pole position with Reg Parnell fourth in our cars. The first race, the Chichester Cup, was run on a very wet track. This did not suit the BRMs; with so much power and a light fuel load for a 5-lap sprint race, wheel spin was inevitable, Ken finishing second and Reg fourth. The track had dried for the start of the later race, the

Glover Trophy, thus allowing better tyre grip. Ken won at record speed but Reg retired.

On 23rd May one car raced at Charterhall driven by Ken Wharton. This event was something of a nuisance to the mechanics as the following week we were due to race once more at Albi. Even more disappointing we were beaten into third place again by two pre-war, Bourne-built ERAs driven by Ron Flockhart and Bob Gerard. After a hasty drive back from Scotland the car was quickly prepared to join the other two ready for departure to Dover.

As this was to be the first overseas venture under the Rubery Owen banner, all personnel were again required to sign a document acknowledging they were ambassadors for Britain, and bound to be of good behaviour under penalty of dismissal. The convoy of the Commer workshop vehicle, this year driven by Jack Heward, together with the three Austin transporters, always looked very impressive. Maurice, Cyril and I again crewed one of the Austin Lodestars. The week following our departure HRH Princess Elizabeth became Queen and many flags and decorations were already in place along our route in anticipation of the Coronation celebrations, making us feel very proud to be British and recently designated an unofficial ambassador for Britain! Crossing to Dunkerque on the ferry we travelled via Paris for an overnight stop south of Orleans. During a refreshment

Alberto Ascari in the 4½-litre works Ferrari at Albi. Compared to modern-day steering wheels the Ferrari version looks enormous.

break near Paris a small, weather-beaten little man in riding breeches was strolling round our vehicles with an inquisitive look on his face. I jokingly said to Cyril "There's Gordon Richards" (the top English jockey of that period). To our surprise the little fellow came over to us and said in a strong cockney dialect "Wot you got in there, mate? Horses?" It turned out he *was* a British stablehand working at Chantilly.

British registered cars were very few on the Continent in those days, giving rise to a flash of headlights, friendly wave and 'hail-fellow well-met' response whenever one was encountered on the roads. On Wednesday evening we arrived at our destination to be warmly welcomed for a second time by the good citizens of Albi, Raymond Mays once again travelling in his Bentley with the inevitable male companion.

Juan Fangio looking most composed and ready to practice for the Albi Grand Prix.

Race opposition included a works-entered Ferrari for reigning world champion Alberto Ascari, and Guiseppe Farina driving Tony Vandervell's Thin Wall Special. The race was to consist of a 10 lap heat followed by an 18 lap final, the finishing order in the first heat determining grid positions for the final. Practice, by BRM standards, was fairly uneventful mechanically although Gonzales had a tyre throw a tread which caused some concern. Juan Fangio took pole position with Alberto Ascari alongside, Froilan Gonzales third, and Ken Wharton fourth. Despite our good grid positions it was still necessary to work long into the night. Fangio complained of a misfiring engine, diagnosed as sticking valves, which required removal and replacement of the cylinder heads, a time-consuming task. Raymond Mays gave us a little pep talk, saying that our backs were to the wall, to which Cyril was heard to murmur "Safest bloody place, mate"!

Completion of the first lap brought a thrilling sight to the BRM team and its supporters with Fangio leading from Ascari. Within three laps of the start of heat one, both Ascari and Farina had succumbed to the furious pace, leaving Fangio to lead and win the heat with Wharton taking second. Gonzales, unfortunately, had a second tyre throw its tread. Maurice Dove and I were the nominated wheel-changing crew as only two people were allowed to work on a car at any one time during a pit stop. With the replacement wheel successfully fitted, we attempted to push-

A vivid memory remains. Juan Fangio's BRM leads Ascari's Ferrari at the end of the first lap at Albi. Watching from the pits are me, Maurice Dove, Peter Berthon and Tony Rudd.

Tony Rudd with stopwatch discusses progress with Ken 'Flojo' Williamson and myself.

start the car; no electric starter motors fitted then. On the slight gradient at the pit exit we were having difficulty gaining momentum. Realising the situation, Gonzales jumped out of the car and helped to push, on achieving sufficient speed he jumped back in and the car restarted. Had we realised that some of the rubber fragments from the failed tyre had penetrated between the brake calliper and the disc, then rotating the wheel backwards before trying to push-start it would almost certainly have removed the offending rubber.

For the final, Fangio and Wharton shared the front row of the grid, with Gonzales on row three. At the end of lap one Fangio and Wharton came through in first and second with Gonzales quickly making up ground, BRMs in first, second and third places. What a glorious and thrilling sight for the men of Bourne! Our joy was shortlived, however, because on lap eight it was the turn of Wharton's car this time to throw a nearside rear tread. Better prepared now, Maurice and I changed the wheel, after which Gordon Newman and Cyril Bryden replaced us to push-start the car – in that way we were still within the rules of only two men at a time working on a car. Barely had Wharton gone on his way when Fangio came in with the same problem, but this time the

flailing tyre tread had damaged the brake system, causing him to retire. Gonzales was now leading the race, only for the tyre gremlins to strike yet again. A new tyre fitted, Gonzalez set about trying to overhaul leader Louis Rosier in his privately-entered blue Ferrari.

Meanwhile, Ken Wharton had gone missing! Tom Cole, a fellow driver and member of the Echo radio family (E K Cole), reported seeing the debris of the crashed car and was of the opinion that Ken would be lucky to have survived. Fortunately, he was wrong. By something of a miracle, Ken had been thrown from the car and landed in a ditch, the car then hit a stone wall and was completely destroyed. Ken unbelievably suffered only minor injuries and was detained in hospital for two nights.

Gonzales, in the meantime, was still pursuing Louis Rosier but in vain, the Frenchman going on to claim a popular victory on his home ground. After investigations and deliberations it was concluded that Wharton's accident was due to driver error; possibly Ken had been trying too hard after being led by Fangio

Juan Fangio receives the chequered flag to win heat 1 of the Albi Grand Prix.

Below left: The start of BRM's tyre troubles as Froilan Gonzales arrives at the pits with a stripped tread.

Below: Maurice Dove and I replace the rear wheel watched by Tony Rudd and a concerned Vic Barlow, the Dunlop tyre representative (in blazer).

The wreck of Ken Wharton's BRM following his terrible crash at Albi. Ken was fortunate to suffer only minor injuries after being thrown clear into a ditch.

earlier in the race. After recovering the wrecked car and loading our vehicles ready for a morning departure, we were invited to Fangio's hotel where he was putting on a little celebration. On arrival we found Fangio standing by a table laden with ready-filled glasses of various spirits, and a good time was had by most, Ken Wharton being the exception. Despite failing to secure the overall victory we had hoped for, our result ranked as the best performance by the BRM cars to date. The engineering status of BRM had been enhanced although, sadly, the extremely hot weather and power of the BRMs had proved too much for the tyres. So we left Albi, a town we had enjoyed visiting and where we had been made so welcome, never to race on the circuit again. As far as I am aware, the lap record is still held by Fangio's BRM.

Despite his horrific accident, Ken was only briefly detained in hospital. Three weeks later he was back driving a Frazer Nash at the British Empire Trophy sports car meeting on the Isle of Man. The wrecked BRM was returned to Folkingham where any serviceable parts, of which there were few, were salvaged, inspected and crack tested for future use.

On Monday morning we departed on our journey back through France making an overnight stop at Vatan, a small town south of Orleans. Arriving there late it was not easy to find accommodation for twelve people and we had to settle for quite grotty hotels, hunting for cockroaches in our bedrooms. The next matter on our mind that evening was food. Although late, we succeeded in finding a restaurant which was still open, but what the kitchens were like is perhaps something we did not want to know. What arrived at our table was a type of sausage which Cyril was the first to attack. After he had sliced it he quickly withdrew, saying "Phew, I've smelt better bloody sewers," a statement which put everyone off with the exception of Bagwash, who would eat anything. The remainder of us survived on chips! The following morning we departed with Tony Rudd, intent on having lunch in Paris where we witnessed throngs of people watching the Coronation of our Queen on television sets in shop windows. Once back across the English Channel many celebrations were taking place, Cyril occasionally joining in by opening the window of the transporter to give his rendering of *God Save the Queen* as we passed through London, much to the amusement of the citizens en route.

Raymond Mays had been persuaded to send a V16 car to the Isle of Man to make a demonstration run round the TT circuit during the British Empire Trophy meeting on 18th June. The personnel chosen to go were Tony Rudd, Maurice Dove and myself. We were delighted and imagined it was going to be a picnic after Albi: no all-night sessions, no pre-race checks, no pit panics. Oh what joy! However, things have a nasty habit of turning out somewhat differently to what's anticipated … On 15th June we drove the Austin transporter on an uneventful journey to Liverpool where we stayed overnight in a rather dingy hotel. The following morning, arriving at the ferry terminal we were told the crossing was going to be calm, but the interpretation of calm weather differed slightly between the forecasters and the three non-mariners from Bourne. The sight of Douglas, with our breakfasts intact, was greeted with relief and gratitude that the TT race was not held during the severe weather of the winter months.

Reg Parnell had been nominated by the race organisers to drive the car. He was also to drive an Aston Martin DB2 sports car, an official entry by the manufacturer, in the main race. The BRM ran trouble-free during a 6 lap practice run. Reg was happy, we were happy, what a gay day! However, the Aston Martin suffered problems with the transmission drive during official practice. Unless new parts could be obtained urgently the car would have to be withdrawn so new parts were to be flown out from the Aston Martin factory. BRM shared the same garage as the Aston Martin team and, as we had put our car to bed, an early night beckoned. The parts for the Aston were due to arrive somewhere around midnight. It was not usual for racing mechanics to work late into the night, unless they were the BRM boys, of course, who did all-night stints, a tradition we were determined to maintain! Forfeiting our early night we set to work and assisted the Aston Martin lads to rebuild the car – such was the camaraderie between motor racing people in those days. The Aston was repaired in time and Reg duly went on to win the Tourist Trophy. Although our 'picnic dream' had been partly shattered, everyone was delighted.

The BRM crew, along with Reg Parnell, were staying at The Queen's Hotel on the seafront at Douglas. However, the celebrations were to be held at The Majestic Hotel at the other end of the promenade. We were invited to attend and decided to make the journey there by the famous horsedrawn tram which ran along the seafront. During the journey Reg, sitting at the rear of the tram, gradually applied the brake. This adjustment did not please either the horse or driver, particularly the horse, the clip clop gradually getting slower and slower until the driver walked casually to the rear and, without uttering a word, released the brake – something he had done many times before, I suspect. Ken Wharton was staying at the Majestic and during the evening Reg had somehow obtained Ken's room number. Now Ken was not the happiest man on the island as he had wanted to drive the BRM, being at that time one of the regular works drivers

but, after some deliberation, to Ken's disgust, the race organisers had insisted on Reg being at the wheel. Cordiality was probably not enhanced when Reg booked a number of drinks to Ken's room number. How that little problem was resolved I do not know but I imagine Ken was not best pleased.

Back at the Queens I woke in the morning to find the bed damp. Being mid-June, bedroom windows had been left fully open but during the night the sea had blown up very rough and spray was blowing across the promenade and through the window, with bedclothes and personal belongings getting wet. This weather did not augur well for the return passage later that day, but it had to be faced. Our fears were realised and Tony Rudd spent the entire crossing on a bunk in the cabin of a ship's officer. For my part, I was in the company of the Ferodo brake representative who advised me that the best thing to combat seasickness was brandy, and would I care to indulge with him? Not one to disregard such sound advice, I gave it a whirl. To this day I am not sure if it was good advice or not. All I know is I was not sick, the brandy was very pleasant, and we eventually arrived at Liverpool rosy-cheeked and happy.

Reg Parnell was delighted that he had won the previous day's race and invited us to take tea with him at his farmhouse near Derby on our return journey to Bourne. Ham salad, followed by strawberries and cream: delicious!

"It's aye soor milk when they B.R.M.s ur stoorin' round Charterha'!"

"Fangio, B.R.M. * * * * !!!"

After tea we were taken on a conducted tour of his farm, which had been left in the hands of his son Tim whilst Dad was away. It was a responsibility which apparently had not been undertaken to Reg's satisfaction and Tim received a bit of a rocket for spending too much money on animal feeds. The farm was largely for the breeding and rearing of pigs, which may have accounted for the ham! During the tour Reg offered to give us an eight-week-old pig as a reward for our efforts back on the island. We gladly accepted his offer, giving little consideration to what we would do with the wretched thing back at Folkingham. In fact, the pig did initially protest about leaving Derby, but we persuaded him it was really for the best and he could become something of a celebrity if he stuck with us.

Transporting a live pig from Derby to Bourne was a new experience to us all. We just did not race pigs although, some years previously, I had mischievously told colleagues that I was going to watch some pig races the following weekend, an idea which backfired slightly when a number of people began to show an interest in coming, too, and requested directions and details. In order to escape a lynching the fictitious racecourse on which the racing was to take place was deemed unfit for use.

Deliberations ensued over how we should solve our problem. We liked the wee creature and he seemed to be getting quite fond of us. We could not leave him loose in the back of the vehicle; he would not have enjoyed being in there alone with a racing car and, no doubt, the car would also have felt it a bit degrading. Reg was most helpful by saying "Surely you can manage a little bloody pig, after all you have 500 horses under that bonnet in the back." To resolve the problem the pig was put in a hessian sack with its head protruding out of the top to enable it to breathe. It was my turn to drive. Tony sat in the centre and Maurice took charge of our extra passenger, which he placed on the cab floor by his feet. Unfortunately for the pig, the exhaust system ran underneath the foot well causing it to get rather hot. Now you must appreciate that the pig was only in a thin sack and, unlike Maurice, had no shoes on. Had we proceeded like this there was the distinct possibility that we would be stopping in a lay-by to have a hog roast. As we had already enjoyed a good tea

we decided against this, Maurice deciding to nurse the bag with the pig inside and hold its head out of the side window to get some fresh air, much to our amusement and, even more so, the astonishment of passers-by. Although the laughter coming from within the vehicle at the predicament of the poor creature was very distracting for me, the driver, the reaction of fellow motorists and pedestrians while passing through Derby, Nottingham and Grantham was hilarious. I recall being stationary at traffic lights when a couple out for a stroll appeared to be looking at the BRM logo on the side of the vehicle, when suddenly the man's eyes were diverted. Although I am unable to lip read I feel sure he casually remarked to his lady companion "Oh look at that sweet little pig." Realising that it was not an everyday occurrence to see such a face peering out of a vehicle window, he stared in disbelief before both he and his companion roared with laughter and passed some comment about ugly mechanics. Similar reactions were encountered on numerous occasions on our journey and I swear I once saw the pig laugh!

The poor creature eventually arrived safely at our Folkingham base where we housed him in one of the derelict buildings on the airfield near to where our workshops were situated. Maurice and I fed and watered the animal for some weeks with the assistance of the animal-loving Jock. He had a varied menu which included greenstuffs, old sandwiches, and occasionally orthodox pig food! During the period of his stay we often worked a night shift and on the far side of the airfield we had discovered a field of kale. If we were there we would take a van and collect a stick or two of the kale which supplemented the pig's diet. He was also very partial to Riley's Caramel Toffees and would sniff round to see if I had any in my pocket, giving me a gentle nudge if he thought he was onto a winner. He also loved having his back groomed gently with a wire brush. Alas, he was like Topsy who grew and grew until, sadly, he went the way of most pigs and was eventually loaded into a BRM van and taken to Bourne cattle market to be purchased by a local butcher. I suppose in a funny sort of way he had been lucky. As a pig his life had been unique; how many other pigs had been fortunate enough to see the streets and sights of Derby, Nottingham and Grantham from such a lofty

grandstand seat? He had been admired and, yes, even cheered as he passed along those streets, had watched as racing cars were tested and had been a friend to all. I have little doubt the end product tasted a little bit superior as a result!

Our next event was a Formule Libre race at Silverstone on 18th July following the British Grand Prix. Two BRMs were entered for Juan Fangio and Ken Wharton. A good practice session resulted in Fangio fastest with Wharton third and the Thin Wall Special of Giuseppe Farina second. All was not well, however, with Fangio complaining of power loss. Back in the garage at Brackley the decision was made to remove the cylinder heads to resolve what seemed to be a recurring sticking valve problem. The team was now well organised in this operation, albeit it meant another all-night session, and under normal circumstances the car would be ready in good time. Unfortunately, one of the cylinder heads was negligently re-fitted with two sealing rings, resulting in a massive coolant leak which left us with no option but to remove

the problem head again. This resulted in a tremendous race against time to reassemble the engine. With little time left before we were due on the starting grid, the rebuild was complete. To save time and also to prove the car, RM decided to drive it along the A43 from Brackley to Silverstone, a task he glorified in, the police graciously turning a blind eye. Following in a car, I can recall seeing a herd of cattle stampeding away from the road, scared by the tremendous roar of the BRM.

Disappointingly, although victory eluded us, our overnight efforts were not entirely in vain as Fangio finished second to Farina with Wharton third. Farina achieved the first 100mph (162kph) lap of Silverstone in his pursuit of victory. Who was at fault for the sealing ring mistake was never established, but most fingers pointed to the same man …

On 25th July one car was entered in two races of 15 and 10 laps respectively at the Snetterton circuit in Norfolk, which had been an American Air Force base equipped with B-17

Opposite: Ken Wharton explains to Raymond Mays how he won the USAF Trophy at Snetterton.

Ken Wharton seated in the V16 BRM at Charterhall, Scotland. With Maurice Dove, Arthur Hill, me and Raymond Mays at rear, RM's Continental Bentley alongside, and Austin Lodestar transporter in rear.

Flying Fortress bombers during the war. Ken Wharton had been selected to drive, but entries were few and of a poor standard, leaving him to win both races easily.

Following that simple exercise was another trip to Scotland for a meeting at Charterhall on 15th August where two cars were entered in a 100 mile race to be driven by Ken Wharton and Reg Parnell. Unfortunately, Reg had a brake lock in practice and crashed his car, causing sufficient damage to necessitate its withdrawal. Ken made amends by winning the race on the following day.

There was now a five week break until the next meeting at Goodwood on 26th September. However, a new V16 car was being built at Folkingham and so work was plentiful. This was to be a sprint version with a lighter chassis to compete in the short Formule Libre races of 1954. Coinciding with this project, work continued on the development of the new 2.5-litre engine to meet the requirements of the new Formula 1 specification.

Although Folkingham airfield was a rather isolated place, due to our captivating occupation we frequently received unexpected visitors – not least members of the Lincolnshire Constabulary who seemed to find numerous excuses to pay us a visit. Even so, it was something of a surprise one day to receive an unscheduled visit by a member of the Royal Canadian Air Force who had made a forced landing in a Sabre Jet Fighter plane from the base at North Luffenham, some twenty miles distant. The pilot telephoned his HQ and a ground crew came out and, in Willie's words "Gave the old thing a little tweak" and it was hopefully airworthy once more. Willie became quite excited and fascinated by this turn of events and very soon got himself involved. Jumping into the Standard Vanguard he escorted the pilot back to the main runway, the plane now ready for take-off. He was advised to keep clear of the rear of the aircraft due to the blast from the jet engine but alas, the advice fell on deaf ears. Typical of Willie he seemed reluctant to see the Sabre depart and followed it along the runway, resulting in the van looking as if it had been shot blasted!

Two cars were taken to Goodwood for Fangio and Wharton,

where again two sprint races were to be contested. The Woodcote Cup was easily won by Mike Hawthorn in the Thin Wall Special with Fangio second and Wharton third after spinning at the chicane. Mike was having a good day and went on to win the second race, the Goodwood Trophy, after Fangio retired with gear selection problems. Ken finished second.

One week later was our final race of the season at the little airfield circuit near the lovely Wiltshire village of Castle Combe. Ken Wharton started from pole position and won with ease from Bob Gerard's ERA; revenge for Charterhall earlier in the year. Taking part again that weekend was the young Scottish driver, Ron Flockhart, in his ex-Raymond Mays ERA. RM liked what he saw and also thought he was quite a good driver. Following that event he persuaded Alfred Owen to sign him as a BRM team driver for 1954. It was a weekend of much fun, staying in Chippenham at the Bear Hotel, with the cars in Garnsey's garage. Also at the same garage was a privately-entered Maserati driven by a happy-go-lucky – but very slow – D G Ross. Were he to win we would have been looking for pigs flying over Chippenham! As usual there were many autograph hunters, D G Ross signing as Stirling Ross, whilst I signed as Peter Out. Post-race, a wonderful party was given by the Garnsey family where D G Ross, a versatile individual, seemed to be in charge of dispensing drinks. Should one be drinking gin he would ask what you would like added and, before receiving a reply would say "I know, more gin." It was one of those sorts of party!

So, another racing season came to an end. On reflection, it had been only moderately successful and we looked forward and hoped for a better future. However, there was still much work to be done. The new lightweight version of the V16 car was completed and successfully tested at both Folkingham and Goodwood. One of the old V16s was on its way to New Zealand in the care of Willie Southcott and Gordon Newman. Ken Wharton was to drive the car in the Grand Prix and would follow later. Gordon so liked the country he vowed to settle there eventually – a vow he later fulfilled.

THE ITALIAN JOB

When high performance counts

you can rely on

MINTEX
BRAKE LINERS

MINTEX brake and clutch linings are manufactured by British Belting & Asbestos Ltd. and are available from our stockists and at leading garages throughout the country.

January 1954 was a busy month with modifications and updates carried out on the new Mk II V16 sprint car. A second chassis was also being made, and parts cannibalised from the older cars were prepared in readiness for assembly – all to be completed ready for the Goodwood Easter meeting on 19th April. Preparations entailed many days' testing, not only proving the car, but also giving new driver Ron Flockhart, and retained driver Ken Wharton, valuable experience in the handling and setting up of the car.

The majority of this testing was done by Flockhart once Wharton had left for New Zealand, where success was not as good as had been expected, Ken finishing third in both the New Zealand Grand Prix at Ardmore and The Lady Wigram Trophy at Christchurch a month later, having initially taken pole position for both races.

At this time the Bourne works was working flat-out on the new 2.5-litre, 4-cylinder engine for the new Formula 1, and so a greater variety of work was being undertaken at Folkingham. It was during this period that I learned to be wary of the practice of certain individuals of wrongly directing blame. For instance, I was assisting Dave Turner re-assemble a V16 engine, where the usual practice was to segregate nuts, etc, taken from the various components during dismantling, thus ensuring they could all be accounted for on rebuild. On this occasion, Dave remarked that one of the camshaft nuts was missing, seeming to infer I must have dropped one. I certainly knew I was not guilty of this and, to my surprise, he quickly located the missing nut lodged precariously in the lower bowels of the engine, where it could have caused serious damage. Dave's attitude led me to believe he had dropped it and knew all along where it was. Fortunately, the nut was safely retrieved but thereafter I was cautious in the extreme.

The second Mk II car was not ready in time for Goodwood, so a Mk I was taken to complete the two-car entry. Ken Wharton drove the new car in the Chichester Cup, starting from pole position and winning the race. Ron, making his debut race for BRM, drove the Mk I and finished fourth. For the Glover Trophy the two drivers changed cars, Ken again winning, this time in the Mk I with Ron again fourth with a misfiring engine.

On our return journey Willie was stopped for speeding. Spouting his usual 'flannel' with a friendly smile he quickly overcame the problem by opening the back doors of the Austin and showing the officers the BRM. Maurice who was driving the second transporter, with myself as passenger, stopped at the rear of Willie's vehicle and we watched the proceedings with amusement. One of the officers looked at Maurice and remarked "You shouldn't laugh, you know, you're next, you have no tax disc." Unbeknown to us the disc had fallen off, but the observant officer had quickly spotted it.

On 24th April Ron Flockhart won his first race in a BRM, driving the Mk II and beating a poor field from pole position in a 10 lap event at Snetterton. A hasty overhaul of the original Mk II and we were off to Ibsley, another airfield circuit near Ringwood in Hampshire. Whilst travelling down with Tony Rudd and Arthur Hill on Thursday 6th May for the race on the 8th, we were listening to the commentary on the radio of Roger Bannister making history by breaking the four-minute mile during an athletics meeting at nearby Oxford.

The best cars opposing us at Ibsley were a pair of C Type Jaguars – we were really in the big time now! Ron Flockhart took pole position and won the race. Had he not done so we would probably have lain low for a while and left under cover of darkness!

The second Mk II car was now complete and ready to attend the new motor racing circuit built around the Grand National horse racing course at Aintree. The circuit ran in an anti-clockwise direction, as opposed to the one taken by the horses, with the exception, that is, of the ones I bet on: God knows which way they went!

One BRM was taken to Aintree on 19th May to take part in the opening ceremony the next day, at the invitation of owner Mrs Mirabel Topham. Ten days later on 29th May the first motor race

meeting was held there, Ken Wharton and Ron Flockhart driving the BRMs. The race, the Aintree 200, was to consist of two 50 mile heats and a 100 mile final. In pouring rain Ken came fourth in heat 1, making the race debut of the second sprint car. In drying conditions Ron won heat 2. The final was not a great success for BRM as a rather disillusioned Ken Wharton retired with faulty brakes,

Ron Flockhart lines up in pole position in the Mk II V16 BRM for the Glover Trophy at Goodwood. He could manage fourth place only with a misfiring engine.

whereas Ron Flockhart lost considerable time due to performing his habitual spin, though still managing third place.

To keep Ken Wharton happy, maintain contact with supporters and ensure the Owen Racing Organisation's flag kept flying in Formula 1 prior to the new 2.5-litre BRM being ready, Alfred Owen had been persuaded – mainly by Ken Wharton – to purchase a new Maserati 250F from the factory at Modena in Italy. After much delay Raymond Mays was advised the car was ready for testing on the Modena Autodrome and, at the end of May, the car was test driven there and approved by Ron

Flockhart. Arthur Hill, who had graduated from the same garage as I prior to his military career, was nominated as its mechanic, to be assisted by one other at each event. Though the Maserati 250Fs were proving quite competitive in races, the cosmetic standard of engineering was considered inferior to that of the BRMs. For example, where Maserati used a rather ugly-looking plain nut and common spring washer, BRM used a neat-looking self-locking nut like those in aircraft construction. Cleanliness was also of a higher standard on the BRMs. Despite their lack of success, opposing teams – and the public in general – invariably complimented the BRM team on its standard of workmanship; even so, it was Maserati that was winning races …

The next meeting for the V16 was on 5th June when two cars would run in the Whitsun Trophy at Goodwood. Ron Flockhart finished second to the Thin Wall Special driven by Peter Collins, and Ken Wharton came fourth, a full minute behind the winner. Ken now seemed to be forever finding fault and gave the impression of increasing disillusionment by being so often out-driven by his younger colleague.

Whilst the V16s were still to run in minor Formule Libre events around the country to keep the BRM name in the public eye, the main objective was to build the new Formula 1 car. This was consuming everyone's time at Folkingham with the exception of Arthur Hill who was preparing the Owen Maserati, now painted in BRM's particular shade of dark green ready to compete in the French Grand Prix at Reims on 4th July. Accompanying Arthur Hill were Tony Rudd and Maurice Dove. It is worth noting that, in 1954, in contrast to the 200 mile Grand Prix of today, all World Championship Grands Prix were run over three hundred miles, or three hours, whichever was the shorter.

The Maserati's performance was little short of disaster: the car suffered massive vibration due to propshaft misalignment, which resulted in a different type of vibration between Bourne and the Maserati factory! Ken qualified a dismal 16th, which put him on row seven of the grid, and he retired midway through the race due to the vibration, having been anything up to 10 seconds a lap slower than race winner Fangio in the new Mercedes-Benz W196 'streamliner.' After the dust had settled it was agreed that a Maserati works mechanic would come to Folkingham and attempt to rectify the car's shortcomings.

If the French Grand prix had been a near disaster, that was as nothing compared to the Maserati's next outing at the British Grand Prix at Silverstone on 17th July. On a wet track Ken Wharton could not compete with the flying Mercedes and Ferraris, lapping some 12 seconds slower than Fangio. Prince Bira, a friend of both Raymond Mays and Tony Rudd, had entered his own blue-painted Maserati 250F but was feeling unwell and so, on the recommendation of RM, Ron Flockhart was nominated as his reserve driver. Ken had qualified 9th on the grid, with Bira alongside and, after a lengthy pit stop with a misfiring problem, he went on to finish 8th, four laps behind the winning Froilan Gonzales in a Ferrari. Meanwhile, Bira had pulled into the pits feeling quite ill and handed over his car to Flockhart. On a still damp track Flockhart – hoping to impress and probably trying too hard – lost control at Copse Corner, overturning and severely damaging the car. Fortunately, Ron escaped serious injury.

I think the shock of what had happened to his car partially cured Bira's illness; he was furious and, as the damage had been caused with a BRM driver at the wheel, he insisted BRM repair it. To pacify Bira – and probably unknown to Alfred Owen – his car was exchanged for the Owen Maserati. Thus, at least Bira was happy and, as was eventually proved, got the better of the bargain. The car now in BRM's possession was to be repaired and run by us. Due to the propshaft vibration problem encountered at Reims which was still evident, it had been decided to make a replacement propshaft at Bourne to our own high standard. This was completed and would be ready for fitting after the Silverstone meeting. Unfortunately, when it came to this, the shaft was too long and a mini panic ensued because no-one had realised that the Bira car was the earlier, slightly shorter wheelbase version. To rectify the problem the engine was moved forward to accommodate the propshaft. In addition, the car was fitted with Dunlop disc brakes in place of the original drums, and Dunlop light alloy wheels to replace the Pirelli wire wheels. An increasingly discontented Ken Wharton was not told of the short chassis problem, but would he notice the difference?

The next race for the Maserati was the Swiss Grand Prix at Berne on 22nd August. It was my turn to travel with Tony Rudd and Arthur Hill. and the journey and subsequent events proved interesting. We were at last using the faster channel crossing route from Dover to Calais; much more pleasant and less tiring than the slow overnight haul to Dunkerque of earlier days. After a rather ordinary journey across northern France we entered Switzerland after nightfall, with me driving. In the prevailing dark and gloomy weather I saw orange flashing lights ahead and approached at slow speed. Seeing no apparent reason for the lights, I imagined they merely signified 'proceed with caution,' probably for road works, and was about to accelerate past when an express train thundered across an unmanned level crossing, almost taking the nose of the Austin with it – a very frightening experience! But why had a safety-conscious nation not installed red lights or barriers? After visiting the nearest toilet we pressed on, this time with Tony driving.

As we neared our destination, I remarked that the road signs were marked Bienne. Tony, never lacking an answer, assured us that this was the continental spelling of Berne. So we arrived, enquiring from passersby for directions to our hotel. Our request caused looks of bewilderment; there was no hotel of that name in the town … After various gesticulations to try to convey to the locals that we were here to compete in the Swiss Grand Prix, the penny dropped. "Ah, you must go to Berne, this is Bienne, you must go another thirty kilometres." At about midnight we finally arrived at our hotel, with Tony frequently being reminded about his lack of navigational 'skills.'

The Bremgarten circuit was one of the most picturesque I had yet visited, set in a wooded area on theoutskirts of Berne. The circuit consisted of a seven kilometre conglomeration of fast curves, sharp bends, short straights and undulations, often on a cobbled surface, and a short section of it was normally the main road to Geneva. Once again Wharton and the Maserati could not compete with the Mercedes and Ferraris, achieving only a place on the third row of the grid. During official practice a local refreshment vendor decided to cross the track with a box of bottles and, in best Buster Keeton style, fell with his wares in the middle of the track. Miraculously – and luckily for him and everyone else – the bottles did not break. Although cars were running the mishap coincided with a relatively quiet period and no damage was done.

Practice completed, we made to return to our allocated garage. A gentleman was directing me as I reversed the transporter through the crowds, but his directions resulted in my hitting a car. Now, if you're going to damage a car why not pick a good one? Regrettably, I 'modified' a Super Porsche entered in the sports car race and owned by local restaurateur Walter Ringgenberg! He was understandably less than pleased and tried to enlist the help of Stirling Moss to have me cast in the dungeons. "You remember me, Mr Moss, please?" he asked. "Yes, I bloody well do," replied Stirling, "We had trouble with you last time we were here"! To what Stirling was referring I have no idea, but Ringgenberg's plea for help fell on deaf ears. During the argument a large man arrived and instructed me to get out of the vehicle, saying he was a police officer. I doubted this and, being reluctant to leave my seat, enquired why he was not in uniform, whereupon he turned back the lapel of his jacket to reveal a large sheriff-type badge, at the same time reaching across to remove the ignition key from the Austin. It was the local Chief of Police; not one of your "'ello, 'ello 'ello, what 'ave we here, then?" types, but the top man himself! I felt quite honoured to be escorted to the local 'nick' by such a high-ranking officer and, I must say, was treated very well whilst detained, even offered tea and biscuits. Eventually, Tony Rudd arrived and, between us, we managed to satisfactorily explain that it was an unfortunate accident. After producing valid insurance cover, we were allowed to go. Sadly, the same cannot be said for the unfortunate Walter Ringgenberg: not only had his pretty little Porsche been damaged but, apparently, he was later charged for failing to produce an

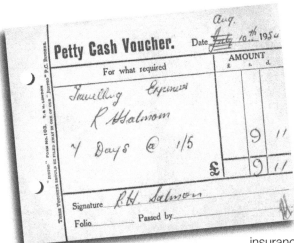

A serious-looking Juan Manuel Fangio with partner Donna Andreina.

insurance certificate!

In rather wet conditions the race was easily won by Fangio in the Mercedes, with Gonzales second in a Ferrari, both having lapped all the other cars. Ken had a confrontation with Sergio Mantovani's Maserati on lap four and eventually finished sixth, the best performance of the car to date. As far as we were aware, Ken had not realised that the car he had driven had the short wheelbase. The motorcycle Grand Prix was run on the same day and was won by Englishman Geoff Duke riding a works Gilera.

Sadly, we had just witnessed the last Formula 1 Grand Prix to be held in Switzerland. The Swiss government banned all circuit motor racing the next year following the disaster at Le Mans when eighty-five spectators died in an accident. The beautiful Bremgarten circuit was lost for ever …

On Monday 23rd August we commenced our journey back to England and, as it turned out, much to the displeasure of Alfred Owen and Ken Wharton. A late entry had been granted to run the Maserati in the Italian Grand Prix on 5th September. In view of this we were to be rerouted direct to Monza but, due to a typical cock-up in communications between Bourne and Berne – no mobile 'phones then – this information had not been conveyed to Tony Rudd. This was unfortunate because we would have had the assistance of the Maserati works personnel at their home event.

The Owen Maserati was still considered a secondary piece of equipment in some quarters and probably quite rightly so as the company's prime objective was to race BRMs. The V16s were still competing in Formule Libre events. On 14th August one car (a Mk II) was sent to Snetterton for Ron Flockhart to compete in a 40 lap race, once more to take on the Thin Wall Special driven by Peter Collins. Ron had a race he would wish to forget, running out of road on two occasions and being lapped by race winner Collins to finish a distant third.

Lincolnshire was the habitat for many country characters, one of whom was Reg James, the workshop cleaner at Folkingham. Reg was very proud of the giant onions he grew in his garden, bringing in to Folkingham a sample weighing some 2lb for all to view, exclaiming proudly "I growed 'em meself, growed 'em from seed." Of course, he immediately left himself open to a 'wind up,' in this case the 'winder' being Danny Woodward. Examining the onion, Danny remarked "Not bad, Reg, about the same size as some I thinned out," causing Reg to go off, chuntering something about a "clever bugger." Incidents such as this were frequent and added to the fun we had.

Castle Combe was the next venue for the V16, a race of only 27 miles. These

Peter Berthon and Raymond Mays pictured beside Lac Leman in Switzerland during their journey to Monza with the Ford Zephyr.

Raymond Mays with the Ford Zephyr on the Monza circuit. The car was driven to Italy on the pretext of a publicity and proving run for the Raymond Mays cylinder head conversion fitted to that car. Ken Wharton and others successfully raced a number of cars fitted with this conversion.

minor events were hindering progress on the build of the new Formula 1 car, the more so when, once again, the Mk II (which was raced for the remainder of the season) was beaten into second place by Bob Gerard's Cooper-Bristol. The main reason for attending these events was Alfred Owen's desire to keep the BRM name in the public eye, but not with the disappointing results we were achieving of late, I fear.

It was becoming increasingly apparent that BRM required the services of a gremlin catcher, for another ludicrous incident was about to overtake us. Following Castle Combe, one car was entered in a 40 mile race at Charterhall on 4th September to be driven by Ron Flockhart. If it had been a 400 yard race he might possibly have won but, after starting from pole position and only yards from the starting grid, a stone jammed the carburettor mechanism and Ron was forced to retire. If variety was the spice of life we had it in abundance!

Back to Goodwood for the traditional autumn meeting on 25th September, where two of the Mk II V16s were entered for Ken Wharton and Ron Flockhart to contest the Formule Libre race, once more competing against our old adversary, the Thin Wall Special driven by Peter Collins. Again, we were unable to overcome that rival, Wharton having to be content with second once more. Ron continued with his (increasing) habit of not completing a race, on this occasion running out of road on the first lap to retire with damaged front suspension. Travelling to the circuit one day from Bognor Regis during this meeting Raymond Mays became quite agitated when, negotiating a roundabout near Chichester, he attempted a manoeuvre of which a young fellow motorist did not approve. RM equally disapproved when the motorist concerned opened his window and advised him to "Take a bloody driving test," eliciting the response "How dare anyone criticise my driving; does he realise who I am?"

The final meeting of the 1954 season for the V16s was a 50 mile race at Aintree on 2nd October where two cars were entered, again to be driven by Ken and Ron. A good practice saw both cars sharing the four-car front row of the grid with the Thin Wall Special of Collins, and Moss in a Maserati 250F. In the race Wharton collided with Schell when duelling for third place

and was forced to retire whilst Flockhart improved on his recent performances by finishing third.

And so another season ended for the V16s though not quite for the racing team as the Maserati was entered in the Spanish Grand Prix at Barcelona on 24th October. Ken did not perform well in practice, managing only a dismal fourteenth place on the grid. He daily became more and more disillusioned, exacerbated further when, during the meeting, he learned about the original Maserati chassis being exchanged for the short wheelbase one after the Silverstone crash. He showed little enthusiasm in the race, finishing a distant eighth. I imagine his pride had taken a knock when he realised he should have recognised the different handling characteristics of the two Maseratis.

Although Ken anticipated driving for BRM in 1955, the Spanish Grand Prix was his last race for the team. He had been a good servant and had carried out some valuable test driving, but increasingly he seemed at loggerheads with some members of the management, and was apparently negotiating with both Vanwall and BRM for a drive in 1955. Eventually, whether by choice or circumstance, he signed to drive the new Vanwall.

Towards the end of 1954 improvements were made to the facilities at Folkingham with the erection of a new body and chassis shop. An agricultural-type building was supplied and erected by Salopian of Shrewsbury, one of the Rubery Owen group of companies. This allowed Stan Hope and all his merry men to work under the same roof, at the same time enabling the Folkingham stores to be enlarged by moving it into the old panel shop. All Folkingham personnel were involved in introducing the changes, and moving equipment, making workbenches and installing airlines made for a very busy winter, particularly as work was also proceeding apace with the new formula cars.

FAREWELL THE V16

For 1955 Peter Collins replaced Ken Wharton as No 1 driver, with Ron Flockhart retained as both No 2 and test driver. Activity at Folkingham was intense. Minor modifications were still being introduced for Collins on the BRM Mk II V16 and the Maserati was also undergoing modifications and updates, but the majority of working hours – of which there were many – were spent constructing the new Formula 1 car.

On the night of 15th February, 1955, Peter Berthon was badly injured in a car accident. Returning from London with his secretary, he lost control of his Ford Zephyr on the A1 near Stilton, and came off second best after coming face-to-face with a tree. He suffered a broken jaw and injuries to his chest and both he and his passenger were admitted to hospital in Peterborough. His problems were further compounded when wife Lorna, visiting him in hospital, learned that his secretary had been travelling with him that night in the direction of Folkingham, and was a patient in a neighbouring ward. I fancy the fact that he had a fractured jaw, now wired up which made talking difficult, may have ironically worked in his favour. It may also have temporarily affected his hearing …

Too many valuable working hours were being spent on the V16s and the Maserati, hours which, in the opinion of most of the staff, could have been better spent on construction of the new cars. It did, however, go some way towards keeping Peter Collins happy, together with the British public, which was still loyal to the BRM despite so many failures. Peter Collins spent time testing both cars at Folkingham and, with all due respect to Ken and Ron, it was obvious we had gone up a grade in driver ability. Unfortunately, Peter Berthon's recovery was taking longer than anticipated and, due to the damage caused to his chest and lungs, he had now contracted pneumonia.

The opening event of the 1955 season for the Mk II was the Easter meeting at Goodwood. First up was the Chichester Cup where Peter Collins started from pole position and went on to win the race. The second race was – unusually for the 1950s –

Gordon Newman – 'Bagwash' – in one of his favourite situations, and enjoying two of his favourite pastimes: playing bar billiards and drinking, this time at the Griffin Inn at Irnham.

a handicap event. Starting from scratch, the handicap imposed by the officials was far too great to overcome in a race of five laps, a distance of only twelve miles. In achieving a fifth place finish we considered Collins had done remarkably well.

At last the build of the first chassis for the new Formula 1 car was nearing completion – it had wheels and gearbox fitted and was awaiting a power unit. Development of the engine had proved more time-consuming than anticipated, resulting in many long days and nights at Folkingham. Phil Ayliff, who had recently completed his RAF service, had joined Willie in the test house. Phil was the son of Harold Ayliff, a pre-war ERA mechanic with Raymond Mays. With introduction of the new car imminent, a frequent visitor to Folkingham was A F Rivers-Fletcher. 'Rivers,' as he was more usually known, was the Public Relations Officer for the Owen Racing Organisation and spent many hours filming our activities and happenings at race meetings. He was a charming and dapper man who had raced various cars pre-war, one such being his famous Alvis.

Although not technically minded, RM was taking a more active part in the proceedings due to PB's long absence. Lack of his technical knowledge was highlighted on one occasion when he reputedly enquired why an engine sitting on the test bed was not running. On being told it was awaiting a camshaft, he replied, "Bugger the camshaft, let's get the engine running"!

P25 chassis under construction in the fabrication shop at Folkingham.

A pre-fabricated front cross member for a P25 chassis being fettled after assembly and welding.

The prototype P25 BRM built for the 2½-litre formula on display at Folkingham airfield.

Rear view of P25 BRM, showing the massive exhaust necessary to cope with the large bore 4-cylinder engine and the sweeping lines of the original tail cowling.

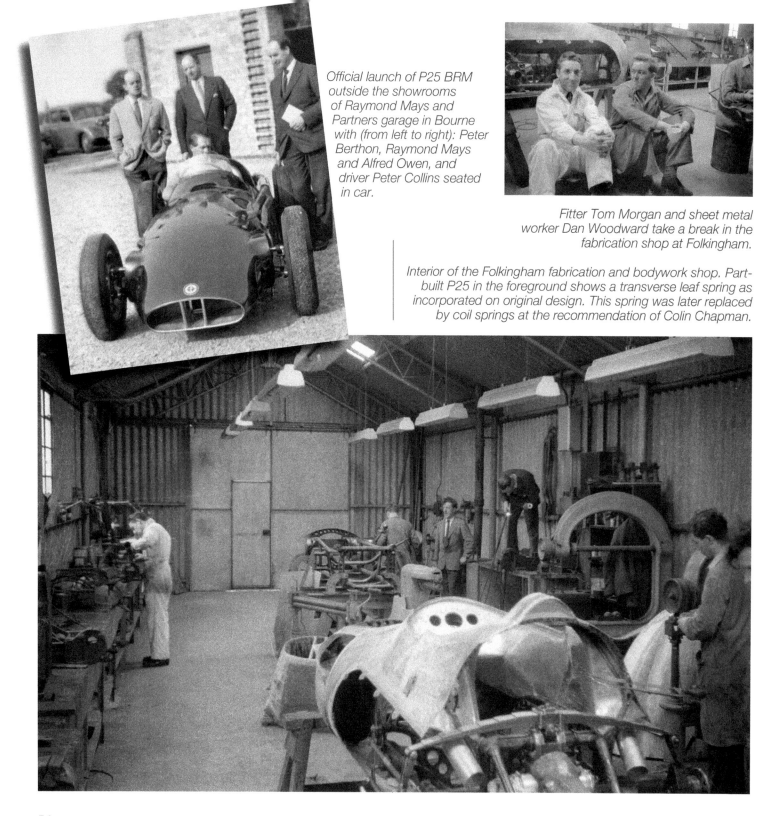

Official launch of P25 BRM outside the showrooms of Raymond Mays and Partners garage in Bourne with (from left to right): Peter Berthon, Raymond Mays and Alfred Owen, and driver Peter Collins seated in car.

Fitter Tom Morgan and sheet metal worker Dan Woodward take a break in the fabrication shop at Folkingham.

Interior of the Folkingham fabrication and bodywork shop. Part-built P25 in the foreground shows a transverse leaf spring as incorporated on original design. This spring was later replaced by coil springs at the recommendation of Colin Chapman.

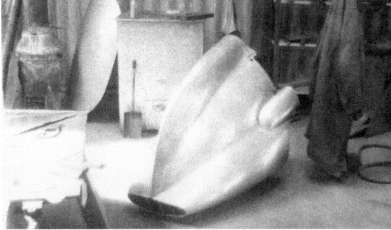

However, he was useful in progressing parts and one occasion comes vividly to mind. Dave Turner was grudgingly working late one Saturday evening when he required some items from the stores to complete an engine rebuild. RM told him to find the material controller, Clarrie Brinkley, and get him to come and open the stores and issue the required parts. Dave, although not a great buddy of 'Brinks,' knew where he was most likely to be on a Saturday evening, and that was in Arthur Ambrose's pub, The Golden Lion. Once found, 'Brinks' was told of RM's request whereupon – probably influenced by having indulged in a few beers, or maybe to impress his drinking friends – he suggested Dave tell RM what he could do (which would require that RM visit a taxidermist!). Dave, being the man he was, repeated these words verbatim, which was not the reply RM was expecting. Needless to say he was far from amused, describing 'Brinks' as "that odious man." Brinkley was subsequently suspended from work for one month, unbelievably on full pay, allowing him, a keen angler, to enjoy a month's fishing with no financial loss. I imagine if one could suffer the humiliation of such a penalty, it was a pleasant one to endure.

Exceptionally long hours were being worked at Folkingham, and the stress and pressure imposed on staff – combined with the resultant irregular eating habits – were becoming evident in a variety of ways. Men became irritable; faces looked tired and drawn. The most common ailments were stomach problems, including gastric ulcers, and they became a somewhat jocular topic of discussion. Meggeson or Rennies indigestion and dyspepsia tablets were in abundance, Willie and Bagwash in particular becoming somewhat addicted to these remedies. In the case of Bagwash, whilst he was supposedly gaining relief from this medication, a combination of the previous evening's intake of beer followed by the tablets appeared to exacerbate an already obvious flatulence problem. It was not unusual for someone to say "I shouldn't go down there, mate, Bagwash has just dropped one," the latter individual a lone figure by his workbench, wearing

Stanley Bernard Hope; master metal craftsman and would-be actor.

A newly completed tail cowling ready for painting for an early P25 BRM in the fabrication and bodywork shop at Folkingham. The coke-burning stove in background was the sole means of heating the workshop; hardly sufficient on the cold and bleak airfield during winter days.

a wry smile. Remarkably, he seemed able to fart at will, and it was not unknown for a fellow member of staff to approach him only to beat a hasty retreat! I recall the occasion when he and I had taken a BRM to display at Sutton Coldfield, walking down the street whilst he noisily emitted wind continuously for fifty yards, with people obviously wondering why we were both laughing. Why such a natural function causes so much amusement I do not know, but had there been such an event in the Olympic Games I feel sure he could have farted for England.

Bagwash objected to people looking over his shoulder whilst he was working and, to deter this, had another weapon in his armoury. Whilst oxyacetylene welding – at which he was adept – he would intentionally create a shower of sparks or a mini explosion to put off the unwanted spectator.

Following the winter overhaul and modifications, the Maserati was ready for its first event of the season and the first race for Peter Collins in the Italian-built car, the *Daily Express* International Trophy race at Silverstone on 7th May. Though managing only fifth fastest time in practice, this put Collins on the second row of the grid, the car sounding fantastic. Faced with two new Vanwalls driven by Hawthorn and Wharton, and the Maseratis of Moss, Salvadori and Fairman, Peter Collins drove an exceptional race to win by a margin of 35 seconds and, at the same time, record the first win for the Owen Maserati. What Ken Wharton's thoughts were at this result we can only guess. Whilst we were tremendously encouraged and delighted with this win, it was regarded by both Folkingham and Bourne staff as something of a hollow victory, far removed from a BRM win. a sentiment no doubt echoed by Alfred Owen.

Tony Rudd's workload, due to Peter Berthon's absence, was enormous, leaving him with overall responsibility for the

development of both engine and chassis. Answering numerous queries and solving the many day-to-day problems left him little time to enjoy recently-married life with Pam, daughter of the legendary Bourne dentist Roy Carvath. Life was hectic for him, to say the least.

In addition, two Mk II V16s had been entered for a 10-lap Formule Libre race at Snetterton on 28th May. Unusually, and for some unknown reason, the starting grid positions for this race were drawn by ballot, making the front row look like a secondhand car sales lot, shared by Collins' BRM, two Lister Bristols, a Jaguar C Type and an ancient Maserati 8CM. Collins sped away to lead the race and break the existing lap record until he came to lap one of the Lister Bristols with which he collided. The driver of the Lister appeared to be out for an afternoon's pleasure drive and, looking over adjacent farm crops, had not seen the BRM looming behind. He took the leader's line and put the BRM out of the race. Flockhart finished in second place to Salvadori's Maserati.

Only two days later Collins was entered in the Owen Maserati at Crystal Palace, a new venue for the BRM team. It was a two-heat event, the driver with the fastest aggregate time declared the winner. Again, Peter Collins won, but this time against minimal opposition.

Excitement was now mounting at Folkingham as the day neared for the new car to make its first track appearance. Raymond Mays was spending a lot of time there, asking endless questions and getting very fidgety. Peter Berthon was at last back in circulation, albeit in a wheelchair. The historic day came on 5th June when the car, to be known as the P25, made its track debut at Folkingham with Tony Rudd driving. Initial impressions were favourable, though it was obvious much development work was still necessary. One unique feature on the car was the single rear brake disc situated behind and driven through the gearbox, a feature which become universally known as the 'bacon-slicer.' Such an unusual configuration was the subject of much discussion by opposing team members and the motoring press. It would certainly reduce the unsprung weight, but would it have the stopping power of a conventional four-wheel brake system? The most obvious problem encountered was the slow throttle response of the fuel injection system and, secondly, severe vibration throughout the car. The initial response was to replace the fuel injection system with carburettors and pursue the injection problem later; this would at least get some roadwork completed and was duly achieved by fitting two Weber carburettors. A combination of engine movement and the one-piece propshaft was probably causing the vibration. PB reluctantly agreed to the manufacture and fitting of a two-piece shaft with centre bearing. These modifications showed some improvements and the handling quality of the car gradually improved.

A week after the P25 made its first run, motor racing was dealt a major blow when tragedy struck during the Le Mans 24-hour endurance race. The circumstances of the accident are well known and hardly need repeating here, but suffice to say more than eighty spectators died when Pierre Levegh's Mercedes-Benz flew into the packed terraces opposite the pits in the early stages of the race. The race was allowed to continue to avoid creating mass panic and a general exodus from the circuit of the huge crowds, which would have impeded the work of the medical teams. The repercussions of the accident were felt around Europe and beyond.

Fortunately, the British Grand Prix at Aintree on 16th July went ahead unhindered and Peter Collins was entered to drive the Owen Maserati. Engine failure in practice resulted in a back row starting position. Peter put on a dazzling display of driving to get up to fifth place in a very large field before con-rod failure brought him to a halt at one-third distance. The race was won by Stirling Moss in a Mercedes, whose cars filled the first four places. Whilst not underrating Stirling's performance in any way, the thought does occur that Fangio, who was second, being the gentleman we all knew he was, graciously let Stirling win his home Grand Prix.

The meeting of the West Essex Car Club at Snetterton

on 13th August is a best-forgotten occasion in BRM history. Only one car, a Mk II V16, was entered, for Peter Collins. Whilst proving very fast in practice, it broke a driveshaft on the first lap of the race and was forced to retire. These frequent failures in minor events were becoming very embarrassing and brought extremely critical comments from many directions, not least the national press. Some reports suggested the entire BRM enterprise should be abandoned, ignoring the fact that this was now the private venture of Alfred Owen. It was one thing to fail in a full Grand Prix, but humiliating not to be able to complete a sprint race! The general feeling among the workforce was that the sooner the V16 cars were mothballed, the better for all concerned.

Aintree on 3rd September – the sixteenth anniversary of the outbreak of World War II – was the scheduled race debut for the P25 in the *Daily Telegraph* meeting following a press presentation at the Raymond Mays & Partners garage showrooms in Bourne held the previous Monday. One Mk II was also entered in the Formule Libre event on the same day, both cars to be driven by Peter Collins. Sadly, we had not yet been able to enlist the services of the gremlin catcher we so badly needed, so these were still in evidence at Aintree. The handling of the new car showed promise, and it was very fast. Unfortunately, while performing at racing speed during official practice on a twisty circuit, the engine oil scavenge system was not able to cope, causing oil to be blown out of the engine breather and onto the rear tyres, resulting in Collins spinning off the road. As a modification could not be introduced overnight, sensibly, the car was withdrawn and taken back to Folkingham. We had certainly discovered the cause of this problem the hard way. One small point in our favour was that the new car was, quite rightly, unanimously considered the prettiest of the day, though in this instance beauty was only skin deep. Collins received some small recompense for our efforts, winning the Formule Libre race in the Mk II V16.

Modifications and testing went on apace in preparation for the Gold Cup at Oulton Park on 24th September. Happily, I had

other things on my mind at this time, as on 17th September I married Mary Stubbs, the second daughter of Wilfred and Edith Stubbs, a former Bourne police inspector and his wife, natives of Horncastle and now living in Bourne. Mary's elder sister Joan, a BRM employee, had previously married Cyril Bryden. Our week-long honeymoon was being spent touring North Wales and Cheshire – no Caribbean honeymoons in those days. Having breakfast in an hotel in Whitchurch, I was summoned to the phone to take a call from Tony Rudd: would I go to the Oulton Park circuit as soon as possible? On arrival I was asked if I would help for a few hours as the majority of the men had been working all night. Like a loyal servant I did so, my reward two free tickets for the race. One thing has always mystified me about this, though, how did they know which hotel we were staying in?

I was pleased I was going to witness the first race of the P25. Due to various problems and propshaft changes, little had been possible, resulting in Peter Collins starting at the rear of the grid. Driving brilliantly, by lap ten he had moved up to third place, overtaking a high-class field made up of the new Lancias and also Maseratis, Vanwalls, and a Ferrari. Sadly, it was not to last and, when closing on Luigi Musso's Maserati, Collins was obliged to pull into the pits with a low oil pressure reading. After exciting the large crowd – which gave Peter Collins a great

ovation – the car was retired for fear of totally destroying the valuable engine. Investigations on returning to base showed once again that sod's law had been at work: the oil pressure gauge had succumbed to the effects of the vibrations and was the only thing at fault!

The final race of 1955 was the international meeting at Castle Combe on 1st October, to include both Formula 1 and Formule Libre races. Peter Collins was to drive the Owen Maserati. Originally, it had been intended he should drive the P25 but it was rightly decided that the development work should be given priority and would be better achieved with testing at Folkingham and Silverstone. A broken de Dion tube forced the Maserati to retire on lap thirteen. The Formule Libre race saw the last appearance of a BRM V16 as a works entry, and it seemed fitting that the drive should be given to Ron Flockhart who had probably driven more miles than anyone in testing and racing that car. Ron drove a good race to finish second but was unable to contain the runaway winner, Harry Schell in the Vanwall.

Yet another racing season drew to a close in a year which had witnessed some mild success, unfortunately counterbalanced by plenty of disappointment. Hopefully, future prospects would be brighter with the introduction of the P25 car.

With racing completed we were by no means left idle; on the contrary, we were approaching what was probably the busiest time of the year. In November and December extensive testing was taking place for both cars and drivers in addition to the construction of more P25 cars ready for 1956. Stirling Moss was looking for a car for that year. Mercedes Benz felt it had proved a point, one which no-one could dispute, and decided to quit Formula 1 now that Fangio had won the World Championship for the last two years in a Mercedes. This vast organisation demonstrated quite ably how it could develop and successfully race a car in a short period of time.

Alfred Owen would have dearly liked to see Stirling Moss in a BRM and, along with Peter Collins and Mike Hawthorn, many days were spent testing during this period, along with lesser experienced drivers Ivor Bueb, Jack Fairman, Tony Brooks and Tony Marsh. These tests were taking place at Folkingham, Oulton Park and Silverstone in fair weather and foul. Rumours abounded about where drivers would go. Eventually, Moss signed for Maserati, Collins went to Ferrari as number two to Fangio, and BRM was delighted to have Mike Hawthorn on board, joined by up-and-coming young English driver Tony Brooks, who had recently won the Syracuse Grand Prix in Sicily driving a British Connaught.

Mike was known to most of the BRM team. He was a popular and cavalier type of person and great fun. Invariably he would greet his friend Peter Collins with the words "mon ami, mate" and was famous for his bow tie, which earned him the nickname 'Le pappilon,' meaning the butterfly. He liked his pipe of tobacco and, once in a Brackley hostelry, removed a post horn from the wall and duly gave it a quick blast. Tony Brooks was a much quieter and studious person, very much a perfectionist, but both were equally nice men.

Mike Hawthorn, understandably, wanted to take part in the 1956 World Championship races, the first event in which was the Argentinian Grand Prix in Buenos Aires on 22nd January. The decision was made that the P25 cars were not sufficiently developed to warrant sending them to such a distant event. As a compromise and to enable Mike to take part, it was arranged to send the Maserati. In order to maintain a full complement of staff to concentrate on the build of P25s, Reg Williams, a former Prince Bira mechanic known to Tony Rudd, was hired to accompany the car. He would seek the help of voluntary local labour as required. The car was duly prepared and shipped to South America in readiness for the first of two races.

The Maserati's performance was anything but spectacular. Mike gained four Championship points in the Grand Prix at Buenos Aires, but that was due more to the misfortunes of others than the performance of the Maserati with Mike nursing an ailing car home into third place. Worse was to come in the second race two weeks later at Mendoza, a non-Championship event, when failure of the steering box mounting caused Mike to trail in seven laps behind the winner Fangio in a Lancia Ferrari.

HUMILIATION AT MONACO

Whilst the engine shop and test house were exceptionally busy, the early days of 1956 at Folkingham were fairly quiet for racing shop personnel. Once the routine maintenance and overhaul of existing cars had been completed, we were often waiting for engineering drawings, new parts, etc. Tools and equipment were being maintained and improvements made where possible.

Roy Foreman, a Bourne man, had recently completed his RAF service and joined the company. Roy had worked in Raymond Mays & Partners garage in Bourne prior to his national service, intending to return there on demobilisation. Henry Coy, the garage manager, recognised Roy's skills and very generously advised him to try for a job with BRM. Having been on Rolls-Royce training courses, Henry concluded his skills could be better utilised at BRM, which would also offer him a more promising career – and so it proved. He was engaged by PB to work with Willie Southcott and Colin Atkin in the test house and engine shop as required.

Whatever the situation, there was still time for a little mischief! Around this time the copper inserts in the wheel knockers had been replaced with some made of plastic; as a cost-cutting exercise, it must be assumed, as they were far less efficient (or was it simply because Arthur Hill had misdirected a copper-headed knocker and accidentally broken a spoke on a valuable wheel?) The racing workshop was heated by slow combustion, coke-burning stoves, and it was discovered, quite by accident, that if a small piece of the plastic material from the wheel knockers was placed on the hot stoves, it would emit a pungent smell similar to dog droppings. PB had a poodle called Clooney and, during those cold winter days, it was not uncommon for RM and PB to stand by one of the stoves with Clooney lying nearby. Now, having discovered the olfactory effect of the melting plastic, and seeing the proximity to the stove of the two men and the dog, there was only one course of action ... I managed to manoeuvre myself into a position where, unseen, I could drop a

The large camshaft and air intakes of the twin Weber carburettors, and air deflection panel on the 4-cylinder P25 BRM engine. The panel, in conjunction with the bodyshell, formed a duct to increase airflow to the carburettors.

small piece of the plastic onto the top of the stove. It soon had the desired effect, RM sniffing the air, shuffling his feet and looking on the soles of his shoes with PB doing likewise, eventually taking the dog outside thinking it was in need of some relief. Meanwhile, we mechanics with knowledge of this waggery continued at our benches looking very busy but finding it difficult to keep straight faces.

Testing was much restricted during the early months of the year although Tony Brooks did manage to break the lap record for the Folkingham track. The first race of the season was the Richmond Trophy at Goodwood, held on Easter Monday, 2nd April. The Easter meeting was always popular with racing mechanics, not least because the

The twin Weber carburettors fitted on the P25 4-cylinder engine.

The old control tower on Folkingham airfield, home to Peter and Lorna Berthon, and caretaker Jock Milne and his pets.

track was closed on Sundays, which meant a little more leisure time, sometimes a whole day off. The P25 was proving very fast, both from a standing start and under running, the most important requirement now reliability. Mike Hawthorn's standing start lap was the fastest yet recorded at Goodwood but, sadly, we still lacked the desired reliability, Tony retiring with fuel pump problems on lap 9. Mike had been overtaken by Moss and was now lying second when, on lap 23, a rear driveshaft joint seized, locking a rear wheel and causing the car to overturn on the infield at Fordwater. Luckily, a very disillusioned Mike was thrown clear of the somersaulting car. The following day on our return journey we called at Mike's garage at Farnham to enquire about his state of health, which – all things considered – was remarkably good apart from bruises. I was also able to return his famous corduroy cap, which had been left with me for safekeeping. On our return to Folkingham, Alfred Owen requested a stringent investigation into these latest failures, particularly the driveshaft problem, which could have cost Mike Hawthorn his life.

The following Saturday, 7th April, was open day at Folkingham for ORMA members, which about 750 people attended. They were able to view the workshops and contents and see the cars being driven by a now recovered Mike Hawthorn as well as Tony Brooks, often asking leading questions of drivers and staff which were awkward to answer. However, it was an enjoyable day for all and, as usual, we had one or two surprises for inquisitive visitors. This year an optical tracking gauge was placed in a prominent position with the

Mike Hawthorn testing the BRM on Folkingham airfield.

A typical 1950s Goodwood paddock scene. Here, Dennis Perkins and Willie Southcott manoeuvre a P25 BRM car, whilst a Lucas technician concentrates on the task in hand.

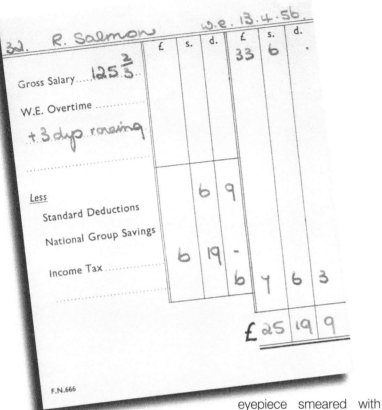

eyepiece smeared with mechanic's marking blue. Curiosity compelled visitors to look into the eyepiece, resulting in several of them wandering round with a blue ring round one eye! Some of the more observant spotted the tax disc in Jock Milne's Ford 8, which was, in fact, a Guinness label – a routine for Jock, who probably thought he had paid enough tax when he bought the Guinness! Oddly, Jock, in contrast to his usual attitude, could be quite friendly toward visitors and seemed really proud to be associated with BRM; he was a great help in preparing for the open day.

Our next event was the Aintree 200 at Liverpool, but prior to that there was testing to be done, this time at Silverstone. Almost every time we tested at Silverstone a small boy would be waiting for a lift in Blisworth village; this was John Pearson who is now well known in motor racing circles and still a good friend. He would come to Silverstone with us and watch proceedings. I still do not know how he got to know we were on our way, but he certainly had a very good bush telegraph system. I wonder what excuse he gave his teacher for his absence?

That particular test day resulted in a second near disaster for Mike Hawthorn. Motoring at speed the bonnet came off his car, almost decapitating him but fortunately inflicting only minor cuts and bruises after demolishing his visor and hitting him in the face! The car was brand new but the bonnet fastenings of such poor design that the front of the bonnet was able to lift when travelling at speed. In this case the vibration released the flimsy fasteners, allowing the bonnet to blow off. It was another unfortunate design error that should not have been allowed to happen but which was obviously quickly rectified. Inevitably, it must have left Mike contemplating whether he had made the right decision in joining the BRM team …

So to Aintree for the race on 21st April where, once again, we were accommodated at The Lord Nelson Hotel in Liverpool, a popular watering hole for sports personalities, actors and press representatives. Amongst the residents on this occasion was *Autosport* reporter John Bolster – a man who was exceedingly critical of the BRM team – famous for his pit lane walking commentaries for BBC radio, his large moustache and deerstalker hat. I suspect his bias may have been due in part to what appeared to be a lack of friendship between himself and Raymond Mays. Little wonder that, to his dismay, his beloved deerstalker went missing from the Lord Nelson one evening; Bolster minus hat would be like a fish out of water. Reasoning that one night's anguish would be sufficient retribution for his critical comments, during the night it was replaced on the peg from which it had gone missing!

Hawthorn qualified second fastest at Aintree with Brooks sixth. Mike got a flying start and was leading on the fourth lap when he suffered brake failure. A clevis pin on the brake pedal was missing; whether it had broken or had not been fitted correctly is a matter of conjecture as no trace of the pin was found. I find it difficult to believe a hardened clevis pin would break, and my opinion is that it had been assembled minus a security split pin, almost a criminal offence. To say Mike was displeased is a gross understatement: like Ken Wharton before him, he was becoming disillusioned, but for different reasons. Tony Brooks went on to finish second, he too having to slow down because of failing brakes after earlier leading the race. Again, the attractive-looking P25 was proving very fast, but without reliability and excellence in preparation we were nothing. Nevertheless, the P25 had achieved its first race finish.

For the next event, the *Daily Express* International Trophy race at Silverstone on 5th May, only one car was entered for Mike as we were scheduled to depart the following day for Monaco. Mike produced a scintillating drive whilst it lasted, leading the race from Fangio and Moss. Sadly, it was the same old story because, after just fourteen glorious laps of a drive that had really excited the vast crowd, he retired, this time with timing gear failure. The disturbing thing for the drivers and mechanics was the fact that the problems causing the retirements were so frequent and varied, but management and design staff were taking too long to react and eliminate defects. One cannot imagine Mercedes Benz taking so long before heads rolled!

There was no time to drown our sorrows as two cars had been prepared and loaded ready to leave for Dover on Sunday 6th May. Once across the English Channel a long journey lay ahead. Our first stop was invariably Reims, where Louis Hatzfeld, a tyre merchant of American origin and an old acquaintance of Raymond Mays, made us welcome and where currency was usually changed, legally or not I do not know! Refreshments were also taken at the adjacent bar, Champagne Jacquesson & Fils, where, over the years, we were to make many pleasant visits.

There was something magical about travelling through France in the spring during the 1950s, despite a rather tiring and bumpy ride on the long straight route nationales of the period, usually lined with poplar trees each side, invariably home to large growths of parasitic mistletoe. Traffic was light and the roadside verges abundant with a host of wild flowers, including lily of the valley, valerian and laburnum bushes. The roadside fence posts were often topped by a lone buzzard, perched as if guarding his territory and waiting for his next meal to pass by, or a heron standing in a dyke on a similar mission. Overnight stops at Dijon and Avignon were made before arriving in Monte Carlo. There we stayed at the Beau Rivage Hotel, which was situated on the hill between Saint-Devote and the Hotel de Paris, and overlooked part of the circuit and harbour below full of exotic yachts, the most famous being the *Christina* of Aristotle Onassis. The Palace garage had been assigned to us for our workshop requirements (not the Royal Palace, I hasten to add!). Here, our allocated

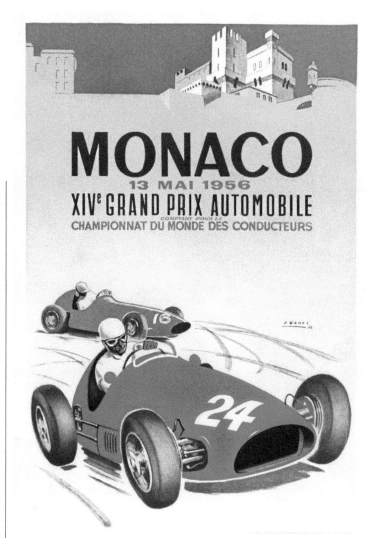

PROGRAMME OFFICIEL   **PRIX: 150 FRS**

working area was on the upper floor served by a rather primitive car lift, the perimeter of which had a narrow gangway with no guard rail. It was quite disconcerting to look down the shaft when the lift was four floors below!

After producing fast laps at Silverstone and Aintree, which demonstrated the acceleration capabilities of the car, we were quietly optimistic; the tight circuit would be an advantage. Before nightfall, however, our dreams were shattered. The extreme contrast between engine acceleration and deceleration on such a twisty circuit with its varying inclines caused the inlet valves

Arthur Ambrose, Frank Moore and Reg Smith take a break on their journey to Monte Carlo for the Monaco Grand Prix.

to stretch. The large inlet valves used at this time had sodium-filled heads, the sodium acting as a cooling medium sealed in by a small, round disc welded to the valve head. After welding, the head was then re-machined, leaving a minimal amount of metal to secure the disc in place. The frequent changes in engine revs on such a twisting and undulating circuit, necessitating many gear changes, caused the discs to come adrift, thus allowing the valve heads to stretch out of shape and lose compression.

Gordon Newman and I talk in the pits at Monaco, with Raymond Mays far right and the ever-present gendarmes close by.

Whilst we salvaged the engines from the spares available, Colin Atkin and Roy Foreman were urgently contacted at Bourne. They hastily removed the engine from a spare car and rebuilt it with old valves. This, together with another spare engine, was flown to Nice airport in a chartered de Haviland Dove, necessitating another all-night session installing the newly arrived engines. Alas! It was to no avail. Despite all this effort, the management and drivers came to the conclusion that the cars would not be competitive and would almost certainly fail to finish the race. Raymond Mays made the difficult and courageous decision to withdraw the cars. Had he been of a more ruthless nature the cars could have started purely to gain the starting money, knowing they would run for only a few laps, a practice not unknown in those days.

So, for a change we watched the race from the balcony of our hotel once the vehicles had been loaded and made ready for departure on Monday morning. Also spectating nearby were some Americans from the film industry advising us to "make

yourselves comfortable, fellas, you know these Grands Prix go on for three whole hours." We were far too embarrassed to tell them who we were and that we were well aware of the time factor!

Back at Bourne it was apparent that the proverbial had hit the fan. What discussions took place behind closed doors we could only guess at, but the outcome was that Alfred Owen decided to withdraw the BRM entries from both the Belgian Grand Prix on 3rd June and the French Grand Prix on 1st July, demanding the utmost concentration to achieve a better performance in the British Grand Prix at Silverstone on 14th July.

At the same time he consented to make an exception and allow one car to run in the 100 mile Aintree race on 24th June to give driver Tony Brooks more running time in the car. Brooks' performance at Aintree did not augur well for the British Grand Prix. After setting a time in practice good enough for pole position, the same stretched valve problem suffered at Monaco reoccurred: the car was scratched and returned to Folkingham.

More and more BRM was becoming the butt of jokes and receiving a bad press. Although time did not allow it to happen often, a thick skin was needed when visiting the local pubs, loyal colleagues closing ranks when ridicule was evident. Undaunted, three cars were taken to Silverstone, Hawthorn, Brooks and Flockhart the drivers. Hawthorn managed third fastest time in practice, putting him on the front row of the grid for the race;

Brooks was ninth fastest and Flockhart seventeenth. After a late night working at the garage in Brackley checking and double-checking the vehicles, one car required starting, which necessitated a tow. We took the car out of Brackley and towed it down the A43 with Tony Rudd at the controls. The engine did not start and he signalled for the tow truck to stop by heavy braking. "No oil pressure" he said. In the semi-darkness he had just been able to see the oil pressure gauge reading zero. Investigation showed oil pressure was there, but not reading on the gauge for the simple reason that the pipe to the gauge had not been connected. The open pipe had pumped oil all over Tony's legs with repercussions which hardly need to be specified!

We arrived at Silverstone on race day with some trepidation: what could possibly go wrong this time; what would be Alfred Owen's reaction if we failed again? Both questions would soon be answered, but not in the way we might have liked.

Mike and Tony both made electrifying starts and, to the delight of the large home crowd, completed the opening lap in first and second places, Brooks having come through from row three! What joy to see our cars leading the works Ferraris of Fangio and Collins, the Maseratis of Moss and Behra, and the Vanwalls of Schell and Trintignant – but could it last? The short answer was "no," Ron the first casualty with engine failure. Mike was proving that the BRM was the fastest car on the circuit and, to the joy of the crowd, a British car was leading in the British Grand Prix; in fact, it was the first time two BRMs had led a World Championship race – a momentous occasion. Disappointingly, after ten laps his times began to get slower, and he eventually retired with a recurrence of the Goodwood problem, a seized driveshaft joint. Again, we had the satisfaction of knowing the car was fast enough to compete with the best, but still the necessary reliability was missing. Brooks was in fourth place until, on lap forty, and now running fifth, he failed to appear on time, eventually driving slowly into the pits with a broken throttle linkage. After a hasty temporary repair he rejoined the race a distant last but failed to complete the lap. At Abbey Curve his throttle stuck open, Tony – not surprisingly – losing control and hitting the spectator bank, which caused a fuel tank to burst. The car overturned and caught fire, fortunately throwing Tony out and clear, in the process suffering a dislocated jaw and chipped ankle. The car was a complete-write off.

Alfred Owen was understandably livid, the telephone lines between Darlaston and Bourne at near melting point. He appeared to doubt the word of Peter Berthon and, to a lesser extent, Raymond Mays. RM was in the difficult position – piggy in the middle – of being responsible to Alfred Owen, whilst at the same time staying loyal to his long-time friend Peter Berthon. Instructions were given to Peter Spear, Director of Research and Development at Darlaston and a man Peter Berthon disliked, to go to Bourne and investigate the cause of these repeated failures and report his findings to Darlaston. As a result of Spear's report Alfred Owen made the decision that the cars would not race again until a 300 mile endurance test, representing a full Grand Prix distance, had been successfully completed. Prior to these extended tests a new throttle linkage was designed and fitted, together with modified rear axle driveshaft universal joints and also engine modifications, interspersed with numerous days testing at Folkingham and Silverstone.

Ron Flockhart did most of the test driving, with additional opinions from Brooks and Hawthorn when they were free of their other commitments. On one of these Silverstone tests Mike took the wheel but, after a few laps, came into the pits looking very, very angry. The throttle had stuck open at Abbey Curve and investigations showed a screw securing the butterfly in one carburettor had come loose, jamming it open. It was a defect in the manufacturer's assembly, and though the mistake was in no way due to the work of BRM staff, it would undoubtedly be unfairly judged as their negligence by the press and public. Although Mike exonerated the BRM mechanics from blame on this occasion, the accumulation of failures resulted in his resignation. It was a decision we all regretted, as he was so well liked by all the team, great fun and an exceptionally good driver. I once heard Raymond Mays describe him as conceited, a statement I totally dispute.

With better reliability seemingly achieved, PB – possibly because of his liking for Italy but also because it would be away from the prying eyes of the British press – persuaded Alfred Owen

The charred remains of Tony Brooks' BRM back in the Folkingham workshop following his crash and subsequent fire at Silverstone.

Entering Italy via the Mont Ceni Pass.

to let us take the cars to Monza for the 300 mile test run. Two Austin transporters and the Commer workshop left Bourne on Friday 28th September for the Dover ferry and, once in France, we made our now traditional first stop at Reims. From Reims we were to take the shorter route across the Alps. This led us south to Dijon through the wonderful wine-producing district of Burgundy and on to Lyon. Wherever we stopped for lunch we would order 'vin ordinaire' which, we were led to believe, was the wine of the district, reasoning that if it was good enough for the locals it was good enough for us.

From Lyon we travelled east through Chambery for an overnight stop at Lanslebourg, eventually to cross the Alps via the Mont Cenis Pass. The beauty of the alpine scenery and the exhilaration of driving round the many hairpin bends, with a sheer drop on one side overlooking the beautiful valleys, was a wonderful experience. The following year, travelling along the same route, we discovered flooding had washed away the hotel of our previous overnight stop. Occasionally, one of the vehicles would have its coolant boil, necessitating a stop to allow engine temperature to stabilise. This gave us a chance to take in the cold mountain air and enjoy the view, and a snowball fight! Descending on the other side of the pass we encountered a further problem – brake fade – forcing another stop to allow the brakes to cool. Eventually we reached the Italian town of Susa. Stopping for a short break we saw a traditional street market with a huge variety of consumables on sale, the main ones appearing to be cheeses and spices, the aroma from which was very appetising. Next was Turin, then via the Autostrada to Milan and Monza, and finally to the now familiar Hotel Marchesi at Villasanta.

Testing commenced at the beginning of October with Tony Brooks driving, to be joined later by Ron Flockhart and Roy Salvadori. Since our last visit in 1952 the circuit had been considerably altered by the addition of a banked section, affording the option of using the old circuit, the new banked one, or a combination of both. For most of our testing only the original circuit was used. Various tests and modifications were tried, lap times comparing favourably with Ferrari which was frequently running simultaneously.

Top: "We'd better wait, he's bigger than us." Taken from one of the Austin transporters whilst waiting for the loco to pass at an Italian level crossing.

The day dawned for the full 300 mile run. Peter Spear had arrived at Monza to witness and confirm the exercise for Alfred Owen. It all seemed too good to be true and so it was because Willie Southcott slipped on a loading ramp, broke his leg and was hospitalised in Milan. We visited him in a splendid hospital, to find him with a pin through the lower part of his leg; he explained how he had watched the orthopaedic surgeon drill the bone with a Black and Decker hand drill to enable the break to be pinned. True or not, it would have been typical of Willie to show such an interest, possibly even to take charge of the operation!

At last we were ready to run the full Grand Prix distance test, a continuous run with the exception of refuelling stops, or, heaven forbid, mechanical defects. With the run going well Ron

The multi-talented Arthur Ambrose demonstrates his skill at operating a teapot in the Commer mobile workshop.

Left to right: Arthur Ambrose, Gordon Newman, Phil Ayliff, Cyril Bryden and I spend a relaxing evening playing dice at Monza.

came round the Curva Parabolica heading towards the pits for an unscheduled stop. Our spirits dropped: please, not another failure! The car came to a rest and mechanics and engineers gathered round fearing the worst, only for Ron to inform us he had a water problem: he needed a pee! PB could barely conceal his anger, tempered somewhat by the fact it was not a mechanical problem after all, but even so hardly the behaviour expected of a Grand Prix driver. But then I do recall Horace Gould once receiving a pit signal at Silverstone informing him "tea up," and stopping for a cuppa, although he was in a very different situation, out of contention and racing for fun.

The outcome was that the management, including Peter Spear, was satisfied with the car's performance and so, after three weeks at Monza, we loaded the vehicles, had a minor celebration and headed back home through the Alpine range, minus Willie who remained in hospital to fly home later.

Back at Folkingham the days were in almost continuous testing, either on our home track or Silverstone. During this period Tony Brooks left BRM to join Vanwall for the 1957 season, whilst Ron Flockhart had been retained and was joined by Roy Salvadori. Both drivers complained about the poor handling qualities of the car and, in addition, Salvadori was also unhappy with the brakes. To try to resolve the problems the opinion of Alec Issigonis, designer of the ever popular Mini was sought, resulting in more modifications but not noticeably faster lap times.

The cars were now being run on BP Energol Corsa 50 engine oil, heavy lubricant unsuitable for the ordinary road car. Jock Milne – in an effort, one imagines, to supplement his weekly pay – had supplied acquaintances in Folkingham village with some of this oil. As the winter mornings were cold, a number of cars – their sumps filled with the thick oil – had to be towed around the village in an effort to start them. How Jock explained that to the owners we would never know. As it was now the season

"I think I might write a book about all this one day." I enjoy a quiet moment of reflection at the Monza circuit.

Past their sell-by date. A sorry-looking set of P25 pistons following a typical engine failure with one valve head still embedded in the piston and one bent below.

"Now, where shall we start?"; the numerous components of a dismantled P25 engine.

of goodwill they probably forgave him; they were certainly in no position to cause a stir in any case.

The year was drawing to a close under yet another dark cloud of failure. Alfred Owen issued an ultimatum to Raymond Mays and Peter Berthon: the motor racing project would be removed from Bourne and Department 31 closed down if suitable progress was not soon apparent. Although everyone went away to enjoy Christmas and hope that our New Year would be more prosperous, this was certainly something to seriously consider during the festive season …

CASABLANCA

Ahappy and – much more importantly – successful new year was what we all at BRM wished for; surely it could not be as disappointing as 1956? In the racing shop the early months of the year were spent making improvements to handling characteristics and the brakes of the P25 car, whilst the engine shop fitters were installing improved valves and timing gears in engines. At the same time it was hoped they were installing the vital lacking ingredient: reliability!

During this period a local butcher's daughter was earnestly pursuing Bagwash, though it appeared her feelings were not reciprocated. The girl somehow managed to acquire the telephone number of the Folkingham workshop and frequently called him at a fairly regular time each day. Getting a bit fed up with this, Bagwash would ask whoever was nearest the phone to take the call and tell her he was not available. Now, that would have been rather impolite so, mischievously, the girl would be told "yes, he's here, just one moment, I'll put him on," much to his annoyance. In the meantime the rest of us would quietly sing a love song nearby, whilst he talked to her. Another joke played on a fellow worker spotted talking to RM, PB or any other person of importance would be to make faces or gestures from a discreet distance, which caused acute embarrassment to the victim. From personal experience I know it was very difficult to keep a straight face.

The early months of the year brought severe weather conditions to Lincolnshire. I was then living at Northborough, a village nine miles south of Bourne I had moved to upon marriage. One January morning I awoke to a heavy snowfall. Undeterred, I drove to Bourne but the hazardous conditions caused me to miss the works bus to Folkingham and I completed the journey in my own car. During the day the snowfall became so heavy I felt it prudent to abandon my car on the airfield and return to Bourne on the works bus. With great difficulty we managed to get the old Leyland to Bourne, the nine mile journey taking about two

BRM workers trying to persuade the old Leyland ex-Greenline bus up Ringstone Hill between Folkingham and Bourne.

Willie, Tony, Phil and Bagwash working on Peter Berthon's Ford Zephyr at Folkingham; don't know anything about the hat, though …

The old maltings in Spalding Road, Bourne, now converted to house the BRM offices, machine shop and drawing office. The tiled building in the foreground is part of the old gasworks, later to be demolished to become part of the site of the new racing shop.

hours of digging, pushing – and not a little swearing. Once at Bourne I anticipated catching the Delaine service bus to Peterborough to complete my journey. To my horror the driver, Derek Tilley, told me the Peterborough bus would not be running due to the weather. On realising my plight he decided to take the bus as far as Northborough to get me home, but would not continue on to Peterborough. This he duly did, such was the devotion to duty in the fifties.

Gordon Newman fitting a brake fluid reservoir on a P25 BRM in the Folkingham workshop.

The first race meeting of 1957, the Glover Trophy at Goodwood on Easter Monday, 22nd April, was fast approaching. After endless days testing at Folkingham, Silverstone and Goodwood, involving driving by Tony Rudd in addition to regular team driver Ron Flockhart and newcomer Roy Salvadori, who had stayed with us after his Monza testing the previous year, that day finally arrived. At last we could go racing again after all the disappointments and frustrations of 1956! After practice at the Sussex circuit both cars qualified on the second row of the grid, behind two Vanwalls and a Connaught, a disappointing performance after the extensive testing which followed our last race nine months earlier at the British Grand Prix. The race was no better, Salvadori retiring with locking brakes and Flockhart finishing a distant third. It was a performance that would not have impressed a frustrated Alfred Owen!

Tony Rudd wore an ancient brown crash helmet for the many miles of testing he did at Folkingham and it was amazing how small amounts of the black, lithium-based grease we used to lubricate the car driveshafts mysteriously got inside his helmet. He was often seen with a black grease deposit on his forehead!

Whether on the instructions of Alfred Owen, the suggestion of Peter Spear, or due to the desperation of Bourne management,

the opinion of Colin Chapman of Lotus fame was sought. At this time Lotus had not yet entered the world of Grand Prix racing, but Chapman was no mean driver. One of his design philosophies was if you can safely cut a corner then cut it, and he had produced very good sports cars famous for their roadholding qualities. He agreed to test drive our car the following day at Goodwood, after which he made his recommendations

A P25 BRM instrument panel as set up for track tests; the driver would be instructed to monitor different gauges on each test run.

regarding suspension changes. One car was modified in line with his thinking and taken back to Goodwood for him to re-test. From these tests he concluded that some improvement in handling had been achieved.

A 1957 P25 BRM by the control tower on Folkingham airfield, the tail now considerably different from the original version.

A P25 BRM stripped of panels and raised on ramps used to ease working conditions. The trestle, which serves as a centre pivot, is clearly visible.

Working conditions in the Goodwood paddock weren't the best, but we always enjoyed being there.

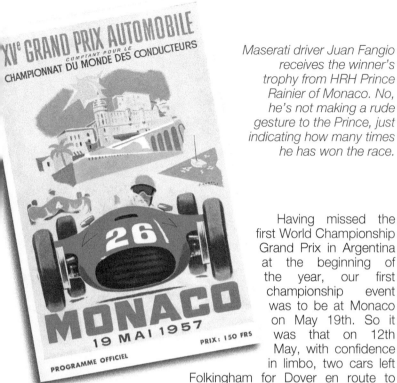

Maserati driver Juan Fangio receives the winner's trophy from HRH Prince Rainier of Monaco. No, he's not making a rude gesture to the Prince, just indicating how many times he has won the race.

Having missed the first World Championship Grand Prix in Argentina at the beginning of the year, our first championship event was to be at Monaco on May 19th. So it was that on 12th May, with confidence in limbo, two cars left Folkingham for Dover en route to Monte Carlo for that circuit's 15th Grand Prix, the painful memory of last year's failure still fresh. Arriving there on the evening of the 15th we found that our hotel of the previous year had been demolished and we had been booked into the Hotel Roma, which we were pleased to discover was much nearer to our garage. It was a pleasant hotel, quite old and high on the mountainside, with panoramic views out to sea from the balcony and an ancient lift serving the upper floors. Like all hotels in Monaco at Grand Prix time it was fully booked.

It had not taken us BRM men long to discover that if the lift was summoned whilst in motion, it would respond to the call without first stopping and allowing the doors to open at its original destination. So, if it was called from the ground floor whilst on its way to the top floor, it would begin its descent without the doors opening at the top. As there was also a group of elderly ladies staying at the hotel, we thought that this presented a marvellous opportunity for some mischief-making. Seeing some of the lady guests enter the lift, we quickly arranged for someone to be at the lift controls on both upper and lower floors, giving the occupants several journeys up and down, peals of laughter coming from within as some of the BRM contingent sang that old favourite about the three old ladies who were locked in the lavatory!

As was usual at Monaco, practice sessions were held on each of the three days prior to the race, the Friday one at the unearthly hour of 6.30am. A total of twenty cars were competing for the sixteen places on the grid. It was soon apparent that Roy

Salvadori was increasingly unhappy with the brakes and handling of his car. The twisty Monaco street circuit, with its curbs, walls, straw bales (before the days of Armco barriers) and lack of run-off areas, was the last place to lack confidence in a racing car; it was therefore no great surprise when he failed to qualify. Roy, a very good driver on the wide, open airfield racetracks back in England, did not appear to relish this tight street circuit.

Ron was also unhappy with his car, managing to qualify eleventh only. The race was memorable for a spectacular crash on the harbourside in the early laps of the race. Race leader Stirling Moss hit the barrier at the chicane in his Vanwall, followed by Mike Hawthorn and Peter Collins in their Lancia-Ferraris immediately behind who ran into the debris. Thus, the three leading contenders were out before the race had really got going. Ron Flockhart managed to get up to fifth place, largely due to retirements, before he too stopped with all too familiar timing gear failure. BRM had the unenviable Monaco Grand Prix record that, of the four cars entered, to date only one had qualified and even that had failed to complete a race. How would Raymond Mays placate Mr Owen this time, and what would be his reaction to yet another failure? As far as we were allowed to know, in fact his attitude was remarkably conciliatory, with instructions that Colin Chapman's suggestions should be completed.

The camaraderie between teams was strong at this time, never more so than between the BRM and Vanwall contingents. Following the race the Vanwall mechanics invited us to join them for a social evening, they having something to celebrate in that Tony Brooks had finished third in their car. They were going to a place in the country and we travelled in their transporter, a converted Bedford bus. It soon became apparent that the driver had already begun celebrating and was the worse for drink, removing a few wing mirrors from parked cars with the Bedford

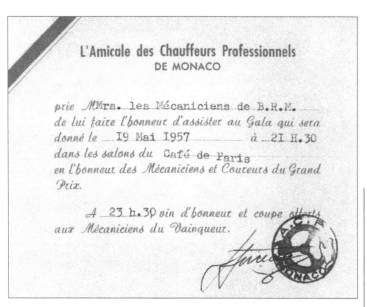

L'Amicale des Chauffeurs Professionnels
DE MONACO

prie *MMrs. les Mécaniciens de B.R.M.*
de lui faire l'honneur d'assister au Gala qui sera
donné le *19 Mai 1957* à *21 H.30*
dans les salons du *Café de Paris*
en l'honneur des Mécaniciens et Coureurs du Grand
Prix.

À *23 h.30* vin d'honneur et coupe offerts
aux Mécaniciens du Vainqueur.

CIRCUIT ROUEN les ESSARTS - 7 JUILLET 1957
ASSOCIATION SPORTIVE DE L'A.C. NORMAND

43e GRAND PRIX DE L'A. C. F.

Programme officiel : 100 fr.

while travelling down the narrow streets. At last in the country we wended our way up a narrow mountain road – and wended and wended and wended, until our Vanwall hosts decided that we must have taken the wrong road. There was no alternative but to turn the bus around and go back the way we had come. This would normally be a simple manoeuvre, but not with an inebriated driver high up on a narrow mountain pass with a sheer drop of about five hundred feet on one side. Seeing the lights twinkling way below was the signal for me and most of the other passengers to evacuate the bus while the manoeuvre was completed. We were more than a little relieved to return to the bright lights of Monte Carlo.

On our return journeys to Calais we were becoming regular visitors to a bar at Hazebrouck, a small town in northern France where we had called one day and discovered that Monsieur le Patron sold English beer. We were now becoming quite well known to some of the local clientele, and during one visit were persuaded to accompany some of them to be introduced to a lady who was the proprietor of a hat shop. She had been a member of the French Resistance during the war and, at considerable risk to herself, had been involved in helping British servicemen escape, proudly showing us a congratulatory letter from Winston Churchill. She and her companions plied us with liberal glasses of wine, and, no doubt with the assistance of the wine, I did what was on reflection a rather foolish thing and bought my mother a hat. Sons just do not buy hats for their mothers! Though reluctant to leave our generous hosts, we made a hasty dash to Calais just in time to catch the ferry. Back home luck was on my side as the hat was a good fit, proudly worn by a very patriotic mum.

During the Monte Carlo weekend Raymond Mays enlisted the services of an old acquaintance, Piero Taruffi, the silver-haired Italian racing driver and engineer, and had invited him to try the car at Folkingham. In my opinion it was a questionable decision for, whilst not underestimating Taruffi's expertise, would it be a case of too many cooks spoiling the broth, I wondered? Would his evaluation further confuse the already confused engineers at Bourne? Taruffi did try the car and – fortunately – his opinion did not contrast greatly with Colin Chapman's; in fact, it may have tended to reinforce Chapman's findings.

As a result of these combined opinions, frantic efforts were now being made to reconstruct two cars to the various recommendations in time for the French Grand Prix at Rouen on 7th July. The changes involved new front suspensions and numerous incidental modifications, but the splined rear driveshafts recommended by both Chapman and Taruffi to overcome the driveshaft problems were not yet available. It was also announced that Roy Salvadori had withdrawn from the BRM team and so the search was on for a second driver for Rouen. With most of the updates completed, Taruffi visited Folkingham again to try the car, reporting the roadholding to be much better, but with still room for improvement to the brakes.

In the meantime, on Chapman's recommendation, a young American driver called Mackay Fraser had been invited to try the car with a view to driving the second entry at Rouen. He visited Folkingham and impressed the management with his ability, and was subsequently engaged to drive the car in France. He was particularly remembered by the staff for spending much of his waiting time sitting in a crouched position on the top of a

A 1950s refuelling system being operated by Phil Ayliff and Cyril Bryden at Rouen, watched by team manager Tony Rudd, while Colin Atkin changes plugs.

Mick Vaughan of Lockheed brakes and a confident-looking author with Ron Flockhart's car at Rouen. This confidence was soon shattered when the car was written off in an accident.

"'ere, you can't park there." How Ron Flockhart's BRM finished up following his crash at Rouen after skidding on oil spilled from Roy Salvadori's Vanwall. Ron escaped with relatively light injuries from such an horrendous crash.

stepladder, reminiscent of a little monkey, watching with a keen eye as mechanics worked on what was to be his car.

Rouen is the capital of Normandy on the banks of the River Seine, probably best known today as the city where Joan of Arc was tried and burned in 1483. The French Grand Prix was being held near the village of les-Essarts, a few miles south of the city, for only the second time on the twisty undulating circuit running through dense woodland; the first was in 1952 when Alberto Ascari won in a Ferrari. The BRM team had been allocated the garage in the BP oil depot, used for the day-to-day repair of commercial vehicles and with very basic facilities – hardly the place to prepare racing cars. The weather was unbearably hot, so much so that RM spent some time spraying the roof of the workshop with a hosepipe in an effort to cool the place; a fruitless effort but he thought it was great fun.

Despite the front suspension improvements practice times were mediocre, Ron Flockhart qualifying eleventh with new boy Mackay Fraser twelfth. On a hot and sunny afternoon Raymond 'Toto' Roche started the race. To the amazement of everyone Mackay Fraser was up into sixth place on completion of the first lap and really mixing it with the big boys. The unfortunate Flockhart hit a patch of oil spilt from Roy Salvadori's Vanwall when the oil filler cap came off, got into a slide and crashed badly, breaking his pelvis and writing-off a new car. Meanwhile, Mackay Fraser was still circulating well when the telltale signs of oil were noticed coming from the rear driveshafts. After a very encouraging performance, on safety grounds he retired, leaving us wondering what he might have achieved had the new driveshafts been ready and fitted …

In Rouen we had found an excellent rooftop restaurant where, to our delight, the fixed menu was accompanied by three bottles of wine per table, red, rosé, and white. Bagwash had a philosophy: you must not mix grain with grapes and on

The Commer mobile workshop makes its way through France on the return journey from Rouen.

The works Maserati team cars make their way through Liverpool streets to the Aintree circuit for the British Grand Prix, followed by the BRM team in the Austin transporters.

this occasion we made sure he had plenty of grapes, secretly decanting wine into his always-receptive glass. Leaving the restaurant and taking the night air he began to assume an unusual posture, leaning against a church wall and slowly subsiding, eventually being escorted back to our hotel like a tacking yacht.

Back at Bourne, with the British Grand Prix at Aintree coming up on 20th July, a desperate search was on for a driver to replace the hospitalised Ron Flockhart. The situation worsened when it became necessary to find a second driver after news came through that Herbert Mackay Fraser had been killed driving a Lotus Sports car at Reims. It was a sad end to the career of such a promising and likeable young driver, one who could have had a great future and showed the potential to be an invaluable asset to BRM.

Aintree was little short of a disaster for the BRM team now with no top line drivers available; it seemed we were being hit from all sides! Archie Scott-Brown had been approached and refused the offer, so Les Leston and Jack Fairman had been engaged to fill the vacant seats, neither of whom was familiar with the BRM.

On the Thursday evening following first practice a spare engine was to be brought from Bourne after its test bed run. Willie and Colin Atkin arrived at our Liverpool garage in the early hours of Friday morning with the story that a kangaroo had crossed the road in front of them on the way. Of course, we seized the opportunity to ridicule them about this, asking if they had been in the Yates wine lodge en route, while they desperately tried to convince us. We later learned that wild wallabies had been known to frequent the Derbyshire Peak District!

To add to our problems the new driveshafts still had to be completed, so hopes were not high. Leston qualified a dismal twelfth with Fairman fifteenth. The race followed the now familiar pattern for BRM, both cars retiring with engine failure. However, the race did prove significant as it was won by a British Vanwall driven jointly by Stirling Moss and Tony Brooks, Moss replacing Brooks during the race after his own car had failed. It was the first British car and driver combination to win a World Championship race. The fact that Tony Vandervell's Vanwalls were our greatest – albeit friendly – rivals must have been a bitter-sweet pill for our own long-suffering but increasingly impatient Alfred Owen, hungry for success. Somehow he kept faith with us …

Despite the BRMs' continuing failures, the staff at Bourne was never anything but optimistic. However, thick skin was an undoubted asset to counteract the criticism and ridicule handed

The three BRMs that finished 1, 2, 3 in the International Trophy race at Silverstone, with (left to right): Peter Berthon, Jean Behra, Raymond Mays, Harry Schell, Rivers Fletcher and Tony Rudd. But where is Ron? Has he had a call of nature again?

out by the press and, closer to home, patrons of the local hostelries in and around Bourne. During the Aintree weekend, Raymond Mays had been approached by Frenchman Jean Behra, a first class driver and former French motorcycle champion, asking if there was a possibility of driving a BRM the following Sunday at Caen in northern France? Jean was Juan Fangio's teammate at Maserati but neither was competing in this non-championship race. RM was delighted with the request from such a driver and, backed by an enthusiastic Alfred Owen who felt they could not miss this opportunity, a car was hastily prepared with even more hastily manufactured new driveshafts. A second car was taken as a spare in one of the Austin Lodestar transporters while the updated car went by air, to be towed from the airport to Caen. On arrival the seat and pedals of the second car were quickly modified to accommodate Harry Schell, another refugee from Maserati who had managed to persuade the race organisers to allow him an entry. RM – never one to refuse good starting money – agreed to let Harry drive the car.

The two cars were fastest in practice, and led the race until Harry retired with yet another engine failure, Jean going on to win. Although only a minor event, any victory after Aintree was bound to give us a tremendous morale boost. Furthermore, Behra and Schell were signed to drive for the remainder of the season when available, and possibly for a full programme in 1958.

Shortly after the victory at Caen, I had cause for further celebration. On 3rd August I became a dad, as my son Michael Richard was born in the Thorpe Hall maternity home in Peterborough.

In view of the fact that Behra and Schell were contracted to Maserati for the remaining 1957 World Championship events, and Ron Flockhart had not yet recovered from his injuries sustained at Rouen, we had the frustration of having a winning car we were unable to race for lack of suitable drivers! Therefore, BRM management suffered yet further indignity in having to cancel our entries for the remaining three championship races, in Germany, at Pescara in Italy (a new race in the championship calendar that year), and the Italian Grand Prix. This meant that our next race would be the postponed *Daily Express* Trophy at Silverstone on 14th September. At least this meant we had six clear weeks to bring all cars to the specifications recommended by Chapman and Taruffi.

The workshops at Folkingham were abuzz with excitement once more, there seemed to be a newfound air of optimism after the success at Caen. A new member had recently joined the racing team, Pat Carvath, son of a Bourne dentist. He had joined BRM as an apprentice in 1952, volunteered for three years in the army in 1954, and had now rejoined us at Folkingham. He was a dynamic sort of character with quite a short fuse and an attitude of "Come on chaps, let's get stuck in." During Pat's absence for military service, Tony Rudd had become his brother-in-law after marrying his sister Pamela. Though he was to receive the obvious ragging from his colleagues, there was certainly no evidence of nepotism; quite the contrary, on occasion.

The BRM convoy makes a refuelling stop somewhere in France; the four vehicles that could each hold 45 gallons of fuel were always welcome customers at continental filling stations.

The three cars entered at Silverstone were to be driven by our good friends Jean Behra, Harry Schell and the almost-recovered Ron Flockhart, and had now been updated to the latest specification. Alas, there was little opposition, as the Vanwalls had not been entered because Tony Vandervell considered that the event lacked prestige. This was a great disappointment as, with our renewed optimism, a lively contest had been eagerly envisaged.

The race was to be run in two heats and a final. The three BRMs all claimed positions on the front row of the grid for the final, Behra and Flockhart finishing first and second respectively in heat one and Schell winning heat two. The final became a BRM benefit, our cars occupying the first three places in the order of Behra followed by Schell and Flockhart. Our euphoria at this victory was countered by the fact that, not only did the Vanwalls stay away, but so too did the factory Ferrari and Maserati teams, leaving a field of largely private entrants. Nevertheless, Jean Behra proved once again what an excellent driver he was. Harry was great fun; probably the last of the playboy drivers. On arrival at BRM he and Jean became great pals, though unfortunately this friendship did later deteriorate.

Jean Behra had a detachable artificial ear, acquired after a racing accident in Ireland earlier in his career when he slid down a road and the spare pair of goggles around his neck had removed his natural ear, as a result of which he no longer carried spare goggles. The story goes that Jean always removed the false ear when he went to bed, leaving it on a dressing table. Whilst staying at the George Hotel in Stamford, and sharing a room with Harry during one of their visits to Bourne, the chambermaid arrived with early morning tea and Harry politely asked her "I wonder if you would be good enough to pass my Grandad his ear?" A totally bewildered maid gingerly passed the ear and scampered from the room looking very pale!

Willie Southcott and I were often hand-in-glove over a little mischief, and at this Silverstone meeting we had adopted an Irish brogue, which must have been fairly convincing as a spectator asked Arthur Hill why he had so many Irishmen in the team. Arthur, with his dry sense of humour, replied equally convincingly and with a touch of feigned bitterness, that the Irish would do the job for lower wages.

Raymond Mays had persuaded Alfred Owen to allow two cars to be entered in the non-championship Modena Grand Prix in Italy on 21st September. As Behra and Schell were contracted to drive elsewhere, a second driver was required to partner Ron Flockhart, and RM had approached Stuart Lewis-Evans who agreed to drive the second car. Tony Vandervell, to whom Stuart was contracted even though not required by Vanwall, quickly overruled his decision. Was Tony still smarting from his association with BRM years earlier as a member of the British Motor Racing Research Trust? After numerous enquiries, including the availability of Peter Collins, it was discovered that bearded Swedish driver Joachim Bonnier was available and he was engaged for the drive.

Modena was bread-and-butter with jam to the Italian Ferraris and Maseratis, both camps using it frequently as their test track, and they easily out-performed the BRMs and privately-entered cars. Ron suffered fuel pump failure after three-quarters distance and retired, whilst Jo, as he was generally known, had a driveshaft disintegrate, one piece flying off in front of the Ferrari pit. One of their mechanics rushed out to retrieve it and, not realising it was very hot, did not hold it for long, much to the amusement of his unsympathetic colleagues.

Tony Robinson, a mechanic with Stirling Moss, had spent much time working in Modena at the Maserati factory. He was well known and in turn knew the city well. Keen to impress, he invited us to go for a drink. It was soon obvious he was well acquainted with the chosen venue, a hostelry that looked considerably upmarket. Colin Atkin, now nicknamed Gelati as he was the double of a local Italian ice cream vendor, was presented with the bill for the first round, whereupon his face dropped. By this time Tony Robinson had made his excuses and disappeared and, realising we had been duped, we did the same, informing the

A 1950s continental frontier station. Passing through border customs was often easier in early afternoon – siesta time …

Left: Two of the Austin Lodestar transporters stopped on an alpine pass, probably because of overheating, or maybe overdrinking by the crew!

Bologna-based Maserati brothers were in financial trouble and consequently sold their business to the wealthy Orsis, who eventually moved car production to their headquarters at Modena, retaining the famous trident motif and Maserati name for the cars they continued to build with great success. The Maserati brothers eventually returned to Bologna to build OSCA racing cars. Surprisingly, the Maserati car build area was not quite the environment one would expect to build racing cars in: cleanliness appeared to be a secondary consideration and, as had been experienced with the Owen Maserati, the finished article left something to be desired. However, if the criteria was winning races, they had got something right. Unfortunately, shortly after our visit Maserati went into receivership and its famous racing team was no more.

Prior to our departure for Modena we had been informed of a possible entry for the Moroccan Grand Prix at Casablanca. This was to be a non-championship race with a view to gaining World Championship status in 1958. On our return from Italy the entry was confirmed. Meanwhile, more of the recommendations put forward by Colin Chapman were being introduced, all of which were slowly but surely improving the cars' performance.

In mid-October we left for our first event on the African continent, with the three Austin Lodestars each carrying a car and as many spares as could be safely stowed. Though the race was in Morocco, it was organised by the French, who had indicated they would particularly like to see a French driver in one of our cars. RM was approached and agreement reached, resulting in the dapper and friendly Maurice Trintignant, a driver of small stature but great experience, being engaged to drive the first car. Ron Flockhart, now fully recovered from his accident at Rouen, would drive the second car with the third as spare.

The three vehicles travelled in convoy via Paris down through western France, the occupants admiring the beautiful scenery

management that the popular Mr Robinson would be returning later to pay. Reluctantly, and much to his disgust, he eventually did so! We found a hostelry more suited to our pockets and spent a very pleasant evening there. Walking back to the hotel around midnight, we passed through a large and ancient cobbled square surrounded by even more ancient-looking blocks of high-rise flats. Cyril Bryden, realising there would be a considerable echo in such a location, decided to drill an imaginary body of soldiers with great effect, causing much laughter and a few heads to appear at windows! He would have made an excellent drill sergeant. Quite what the local residents thought I can't imagine; probably just put it down to the mad English!

Following race day we were invited to visit the Maserati factory. The main occupation of the factory, owned by the Orsi family, was the manufacture of quality machine tools. In the 1930s the

of the Poitiers and Angoulême districts, and on through the vineyards and pine forests to our destination, the seaport of Bordeaux. Here, we were to stay for two nights prior to boarding the Moroccan ship, the Ville de Bordeaux, a packet-boat of 2150 tonnes.

The annual fair was in town with its galaxy of stalls and sideshows. We, of course, were tempted to pay it a visit, and everyone seemed able to win bottles of wine there. That's what it said it was on the label although it proved a rather inferior variety of 'plonk.' Returning to the hotel with our winnings, Roy Foreman was almost abducted by an immense coloured lady of the night emerging from an even darker alleyway and grabbing him. Roy quickly made his escape, looking rather frightened after his brief encounter with such a huge specimen of African womanhood.

It had been decided that, to reduce freight costs, all tools and equipment would be stowed in one of the Austins, which would then travel as deck cargo with the race cars stowed within the holds. The two remaining Lodestars were left behind to await our return. The time to embark arrived and we watched with trepidation as the transporter was hoisted high into the air and lowered onto the deck of the ship, hoping against hope that the stevedores had safely secured our precious cargo to the crane. Once loaded and safely anchored on deck, we relaxed for our three day voyage to Casablanca. Phil Ayliff's first priority was to find the bar. This he appeared to do with rapid success for, barely had we cast off, he was shouting in an inebriated voice "Abandon ship. Away all boats." He then went to his cabin to sleep for a while. We were accommodated in two berth cabins, Maurice and I sharing, as usual. Once installed we viewed the scenery from the upper deck as the ship slowly made its way down the River Garonne into the Gironde Estuary and, after a long and serene passage, out to the Atlantic Ocean.

The Austin transporter being lowered onto the deck of the Ville de Bordeaux to travel as deck cargo to Casablanca.

A stevedore watches, probably with fingers crossed, as a P25 BRM is hoisted high above the Ville de Bordeaux.

What a difference once out at sea! The ship had apparently been commissioned to ply her trade in the fiords of Scandinavia and was not fitted with stabilisers. The undercurrents of the coastal waters off Spain and Portugal caused the ship to roll significantly, at times becoming quite scary. During one period we were informed that the angle of roll had been recorded as thirty-seven degrees; consequently not many people were

One of the P25 BRMs is lowered into the hold of the Ville de Bordeaux.

The SS Ville de Bordeaux leaving port for Casablanca.

Dining on board the Ville de Bordeaux before encountering the rough seas along the Portuguese coast.

... and now they lean the other way.

Left to right: Maurice Dove, Phil Ayliff, John Speight, Roy Foreman, myself, Arthur Hill, Mick Vaughan and Gordon Newman lean one way to counteract the roll of the ship ...

seen at the dining tables. Resting in the cabin on the second day, I was aware of a commotion in the nearby gangway. Looking out to investigate I saw the floor awash with water. A rather foolish passenger accommodated on the starboard side, not a BRM employee, I hasten to add, had decided to open the porthole in his cabin. Had he done so as the ship rolled to port he would have viewed the sky, but to compound his foolishness he had opened it as it rolled to starboard, when the porthole was submerged for a considerable length of time. Due to the weight of the water, he found it impossible to close the porthole until the ship rolled back sufficiently for it to emerge above the water level, allowing a great deal of water to be taken in as a result. Roy and Willie shared a cabin next door to this idiot, and Willie realised something was amiss when he found himself standing in six inches of water. Roy, alerted by this, looked out of the cabin door to witness a small baby being washed out of the neighbouring cabin with its mother frantically trying to retrieve it. At the same time the shocked culprit was being called the most uncomplimentary names in a variety of languages. Willie probably thought he was going to be shipwrecked for a fifth time!

Upon arrival everyone was pleased to be on terra firma once again and we were soon installed in the Hotel Alhambra with the cars at the Garage Sami. Stores and equipment unloaded, it was

time to start engines. This meant towing as no starter motors were fitted. Much to the usual annoyance of the mechanics, ridiculous company policy decreed that only Tony Rudd, Raymond Mays or race drivers were allowed to start cars, often entailing long delays waiting for Tony. In Casablanca, however, this rule was welcomed by mechanics. The Arab residents in the nearby flats did not appreciate the noise of racing car engines and persisted in bombarding the noisy beasts with a variety of missiles, including potatoes, pebbles and, most perilous of all, a large brass padlock which surely could have caused a fatality. Subsequently, whenever possible, cars were started only at the circuit. Maurice Trintignant had not sat in his car prior to arrival in Morocco and many minor adjustments were necessary to achieve his desired driving position.

First practice was fairly normal and, after routine inspection checks and maintenance, the cars were garaged, the mechanics retiring for a tour of the casbah and to sample the nightlife. Alas! The following morning on arrival at the Garage Sami a most depressing sight awaited us: all of the exposed bright metal parts on the cars had rusted overnight. The salt air of the seaside circuit had viciously attacked our – and no doubt other teams' – cars. Parts were cleaned as well as possible, but these must have been the tattiest-looking BRMs to see a race circuit. Final practice on Friday saw Trintignant quicker than Flockhart, qualifying in eighth and tenth places respectively.

Saturday was classed as a rest day, a most unusual occurrence in Formula 1 circles. We were delighted to receive an invitation to visit the American Air Force base of 357 Fighter Interceptor Squadron a few miles from the city – and what a base it turned out to be. On arrival we were offered a large steak-filled bread roll, and that was just a snack! After an extensive tour of the

The extent of roll experienced on the Ville de Bordeaux is obvious here as she sails along the Portuguese coast towards Casablanca.

Deck quoits was a popular – though tricky – pastime on the Ville de Bordeaux during the voyage. Here, Mick Vaughan is seen in action watched by Maurice Dove.

base we witnessed a fighter scramble, allegedly to investigate an unidentified aircraft in their patrolled air space. The speed with which the fighters were airborne was very impressive indeed, although there was a slight suspicion that the scramble had been deliberately engineered for our benefit. After a visit to the bar to socialise over a few drinks we were informed that it was time to eat. With the memory of my snack still vivid in my mind, I was

An avenue of date trees on a typical road in the suburbs of Casablanca.

presented with the largest T-bone steak I had ever seen. Apparently flown in from Holland, it was delicious. Those Yanks certainly knew how to live! The final act of goodwill to complete a wonderful day was to make us all honorary members of their squadron.

Phil Ayliff and Dick Salmon with Maurice Trintignant's BRM in the paddock area at Casablanca.

Phil, Mick, Maurice, Roy and myself study a book loaned by a photographer. 'Sergeant Bilko' has spotted something of greater interest …

Arrival of the King of Morocco prior to the start of the race was accompanied by a bevy of motorcycle outriders. Preliminaries completed, we were ready to race. The always-unfortunate Flockhart was again forced to retire early after collecting an even more unfortunate bird in the air intake. Maurice Trintignant drove an excellent race to finish third, with Frenchman, Jean Behra, the winner in his Maserati. French drivers first and third was a very popular result for the race organisers, the victorious Jean later presented to the King of Morocco.

During the race a most bizarre and comical incident added to the entertainment. Jack Brabham, in a works-entered Cooper, experienced gearbox problems during the race and drove straight into the paddock. His mechanics identified the problem, effected repairs and, totally against regulations, Brabham returned to the track and rejoined the race, much to the astonishment of

race official 'Toto' Roche. Inevitably, the excitable 'Toto' went to seek out John Cooper. John, mischievous as ever, said he had no idea where 'he' was and Toto, not realising he was actually talking to the man he wanted, was by now in a state of panic, producing his black flag to show to Brabham, eliminating him from the race. Unfortunately, he had got himself into such a state he showed the flag to Fangio who came into the pits with a look of bewilderment on his face. Fortunately, Fangio was out of contention for the race anyway after an earlier pit stop, which may have saved Monsieur Roche from a lynching!

It was a happy band of BRM personnel which later attended the prizegiving, our temporary driver, now accompanied by his wife, proving most magnanimous, complimenting and thanking us profusely for providing him with such a good car (an experience new to us!)

The following day was free time with the vehicles loaded and ready for the return journey on the Ville de Bordeaux as soon as she arrived in port. The day was spent sightseeing and a visit to the home of a Mr Graham, an Englishman now settled

A cheerful-looking author in the pits at Casablanca with the Ferrari team in the background.

Phil Ayliff, Willie Southcott and the 'Sheriff' in a car emerging from the shade of the Moroccan tents, put there to provide refuge from the intense heat.

Jean Behra winning the Moroccan Grand Prix in the lightweight Maserati.

Following his victory in the Grand Prix, Jean Behra is presented to HRH King Mohammed V of Morocco.

Maurice Trintignant celebrates with his wife and BRM mechanics following his third place finish in the Moroccan Grand Prix.

The P25 gearbox, showing pot joint-type output drive. Bronze blocks on the inner end of the rear wheel driveshafts created a universal joint. The blocks were allowed to slide in the gearbox output coupling, lubricated by an oil-filled rubber boot. At high speeds the lubricant centrifuged to the outside of the boot, causing the bronze blocks to seize in the pot joint, as in the case of Mike Hawthorn's crash at Goodwood in 1956.

A view of the gearbox end of the long-awaited spline and ball driveshafts, introduced to replace the pot joint-type responsible for a number of retirements.

The outer end of the splined driveshaft.

The P25 gearbox and 'bacon slicer' single rear brake disc with Dunlop calliper fitted.

in Morocco, who provided us with a typical Arab meal. The old adage, "fingers were made before forks" was the order of the day, and very enjoyable it was, too!

Seafaring seemed more pleasant on our return voyage. Either the sea was calmer, our sea legs had improved, or it was just that we were homeward bound after a very interesting season's racing, that contained both failure and some minor successes.

Back at Folkingham many days were spent modifying and testing. Colin Chapman was again involved and lap times at Folkingham and Silverstone steadily improved. In addition, Jean Behra and Harry Schell were confirmed as team drivers for 1958. We looked forward to the new year with growing confidence.

A BRIDGE TOO FAR

The year began with something of a bang when a metaphorical rocket was fired from Darlaston in the direction of south Lincolnshire. Although 1957 had seen some progress towards winning Formula 1 races, understandably, this was insufficient to satisfy the Rubery Owen directors, who were also disappointed by the lack of commercial sales from Department 31 at Bourne. So it was that Alfred Owen issued another ultimatum: start winning races soon or Bourne would be closed. Although it seemed unlikely that this threat would be carried out after signing Jean Behra and Harry Schell, it had to be taken seriously, nevertheless.

Two new cars were being built at Folkingham with what would hopefully be an improved chassis, and engines were being updated to comply with new fuel regulations, which specified commercial petrol, 130 octane (ie Avgas). The Grand Prix distance was also reduced to 200 miles or 2 hours which meant that smaller fuel tanks would be introduced. More significantly, perhaps, we were racing not only for a Driver's Championship but also for a Manufacturer's Championship. Team prestige was going to be even more important.

On 6th February the sports world went into mourning over the news that the Manchester United football team had been involved in an air disaster at Munich airport. An air of gloom pervaded the workshop, as more details of the tragedy were broadcast and realisation hit home at the loss of some great sportsmen.

The Easter meeting at Goodwood on 7th April was to be the first race of the season, with two cars entered for Behra and Schell in the 100 mile Glover Trophy, their first outing together as team drivers. They must have wondered what they had done to deserve the atrocious weather that weekend, snow and rain turning the grass-surfaced paddock into a quagmire. Behra qualified second on the grid and Schell fifth with Moss on pole in a Cooper. Moss stalled at the start leaving Behra to lead the race for the first four laps when brake failure caused him to crash into the brick-built chicane wall, luckily without serious personal

Bagwash in conversation with a seemingly unimpressed Harry Schell; Jean Behra looks on.

Social evenings were the norm when time permitted; here, Maurice seems to be enjoying a very sociable evening …

injury. Meanwhile, Schell was circulating at the rear of the field with brakes sticking on and very soon retired. Two entirely different brake problems! After a medical check at Chichester hospital, which confirmed no breakages, Behra took three days' rest in his hotel. Not a very auspicious start for the new team drivers and another disappointment for Alfred Owen who was in attendance. After a few days Behra declared he was fit to drive again – prematurely, it seemed – as he still suffered chest pains. X-rays later revealed he had cracked ribs but his keenness to drive in the next race at Aintree on 19th April was greater than these problems!

Peter Spear was increasingly present at Folkingham, together with his assistant Ian Hankinson, from whom, there is little doubt, an abundance of information was being fed back to an increasingly pessimistic Alfred Owen. Brake problems were becoming something of an enigma, with various systems tried and an assortment of failures encountered. For our next race at Aintree a back-to-basics arrangement was installed; no servo

Garage premises at Chichester allocated to the BRM team when visiting Goodwood. In later years we were relocated to the Ford dealership premises of RM's friend Jim Elwes.

Willie Southcott working on Jean Behra's car in the garage at Chichester; so industrious is he that his hands and face are a blur!

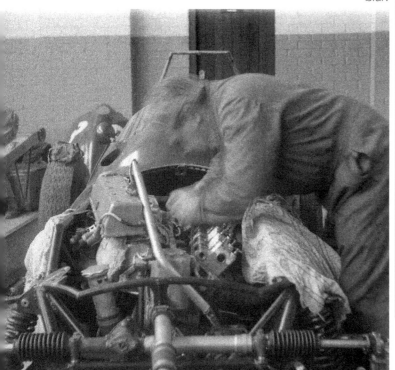

Harry Schell's BRM being towed from the garage in Chichester. Mixed feelings prevailed about tow-starting in towns, often an unpopular necessity.

Tony Rudd warms up Harry Schell's BRM watched by mechanics, the silly rule which forbade mechanics from driving cars as yet not relaxed.

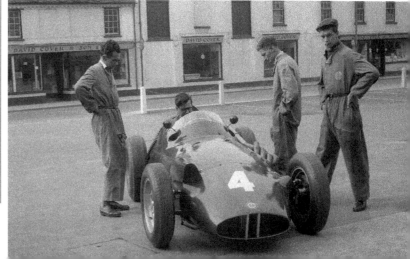

Primitive-looking and fraught with danger: the mobile fuel station in the Goodwood paddock. Both Shell and Esso were located in the same area.

Cars lined up on the starting grid for the Glover Trophy race, with Stirling Moss on pole position in car number 7.

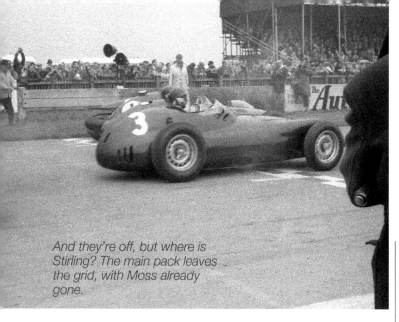

And they're off, but where is Stirling? The main pack leaves the grid, with Moss already gone.

Pumping ale! Me, Maurice and Phil demonstrate our versatility at The Nag's Head in Chichester.

assistance, just two separate front and rear Lockheed systems, so simple nothing could fail – could it?

One car only had been entered for the Aintree 200 to be driven by Behra, if fit. Although his declaration of fitness appeared to belie the truth, Behra decided to drive. Securing pole position, things looked promising but Moss was quickest off the start line and led from the BRM who, in turn, led Jack Brabham and Roy Salvadori, all three in Coopers. After 27 of the 67 laps Behra came into the pits to retire with – you've guessed it – brake failure. The standard Lockheed fluid reservoir had succumbed to the vibration and cracked, losing all the brake fluid.

May 3rd saw us at Silverstone for the 50 laps International Trophy race. Jean Behra was provided with a new car and a considerable amount of time was spent adjusting the seat to his liking, no small operation as he had an acute idiosyncrasy about his seat position and shape. It was disappointing for him to report the car would not perform and suspected it was suffering from flooding carburettors. The car was returned to Bourne and an all-night session worked to make and fit new carburettor mountings to give flexibility, a process repeated the following night. Meanwhile, Ron Flockhart had been circulating in one of the older cars with the result that both would start the race from the second row of the grid.

Race day came and, from the fall of the flag, Peter Collins took the lead in his Ferrari Dino 246, followed by Behra's BRM. On lap four Behra passed the Ferrari and was proving the faster car, taking an increasing lead. On lap eleven the now-famous BRM bogey emerged from the woodwork, a flying stone shattering Behra's goggles. After a lengthy pit stop for facial repairs and new goggles he rejoined the race in spectacular pursuit of Collins, all to no avail, however, and having to settle for fourth place. This is a race he would undoubtedly have won but for this

setback. Ron Flockhart had moved up to third place when, exiting Copse Corner, Bruce Halford's Maserati, being pushed by track marshals, confronted him. In a bid to avoid the marshals Ron took to the verge, hit a bank and overturned. A furious Ron, happily uninjured, was certain no warning flags had been waved prior to the corner, a belief made known to the race officials in no uncertain terms.

On Sunday 11th May, with a feeling of confidence after events at Silverstone, our convoy departed for Monte Carlo for the Monaco Grand Prix the following Sunday. Our travel expenses had by now been revised, though not, I fear, to the advantage of the individual, mechanics now receiving normal pay plus £5 a day with which to purchase their own food and cover incidental expenses. Not many juicy steaks and bottles of wine in traditional restaurants now, instead, mostly dining in Les Routiers establishments, some of which were surprisingly good and economical and much used by French lorry drivers. I doubt if Raymond Mays was surviving on £5 a day, driving down with his young companion and undoubtedly sampling his favourite escargots.

Maurice Dove and I crewed the Austin ETL 615, this time accompanied by Pat Carvath. It had become our regular vehicle and was considered marginally faster than the other two Austin Lodestars, each of which would comfortably achieve speeds of 60mph-plus (100kph). When travelling through France we invariably started our journey early in the morning to get some mileage in while temperatures were reasonable, and allow an early evening stop to locate a suitable hotel. We aimed to travel approximately 400 miles per day. In addition, Tony Rudd insisted

The three Austin Lodestar vehicles parked in France on their journey to Monaco.

Taking a break on the road to Monte Carlo are (left to right): Dennis Perkins, Arthur Hill, Willie Southcott, Gordon Newman, Phil Ayliff and me.

on the racing car wheels being turned daily to eliminate wheel bearing wear in one spot through friction caused by movement in transit. Arriving at Monte Carlo on Wednesday we unloaded the cars at the Palace garage and checked for any travel damage. From there we went on to the familiar Hotel Roma, where we met old acquaintances from the previous year, and were ready to give more ladies a ride in the lift!

After Silverstone, Jean Behra had expressed his pleasure with his car, telling us he thought he could achieve the fastest lap in Thursday's practice at Monaco. He was almost true to his word, sharing fastest time with the Vanwall of Tony Brooks, who would deny him pole position after final practice. Harry Schell qualified eleventh. Everything so far had been too good to be true by BRM standards; no all-night sessions and the cars running well. Was this the dawning of a new era?

Unlike at the present-day location, the starting grid and pits were situated between the central reservation and the harbour, which left mechanics in a precarious situation if working on a car in the pit area during practice. It also meant a 200 yard dash from the start line to the Gasometer hairpin and so a good start by the front men was imperative. It was no place for the faint hearted, with frantic jostling for position taking place by the back markers. Fortunately, Behra made an excellent start, soon to lead the race from the Vanwalls and Ferraris, a thrilling sight to see the dark green BRM hurtling round the tight and undulating street circuit in the lead. Meanwhile, Harry had moved into seventh place. Behra continued to increase his lead for twenty laps, after which his lap times gradually got slower and he pitted with failing brakes and retired. Harry continued to circulate towards the rear of the field

The seafront at Monte Carlo before construction of the swimming pool complex.

I spotted a soldier rather lazily carrying out his guard duties at the gate, probably finding it difficult to keep his eyes open on this warm afternoon.

Harry Schell in contented repose.

On petrol engine vehicles it is quite easy to create a noisy explosion through the exhaust system by switching off the ignition, allowing gasses to build up in the system and switching on again; if timed correctly the noise can be very loud. What an opportunity! The resultant bang was five star, causing the poor GI to leap to his feet looking terrified. Not a prank to play today, I fear …

Our second overnight stop was at Sedan, close to the French/Belgian border. Finding a suitable hotel, we were delighted to make the acquaintance of another resident who insisted on providing us with champagne; he was a travelling salesman for the stuff, what bad luck! Arthur Ambrose, the driver of the Commer workshop vehicle and also, at the time, landlord of The Golden Lion pub in Bourne, struck up a businesslike conversation with the salesman. As a consequence, he was not only plied with free champagne but also received a champagne bucket as a trophy for his hostelry in Bourne. So great was his inebriation it took about half-an-hour to wake him the following morning. Eventually, he surfaced with a very thick head but assured everyone he was fit to drive. Two ensuing incidents went some way toward convincing us that this statement must be correct.

Following the Commer in the Austin later that morning with Pat Carvath driving, a Citroën car was seen coming along a farm road at right angles to the main road on which we were travelling. French law dictated that traffic from the right had priority, but not from a farm track; surely he would stop? He could not fail to see a convoy of four vehicles that had the right of way – or could he? Yes, he could! We had not allowed for the fact he was probably observing his crops, and Pat remarked "That prat isn't going to

after a pit stop to rectify a flooding carburettor and, due to the number of retirements, he finished in fifth place – securing BRM's first two World Championship points.

Investigations into Behra's brake problems revealed a cracked brake pipe flare, causing loss of brake fluid, the failure unfairly blamed on the flare being handmade rather than machine produced. In my experience hand flares were equally as good as machine-made flares if produced correctly, as the latter had also been known to crack. Ever since initial testing of the P25 model, drivers had complained of vibration and continued to do so, leading me to believe that vibration from the 4-cylinder engine – and possibly the propshaft also – caused many of our failures.

Although we had little to celebrate, the usual sampling of Monte Carlo nightlife ensued with visits to Rosie's bar and the Tip Top where Roy Foreman and I managed to win ourselves a jackpot on the one-armed bandits. Car parking was minimal in the Principality with vehicles parked nose-to-tail on both sides of the street. After our evening sojourn, and in the mood for mischief, two or three of us would select a small car and manually turn it round to face the opposite way, laughingly trying to imagine the owner's reaction upon return!

The following day was spent servicing the cars and assessing what spares would be required for our next race, the Dutch Grand Prix at Zandvoort on Whit Monday, 26th May, and to where we would travel direct from Monaco. The journey to Holland proved memorable if only for the unusual incidents en route. The first day's travel was quite normal, passing through Avignon and Lyon for an overnight stop at Beune. Approaching an American base,

stop." I could not dispute that. Arthur must also have realised the prat was not going to stop and his resultant manoeuvre was worthy of Fangio: I am sure that, at one point, the Commer was on two wheels, missing the Citroën by inches. If Arthur was not sober before, he certainly was after!

No sooner had we recovered from this shock than a second and more bizarre incident occurred, again involving Arthur and the mobile workshop. Motoring through a small town we were approaching traffic lights when we witnessed a scene on a par with something from *The Keystone Cops*. The traffic lights were green in Arthur's favour and so he proceeded to cross. At that moment an old lady on a pushbike, evidently colour-blind, decided to cross on red from the right. Observing this we feared the worst but, although having collided with the lady, by good fortune or a miracle, Arthur had somehow managed only to separate her from her bike (which was laying in the road with wheels spinning), leaving its owner looking totally bewildered, but thankfully unharmed, in the road.

The long haul from Monte Carlo had been anything but boring.

Zandvoort is a popular seaside resort near to Amsterdam and a new venue for BRM. As this was the bank holiday season numerous coaches were visiting, many from Germany destined for Zundervaart, a name BRM staff quickly translated into thunderfart. Our hotel accommodation was in the nearby town of Haarlem. We were impressed with the hotel's cleanliness, huge choice at the Dutch breakfast table and, later in the evening, the Oranjeboom beer!

The racetrack at Zandvoort was a twisty and undulating circuit running through the sand dunes. Part of it originated as a road cut through the dunes by the German Wermacht to service its shore batteries during World War II. Later still a group of motorcycle enthusiasts developed it into the present-day circuit no longer used by Formula 1.

Coinciding with our arrival from Monaco was a contingent from Bourne with numerous spare engines and accessories. Jean Behra and Harry Schell, both with replacement engines fitted, were outpaced by the three Vanwalls in practice, the trio

sharing the front row of the grid, with a rather unhappy Jean on the second row and Happy Harry on the third row. Schell made an electrifying start to take third place during the first lap of the race with Behra lying fifth. Harry was going like the proverbial bat out of hell, now in second place behind Moss in the Vanwall, the car sounding perfect. Later, to our delight, he lapped the Ferrari of Mike Hawthorn with Behra now in third place, the order in which they were to finish. Second and third places for BRMs was the best result to date in a World Championship event. Not only was this a success for BRM but also for British motor racing, with green cars finishing first, second and third. At last we had a genuine cause for a minor celebration. Harry was delighted with his race and the performance of the car, which had now completed two Grand Prix with very little maintenance. Sadly, on the debit side, Jean Behra appeared to be somewhat disillusioned, probably due to the fact he had been beaten for the first time by his old friend and rival. This proved to be the first sign of cracks in their hitherto very close friendship.

The Belgian Grand Prix at Spa-Francorchamps was our next scheduled meeting, again, a new venue for BRM and a completely different type of circuit. Contrasting sharply with the twisty tracks at Monaco and Zandvoort, Spa was a very fast road circuit with long, sweeping curves through pinewoods on the Ardennes range of hills. Minor modifications were undertaken during the three week break, primarily to find more horsepower, and included a test run on the long runway at the RAF station at Cottesmore used to simulate the long straights at Spa and, looking further ahead, the French Grand Prix at Reims.

Due to coincide with our visit to Belgium, the football World Cup was scheduled to take place, in which England lost to Russia in a play-off to go through to the quarter final stage, with Brazil beating Sweden in the final in Stockholm. As we were approaching Dover for our crossing to Calais we spotted a ferry leaving the harbour causing 'Bagwash' to jokingly remark "There goes our boat." Little did we realise then how right he was. We caught a later ferry bound for Ostend, a more direct route but, due to the choppy sea, three attempts were required at docking. Safely across the English Channel at last, from Ostend we

The Zandvoort paddock with rolling sand dunes in the background.

Below: In stark contrast to the luxury vehicles of today, based on an OM chassis, this is the Ferrari works team transporter of the 1950s.

The BRM team cars race prepared and ready for action behind the pits at Zandvoort.

travelled along the Jabbecke Highway, a road much used for speed trials in the past, and continued via Brussels and Liége to our hotel accommodation in Spa. Spa is a very pretty town, famous for its reputedly health-giving mineral waters and situated about ten miles from the circuit where our allocated workshops were adjacent to the racetrack.

As expected, our cars were not fast enough to compete against the Ferraris and Vanwalls because of lack of power. Jean Behra had a frightening moment when oil from the engine breather blew out and onto his rear tyre. He spun twice, travelling at maximum speed through the kink on the Masta Straight, somehow without hitting anything, and drove slowly back to the pits for a reassuring cigarette. Not surprisingly, the episode had a profound effect on his confidence and resulted in the team working all night to modify the breathing system, after which Behra could still only manage tenth place on the grid with Schell seventh.

From the start Behra seemed a different man, roaring down into the famous Eau Rouge and up into the woods he somehow

continued page 96

Ferrari mechanics work on a team car at the rear of the pits at Zandvoort.

Harry Schell ready to be push-started to secure a fast qualifying lap during practice for the Dutch Grand Prix.

Mechanics celebrate with Harry Schell following his second place finish in the 1958 Dutch Grand Prix at Zandvoort.

Willie enjoying a cuppa. Seating courtesy of Dunlop …

One of the Austin Lodestar transporters outside the Hotel du Roannay at Francorchamps. The hotel was used by BRM for both accommodation and workshop purposes.

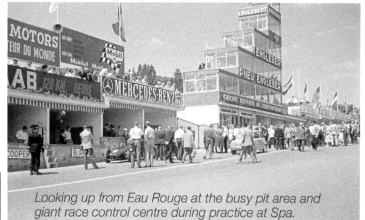

Looking up from Eau Rouge at the busy pit area and giant race control centre during practice at Spa.

Tony Rudd instructs Arthur Hill which pit signals to show to a driver during practice for the Belgian Grand Prix.

The rear of the pits at Spa, with the BRM team mobile workshop in the background, large side flap open for service. The machines and welding equipment carried on the Commer often came to the rescue of fellow competitors.

Looking down at the spectacular Eau Rouge section of the Spa circuit from the hairpin; one of the most exciting places from which to watch motor racing.

Looking back towards the pits at Spa from the exit of the Eau Rouge bends.

Harry Schell is taken on the driver's parade lap in the Alfa-Romeo.

Jean Behra on his parade lap in a Mercedes.

"Honest, it wasn't my fault, guv." A seemingly unimpressed John Cooper listens to Roy Salvadori's comments during practice at Spa.

managed to take the lead, only to be overtaken by a number of cars on the long straights. His gritty determination seen at the start soon evaporated and, disillusioned, he came into the pits to retire after five laps. Meanwhile, Harry gallantly soldiered on to fifth place in one of the most bizarre finishes I had yet witnessed. Brooks' winning Vanwall suffered engine failure after crossing the finish line; second man Hawthorn also experienced engine failure and coasted over the line; Lewis-Evans, third, had a broken wishbone, and fourth man Allison a broken exhaust. It left us reflecting that, had the race been one lap longer, Harry – whose car was still running like clockwork – could have won.

We had gained two more World Championship points from a rather mediocre performance which did not satisfy Alfred Owen. It was generally acknowledged that Behra should not have retired

Champagne Jacques, a favourite watering hole for the BRM boys when visiting Reims.

Vic Barlow, the dedicated Dunlop tyre technician, with his assistant checks the tyre pressures of the BRMs in the Reims paddock prior to the French Grand Prix.

so early because, had he continued, he would most certainly have finished in the points. He was coming to be seen as a man of fluctuating moods …

And so to Reims for the French Grand Prix on 6th July, where our garage accommodation was in Massey-Harris dealer premises adjacent to the Lido bar with which we had already become familiar, our hotel being nearby. The Reims circuit was a virtually triangular track run on public roads with an antiquated grandstand opposite the primitive pits. Good starting money was paid for the race and, in view of this, BRM had entered a third car at the request of the organisers, to be driven once again by veteran French driver Maurice Trintignant.

In first practice Harry was in a mean mood, careering round to record the fastest lap to the surprise of all. This did nothing to inspire Jean; rather the opposite. After final practice, unable to equal Schell's time, Behra put his foot down in a different context and, as number one driver, insisted on taking over Harry's car. After furious arguments between drivers and management, Harry reluctantly conceded and the friendship between the two drivers virtually came to an end there and then. The docile Trintignant was happy with whichever car was left, eventual grid positions for the BRMs being Schell, Trintignant and Behra in third, seventh and ninth places respectively.

Experienced drivers would use a crafty ploy to gain a fast lap at Reims. By going down the escape road at the Thillois hairpin, the corner prior to the pit straight from where the timed laps started, they re-entered the track and could cross the start line at greater speed, thus improving their lap times.

Whether the ex-Harry Schell car was better, or Behra's decision to change had given him new heart, whatever the reason, in the race he drove like a man inspired, competing with Moss and Fangio behind the leader Hawthorn. Unfortunately, he had to retire nine laps from the finish with a failed engine while in second position, after a truly great drive. Sadly, while fighting for the lead, Italian driver Luigi Musso crashed and was killed. Both Schell and Trintignant retired with water and oil leaks respectively, Harry still unhappy he had been forced to give up his own car to

Behra. His mood lightened somewhat when he returned to his hotel to find his small bubble car had been man-handled by some of his fellow drivers and placed outside his bedroom door, his answer being to start it and bumpily drive it down the stairs!

Whilst, to some extent, the performance at Reims had been heartening, we were still chasing that elusive World Championship Grand Prix win. Alfred Owen particularly wanted a good performance in the next event, the British Grand Prix at Silverstone on 19th July. where three cars had been entered for Behra, Schell and the ever-faithful Ron Flockhart. Unfortunately, the latter had been injured in a serious accident in a sports car race at Rouen a few weeks earlier and was out of action for some time. Therefore the American, Masten Gregory, was engaged to drive the third car in this event at Silverstone. Hopes of that happening were dashed on the first day's practice, however, when Gregory crashed his Lister-Jaguar at Becketts Corner and suffered broken ribs. Our entry thus immediately reduced to two cars.

Schell, back in his old car, was again out-driving Behra in practice, claiming second fastest time to the Vanwall of Moss with Behra eighth. The rev counter of the BRMs was fitted with a telltale needle, which indicated the maximum revs used. The needle could be returned to zero by pressing a button at the rear of the instrument. It was suspected Harry, going over the permitted rev limit, had found this button and was returning it to zero, thus concealing any over-revving. I surreptitiously fitted a tyre valve cap over the button on the instrument on his car and,

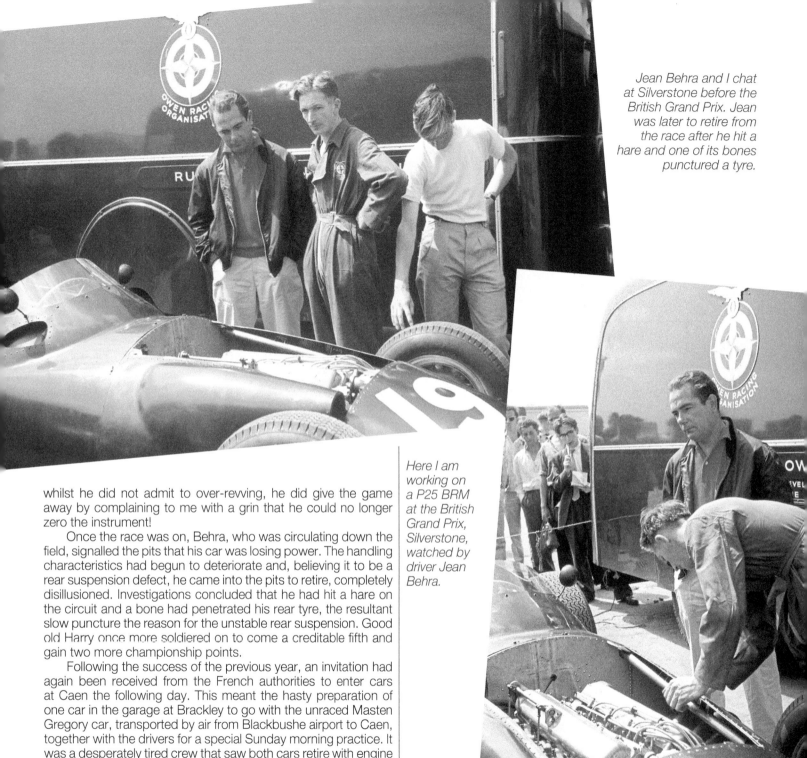

Jean Behra and I chat at Silverstone before the British Grand Prix. Jean was later to retire from the race after he hit a hare and one of its bones punctured a tyre.

Here I am working on a P25 BRM at the British Grand Prix, Silverstone, watched by driver Jean Behra.

whilst he did not admit to over-revving, he did give the game away by complaining to me with a grin that he could no longer zero the instrument!

Once the race was on, Behra, who was circulating down the field, signalled the pits that his car was losing power. The handling characteristics had begun to deteriorate and, believing it to be a rear suspension defect, he came into the pits to retire, completely disillusioned. Investigations concluded that he had hit a hare on the circuit and a bone had penetrated his rear tyre, the resultant slow puncture the reason for the unstable rear suspension. Good old Harry once more soldiered on to come a creditable fifth and gain two more championship points.

Following the success of the previous year, an invitation had again been received from the French authorities to enter cars at Caen the following day. This meant the hasty preparation of one car in the garage at Brackley to go with the unraced Masten Gregory car, transported by air from Blackbushe airport to Caen, together with the drivers for a special Sunday morning practice. It was a desperately tired crew that saw both cars retire with engine failure in a fixture that should never have been accepted.

The notorious Nürburgring, set in the heart of the beautiful Eiffel

Mountains, was the venue for the German Grand Prix on 3rd August. Again, we were breaking new ground, the fourteen mile twisty and bumpy circuit recognised as a severe test of man and machine. Intended to reduce local unemployment, construction commenced in 1925 and it opened in 1927. Although workshop conditions were by no means perfect, they were at least convenient and secure, comprising a number of lock-up garages built to form a guarded compound. Our hotel accommodation was at a small and friendly family-run hotel, the Wilden Schwein, in the nearby town of Adenau half way round the circuit. Official practice was something of a nightmare because of the many bumps, corners and gradients. Setting the suspension to the satisfaction of the drivers proved extremely difficult, the cars bottoming at several places during a lap. The circuit was also prone to spasmodic local rain showers and it was during one of these in the first session that Behra lost control, went off the road and over a hedge. The car was so effectively concealed from view when they went to collect it that Pat Carvath and Maurice Dove initially drove past the spot in the transporter. After all-night modification sessions, a compromise in the suspension settings was reached but the two rather unhappy drivers could still manage only eighth and ninth places, with Harry the faster.

Prior to the start of the race Harry revealed his plan. From his grid position nearest to the pit lane, he intended to come down the pit lane, so would we keep it clear for him, a rather dodgy request that we agreed to undertake to the best of our ability, with fingers crossed for our safety. True to his word, at the drop of the flag, he roared past us and momentarily took second place, only to be overtaken by the faster Vanwalls and Ferraris of Moss, Brooks, Hawthorn and Collins. (The latter crashed later in the race after ten laps and had to be airlifted to hospital in Bonn, where he died from his injuries, the second Ferrari driver to lose his life within three races.) Witnessing the accident, Hawthorn retired. He had lost his greatest friend whom he invariably referred to as "mon ami, mate," and motor racing had lost one of its most popular participants. Brooks went on to win the Grand Prix after Moss retired. Both BRMs retired due to vibration-related problems, Behra complaining of a suspension malady and Schell with brake failure. Had Behra continued in the race, which was possible, he could certainly have finished third, and possibly second. His moods were becoming more and more unpredictable; sad to see from such a talented driver and genuinely nice man.

A new mechanic named Billy Wright had joined our team for the Nürburgring. Originally employed by BRM to work on the now defunct Bowser project, Billy had been seconded to the racing department. He was working under a car in the paddock lock-up garage when he was confronted by a huge black spider heading towards him. "Christ!" he exclaimed. "Look at that!" and made a quick exit, only to find Jack Brabham was up to his tricks once more. He had acquired the thing from a joke shop and was propelling it by air pressure produced by squeezing a bulb at the end of a small diameter tube.

Back at Folkingham a complete stripdown of the cars was necessary to search for cracks and damage after the severe pounding they had recently received. Some minor damage was discovered and reinforcements and repairs made as necessary, but in general the cars had survived well and were now prepared for the Portuguese Grand Prix on 24th August.

At the German Grand Prix Lorna Berthon had arranged a working lunch consisting of bread rolls and wine. Back at Folkingham Maurice discovered a bottle of wine in the Commer workshop vehicle, presumably hidden by driver Jack Heward for later consumption. Maurice invited me to take wine with him, and we sat and indulged, carefully replacing the seal on the now empty bottle: no-one ever complained!

Rebuilds complete, once again the BRM convoy hit the A15 road out of Bourne to begin the 1500 mile journey to Oporto on the west coast of Portugal. This was to be the first leg of

A variety of transporters in the paddock at the Nürburgring.

Helping the opposition: a BRM van preparing to tow-start a Vanwall, demonstrating the comradeship between the teams in that era.

PROGRAMA

CAMPEONATO DO MUNDO DE
CONDUTORES

7º GRANDE PRÉMIO DE PORTUGAL
PORTO 24 DE AGOSTO DE 1958
CATEGORIA CORRIDA
(FÓRMULA 1)

ORGANIZAÇÃO
ACP

BP ENERGOL
O OLEO DOS VENCEDORES

gathered in their harvest, and were threshing the corn by having donkeys trample it, whilst the womenfolk beat it to remove the chaff. It was difficult to see where the corn had been grown on the arid land. Stopping for drinks in an isolated hamlet, we found a small and dingy bar selling warm beer (no refrigerators in 1958), chickens roaming the premises. Fortunately, we had had the foresight and good fortune to refuel the vehicles at San Sebastian, as petrol pumps were as scarce as hen's teeth.

After overnighting at Salamanca we eventually arrived in Oporto, Portugal's second city standing on the banks of the river Douro and famous for its port wine. Large quantities of fish could be seen hanging on racks in the open, presumably being cured by drying in the sun.

This race was Portugal's first World Championship Grand Prix. A very demanding course had been chosen, running through the streets of this ancient city, with kerbs, tramlines and varying road surfaces to test a driver's skill. In first practice Schell put in an electrifying early lap that set the pace for the day, only to be beaten in the closing minutes by Moss and Behra. Final practice saw Behra and Schell placed fourth and seventh. The Portuguese police were like many of their continental counterparts, overly officious, aimlessly marshalling people in and around the pit and paddock areas. With some cajoling and humouring, however, they were soon retrained in the ways of the Formula 1 circus, and allowed us more freedom to move around these areas.

Staying at the same hotel was Maxwell Boyd, then a new and somewhat inexperienced motoring correspondent for the *Daily Telegraph*. He was pleased to be in the company of racing mechanics and was helped by us where possible. We also helped him to an ample quantity of port, after which I recall him having difficulty negotiating the hotel stairs!

Rain showers were prevalent on race day, which, if they persisted, would make the track slippery and dangerous. Happily, fortune was on the side of the drivers and the skies cleared for the race. Moss easily won an incident-free race from Hawthorn, with Behra fourth and Schell sixth. We were still collecting championship points, though, disappointingly, only for the lower places.

an approximately 4000 mile round trip as we were to travel direct from Oporto to Monza for the Italian Grand Prix on 7th September, two weeks later.

It was a fascinating journey. Crossing to Calais we headed south to Paris, a nightmare to drive through, and on via Tours towards Bordeaux and Biarritz where we discovered the cussedness of Spanish customs officers. Eventually, we were allowed to pass, having paid a levy of one BRM lapel badge per officer, and made an overnight stop at the north coast seaside resort of San Sebastian. The next leg of the journey showed us the realities of life in rural Spain where, high on a barren plateau, a primitive way of life was still lived. The peasant farmers had

N.º 1162

CAMPEONATO DO MUNDO DE CONDUTORES - 1958 MECANICO G. P. P.

A primitive method of threshing corn. Seen on the Tierra de Campos plains in northern Spain on the journey to Oporto.

The BRM convoy takes on fuel, whilst someone takes the opportunity to do a bit of maintenance on one of the Austins on the way to Oporto for the Portuguese Grand Prix.

A refreshment stop at a basic-looking café in northern Spain en route to Oporto.

The following morning we departed on the long trail to Monza, prior to which we went to pay our hotel bills only to be told they had already been paid by the race organisers. This news was too good to be true, and this generous gesture was greeted with delight. However, we were brought down to earth when we arrived back at Bourne to find, to our dismay, we had each been billed for the hotel charges.

After an overnight stop in Spain we arrived at the frontier; no problems with the Spanish customs this time, in fact, they seemed pleased to see us leave their country … This time it was the French who were reluctant to admit us – more badges! I suspect there had been some fraternisation between the two sets of officers. A second night stop was taken in southern France near Montpelier, where Maurice Trintignant was resident. Here, I drew

Graham Hill exits the pits at Oporto in the Lotus (20), with Harry Schell's BRM (10) in the foreground. Was this where RM recognised Graham's talent, for two years later he was to transfer to BRM?

the short straw because I had to share a room with Phyl Ayliff. Nothing against Phyl – in fact, we were good mates – but at the time he suffered badly from athlete's foot. Additionally, we appeared to be sharing the room with most of the local mosquito population. To counteract the insect problem, the management provided a deterrent in the form of strips of smoke dispensers. Apparently, the usual procedure was to light one when vacating your room, entering a pleasantly-perfumed, mosquito-free zone upon return. So, before leaving our room for dinner we decided to give the mozzies some smoke. Phil asked how many

Left to right: Dennis Perkins, Jimmy Collins, Phil Ayliff, Arthur Hill and myself take in the mountain air on the summit of a mountain pass en route to Monza.

G. P. D'ITALIA
Lasciapassare personale
CONCORRENTI
Vale per i recinti segnati con la lettera
E
dal 5 al 7 settem. 1958 — non cedibile
№ 848

he should light and, mindful of the odour likely to emanate from his feet, in a moment of light-hearted frivolity I replied "Light the bloody lot," which he did. We had a lovely meal and generous quantities of the delicious local wine but, returning to our hotel in joyful mood, we found our room uninhabitable due to smoke. There was only one thing to do, open the windows for a few minutes to let it clear. Being very tired through travel, and with the assistance of good food and wine, we were soon asleep. I imagine the mosquitoes were outside laughing, just waiting for the smoke to clear because in the morning we both had more bite marks than Dalmatians have spots and the mosquitoes looked decidedly fatter! Another lesson learned and the next three days spent suffering acute irritation.

Arriving once more at the Albergo Ristorante Marchesi at Villasanta, a place we had become quite fond of, the second leg of our triangular journey was complete. Three BRMs were entered for the Italian race, the two regular drivers Jean Behra and Harry Schell to be joined by Jo Bonnier who was replacing the convalescing Ron Flockhart. The Portuguese contingent had now swollen to include more men from Bourne who had travelled out with two more cars and countless spares, an open lorry, referred to as the 'coal cart,' used to transport one of the cars. As cars were stripped and rebuilt with numerous spares strewn about in the limited space available, the scene in the garages at the rear of the Marchesi Hotel was beginning to resemble the yard of an upmarket *Steptoe & Son*. The hotel's 'other' line of business seemed as brisk as ever …

Once more we shared the company of 'Oilio,' who did a roaring trade in waste oil due to the number of engine changes necessary. He also provided us with a rather funny incident. The oil containers were equipped with a pouring spout, the outward end of which was swaged inward giving it a very sharp finish. As man has an instinctive habit of sticking fingers into holes, 'Oilio' arrived in the workshop screaming, his finger firmly stuck in the oil can spout, the inner biting into his flesh. Phil Ayliff eventually managed to cut off the spout after administering an anaesthetic in the form of a large brandy.

Friday practice was held in warm sunshine and Behra's early fast time was soon beaten by the Vanwalls and Ferraris, and again on Saturday, with Behra, Schell and Bonnier eighth, ninth and tenth respectively. If nothing else, they were at least consistent! Schell's race was shortlived. Entering the Curva Grande on the first lap whilst in third place,'Taffy' von Trip's Ferrari collided with Harry and both cars left the road. The jungle telegraph informed us Harry was uninjured, but when he eventually returned to the pits he looked a sorry sight, with numerous small lacerations about his person and a very tatty-looking pair of overalls. He had escaped the crash relatively unharmed but had, unfortunately, landed in a forest of bramble bushes! Meanwhile, Behra was driving an exciting race, dicing with the Vanwall of Moss for second place behind race leader Mike Hawthorn's Ferrari. Eventually, brake problems obliged him to make two pit stops and this, combined with a slipping clutch, forced him into retirement after forty-three laps. Bonnier had stopped earlier with propshaft failure.

Phil Ayliff being towed through the Monza Royal Park to the Monza Circuit. It was not permitted to drive cars through the park.

So our long trek was nearly complete. Monday was spent loading the vast quantity of spares and equipment accumulated during the past three weeks. On Tuesday morning our host, Signor Valentino, saw off the five vehicle convoy, no doubt delighted that peace had broken out once again and happy in the knowledge of more rooms being available for his more lucrative customers! We were equally happy to be returning to Bourne though very disappointed at having none of our cars finish at Monza.

One more race would conclude the racing year for BRM, the Grand Prix of Morocco on 19th October. This year promised to be especially interestinng compared with 1957. Firstly, the event had been upgraded to World Championship status and, secondly, vying for the title were the two British drivers Mike Hawthorn and Stirling Moss. Attracted by the good starting money on offer, Raymond Mays, with his penchant for procuring as much finance as possible, entered four cars to be driven by Behra, Schell, Bonnier, and the now almost fully recovered Ron Flockhart.

The various teams chose a variety of methods of transport and routes to Morocco, the Vanwall team going overland via Gibraltar. In contrast to last year, BRM cars and personnel were to go by air, and a Douglas C54 Skymaster was chartered from the French airline, Transports Aeriens Intercontinentaux, to fly from Stansted airport to Casablanca. Loading degenerated into something of a farce and Tony Rudd, after consultation with the airfreight company, designed a structure, which Stan Hope made to allow the cars to be stacked one above the other in the fuselage. Cars and loading structure were transported to Stansted and unloaded on the airport apron. On seeing this weird piece of equipment the aircrew and freight handling crew looked at each other in a rather bemused manner and threw it on the grass, loading the cars quite easily on one deck. What a pity this was the 1950s because, had it been today, Stan's work would surely have won a prize as modern art.

Billy Wright, the butt of Jack Brabham's spider joke in Germany, was again travelling with us. He was naïve about air travel and excited, as this would be his first flight. We were soon airborne for our direct flight to Casablanca and the lone steward on board served food and wine, the wine sending Billy into a deep sleep, from which he did not wake until we were flying over the southern coast of Spain. Seeing Billy semi-conscious once more, I casually

The Douglas C54 of Transports Aeriens Intercontinenteaux at Stansted airport being prepared for the flight to Casablanca.

Preparing to load a BRM onto the C54 at Stansted.

remarked how hot it had been at Madrid airport, to which he replied "I haven't been to Madrid." "Of course you have" I said. "How could you stay up here without an aeroplane for company? We landed to refuel so don't tell me you stayed on the plane fast asleep." "I must have done," he said and became quite concerned when I told him it was an offence to stay on an aircraft during refuelling, if he was discovered he could be fined, so best not talk about it. To this day I don't know whether or not he ever realised we hadn't landed at Madrid.

Here, I must contradict Tony Rudd. In his book *It Was Fun*, he says two air hostesses accompanied us on this flight. This was not so: one male steward served us food and wine. He also says two transporters travelled to Casablanca via Gibraltar, carrying spares. Again, this was not so because no BRM vehicles went by road.

On the ground at the small airport at Casablanca, our cargo appeared to be breaking new ground for the handlers with maximum supervision necessary to ensure the cars were safely unloaded, after which they were

Loading BRM cars onto the Douglas C54 at Stansted airport.

Almost there, as the last BRM is forklifted into the aircraft.

Sherpas

ENICAR

ULTRASONIC

BRM mechanics boarding the Douglas C54 at Stansted airport.

Below: The garage accommodation allocated to the BRM team at Casablanca with mechanic Maurice Dove entertaining a member of the US air force. His goodwill gesture was probably the reason for our invitation to visit the air force's 357 FIS.

The C54 with cars and mechanics on board.

towed to the Garage Sami by a variety of vehicles provided by the organisers. Settled in our hotel after a tiring day, we were soon disturbed by an hysterical Pat Carvath, appearing in danger of peeing his pants, though eventually managing to blurt out through tears of laughter "You'll never guess what Billy's done, he's only crapped in the bidet!" Apparently, he had met Billy in the corridor

Pat and Phil wait outside the Casablanca garages.

The 'Sheriff' about to hit the trail.

carrying a folded copy of the *Daily Mirror* and looking for the communal toilet to dispose of the contents from the bidet. There were no en suite facilities in those days and Billy was complaining bitterly that the toilets out here did not flush very well!

That year we had done our best to protect the bright parts on the cars from the rust caused by the salty air experienced the previous year. The ridiculous company rule whereby only a selected few were allowed to tow-start and drive the cars had finally been waived, with mechanics now permitted to drive. Nevertheless, the cars still had to be towed to the circuit, with me steering Harry Schell's car which was being dragged along behind an ex-army Dodge 3-ton box van to take part in Friday practice. The main purpose of that session was to adjust suspension settings, gear ratios and carburation. Returning to the garage I was again towed by the Dodge box van, the Arab driver deciding to take a different route, which I had no choice but to follow.

The pits at the Ain-Diab circuit at Casablanca.

Raymond Mays, Ron Flockhart and mechanics in the busy pit area during practice for the Moroccan Grand Prix.

Jean Behra appears uninterested in the Royal cavalcade, but is making a serious point to someone as the entourage of HRH The King of Morocco passes.

Outriders approach escorting HRH King Mohammed V to the Royal box.

Negotiating a slight incline approaching a bridge over the road, I heard a loud bang from the direction of the towing van, quickly followed by an even louder bang. It was at this point that my brain told me to go into self-preservation mode. To accommodate the race traffic a series of three Bailey bridges had been built across our road. Unfortunately for me, the constructors had not taken the incline into consideration and so the first of the bridges came into light contact with the top of the box van, the second bridge gave it a mighty nudge, and the third one ripped the top off completely! Seeing about a ton of metal van roof hurtling towards me certainly sharpened my reflexes; like a rat up a pump I got down into the cockpit as low as possible, the flying roof taking the windscreen off Harry's car and the front of the car disappearing under the back of the van! The van driver suddenly stopped – I can't think why – leaving me with no alternative but to go further

Chariot fit for a champion. Ferrari mechanics wheel Mike Hawthorn's car to the starting grid. Mike clinched the Driver's World Championship by bringing the car home in second place.

under the back of the van, causing even more damage to poor Harry's car. Finally at rest and regaining my composure, I looked up to see a white-faced 'Sheriff' Perkins peering at me, obviously expecting to see a decapitated body. In a state of shock he asked "Do you want a fag, mate?"

Another casualty of this incident was Willie's toolbox, which had been dislodged from the lorry and was lying empty in the road. This meant that its contents – about a thousand items – tools, nuts and washers, split-pins and a whole variety of knick-knacks peculiar to the occupation of racing mechanics, was spread over the ground. We were later given to understand that the driver of the lorry had been instructed not to go that way and he was now looking for another job!

Final practice finished with the front row occupied by Mike Hawthorn's Ferrari on pole and championship rival Stirling Moss alongside, together with Stuart Lewis-Evans, both in Vanwalls. Jean Behra's BRM was fourth on the second row and the other

Here, I'm being towed to the circuit in Harry's car. The return journey almost ended in disaster when the towing vehicle hit a bridge.

Casablancan street scene.

BRMs way back in eighth, tenth and fifteenth positions. Not very impressive. Whilst obviously our priority was the performance of our own cars, one could not fail to be captivated by the impending battle between Stirling and Mike, one of them soon to be the first English driver crowned World Champion. Mike was probably the favourite as he had only to finish in second place to win the title, whilst Stirling not only had to win but also claim the one extra point for fastest lap, with Hawthorn finishing no higher than third.

As in 1957 the race came under the jurisdiction of the French, the inimitable and tubby little Frenchman 'Toto' Roche again dropping the flag in his own farcical fashion. Once the field had sorted itself out Stirling took the lead from the Ferrari of Phil Hill, who then allowed Mike to move into the second position he so desperately needed, there to circulate comfortably for the remainder of the race. A delighted Mike Hawthorn clinched the World Championship by one point from the unlucky and disappointed Stirling Moss.

Meanwhile, the field following was having mixed fortunes, the most unfortunate being Stuart Lewis-Evans whose car crashed and caught fire. Stuart suffered severe burns and was flown to England, only to succumb a few days later. Jo Bonnier soldiered on to finish fourth for BRM with Harry Schell fifth. Ron Flockhart retired early on and Jean Behra, uncompetitive in front of a French-speaking crowd, pulled into the pits at mid-distance in utter frustration and walked away. A disconsolate and disappointed Jean later came to say goodbye, informing us he was leaving BRM to drive for Ferrari in 1959. It was a shame for everyone involved. Jean had great confidence in Tony Rudd and was sure he would one day build a championship-winning car for him to drive. Sadly, fate was to decree otherwise …

Shortly afterwards Mike Hawthorn announced his retirement from motor racing. He had reached the pinnacle by winning the World Championship but I have little doubt that the loss of his friend Peter Collins also influenced his decision to finish with motor racing. It was not an auspicious conclusion to a season of mixed fortunes. Had we improved since last season? Well, yes! Second and third place finishes at Zandvoort had been our best ever result, but we had not yet won a World Championship Grand Prix, which Alfred Owen wanted so badly. He was obviously displeased now the Vanwalls were consistently winning races.

Monday morning saw us at the airport to prepare for our flight back to Stansted. Tony Rudd was not in the best of moods for two reasons: firstly, he had a substantial hangover and, secondly, one of our mechanics was missing. Yes, you've guessed it, Billy again! Pat Carvath took a taxi on a mercy mission and eventually found a frightened-looking Billy, escorting him back to the airport.

Homeward bound. The powerful C54 with a sunset backdrop on the flight from Casablanca.

All things considered it's a wonder that Billy was successful at his job interview as he was rather out of touch with the time. Shortly after take-off we could see the Vanwall transporter far below wending its way to Tangiers for the crossing to Gibraltar and long trek back through Spain and France to London. We did not envy them their long drive; this would be the one race in which we would beat them! Billy, possibly feeling guilty due to the inconvenience he had caused, or possibly because he did not want to miss Madrid this time, stayed awake all the way.

Once back in England meetings in the upper echelons of power at the offices of the Royal Automobile Club in London took place to discuss formation of the new Formula 1 regulations to be introduced by the FIA for 1961, the current specification being due to end at close of the 1960 Grand Prix season. The most important of these considerations was engine size, the units under discussion being either 1.5- or 3-litre capacity. Whatever the choice, BRM would need to develop a new engine.

Meanwhile, we humble mechanics were to spend the winter once more involved in maintenance, modifications – and mischief. Gordon 'Baggie' Newman had become a very disgruntled man, not at all happy with his lot, a mutual dislike having existed for some time between himself and Peter Spear. His frustration caused him to be quite unusually irritable occasionally with a workmate, and one such instance had seen a difference of opinion between himself and Maurice Dove. Sitting having our tea break one day, Maurice ate a banana and, putting the skin on the floor he flippantly remarked "You're supposed to put a banana skin on the floor so that the foreman slips up on it." Sure enough, as if by design, 'Baggie' stepped on it with his heel and came a right purler, which did nothing to improve the temporary rift between them. Fortunately, 'Baggie' bore no malice and they were soon friends again with both seeing the funny side. The

same could not be said of the situation between 'Baggie' and Spear and, when the opportunity came for 'Baggie' to go to New Zealand on a one-way ticket, he was quick to accept. BRM's loss was New Zealand's gain.

113

'BYE 'BYE BAGWASH

The 1959 season started earlier than in previous years, and possibly with a degree of quiet optimism for BRM as it had been placed in six World Championship events the previous year.

One type P25 2.5-litre car was being sent to compete in Formule Libre races in New Zealand in January and February to be driven by Ron Flockhart, accompanied by mechanics Gordon Newman and Roy Foreman. Sadly, Gordon – 'Bagwash' to one and all – was about to leave BRM as he had agreed to go with the car on a one-way ticket. Often having spoken of his desire to emigrate to New Zealand, he was now finally doing so. He would be sorely missed at Folkingham and in motor racing circles generally, also around the hostelries of Bourne and district where bar takings would be considerably down. Although we had had differences of opinion on occasion we had been good workmates; he was a man who bore no malice and I was pleased to have known and worked alongside him.

The opposition in New Zealand included Stirling Moss, Jack Brabham and Bruce McLaren in Coopers, and Jo Bonnier and Harry Schell in privately-entered Maseratis. The New Zealand Grand Prix at Ardmore was the first race on 10th January, the format being two heats and a final. Ron won his second heat but had to retire in the final with oil system failure after a very poor start, largely due to the ineptness of the dignitary assigned to start the race. The next event was the Lady Wigram Trophy held at Christchurch two weeks later. Ron gained pole position in practice and, after a terrific dual with Jack Brabham, won the race, both cars twice lapping the third placed car! Finally, our small team travelled to Invercargill on 7th February for the Teretonga Trophy, comprising two twelve mile heats and a sixty mile final. Again, Ron took pole position for the

final but, after a poor start, was unable to overtake Bruce McLaren and settled for second place. It was a very popular win for the likeable New Zealander on his home soil and rounded off our team's month-long trip 'down under.' Roy Foreman returned to England alone leaving Gordon to spend his future in the country he loved.

In January motor racing suffered a tragic loss when Mike Hawthorn, recently retired from the sport, was tragically killed in a road accident near Guildford in Surrey. Later in the year Maurice Dove and I, accompanied by our wives, were honoured to represent the BRM team at a memorial service in London. I still recall singing the hymn *He who would valiant be*, a most appropriate choice for such a popular sportsman.

In the late spring BRM received notice from the Air Ministry that the leased Folkingham airfield would have to be vacated. It was to be converted into a Thor rocket site, part of the east coast defence network. This was a serious blow to our testing facilities for, not only did we   track test there, but it was also the site of the engine   test beds which had been moved there   from   Bourne

A test day at Goodwood where something is causing Pat Carvath to look very serious and concerned.

some years earlier due to complaints regarding noise pollution from Raymond Mays' neighbours. Eventually, agreement was reached which permitted a new test house to be built 500 yards to the north of the existing site, but still within the boundary of the airfield.

Meanwhile, a new racing car workshop was to be built on the site of the old gasworks next to the existing Bourne premises to accommodate the contents of the rest of the Folkingham workshops. Unfortunately, despite lengthy negotiations with the Air Ministry, we were unable to retain the track testing facility at the airfield, the equivalent, in today's world, of Ferrari losing the Fiorano test circuit at the back of its factory! Later in the year we would have no alternative but to test at other venues, such as Snetterton, Silverstone or Goodwood, although nearby North Witham was used for straight line testing on a disused RAF airfield runway. On the plus side was the fact that administration, the design, machine shop and racing shop would all be together as a compact unit.

Back at Folkingham, development work continued with Phyl Ayliff – a popular choice – promoted to succeed 'Bagwash' as chief mechanic. Prior to the start of the championship season, there were the usual three minor UK Formula 1 events, beginning at Goodwood on 30th March where two P25 cars were entered for Harry Schell and Jo Bonnier, a third car taken as a spare. (Jo had now been taken on as a full-time team driver to partner Harry Schell and Ron Flockhart.) The Goodwood meeting followed the usual pattern: a 100 mile (161km) event in which Harry finished in third and Jo in fourth. Once again minor celebrations at The Nags Head in Chichester were called for and representatives from Shell, who were also staying there, joined us. Very little excuse was necessary to celebrate and our talents were applied equally on both sides of the bar.

With the BRM's performance apparently improving, Stirling Moss was once more showing an interest in driving the car. Arrangements had been made for him to test drive two cars at Goodwood the day following the race and, in so doing, he clocked the first 100mph lap of the circuit. As a result of that impressive outing, Stirling's management approached Alfred Owen with a view to Moss driving one of our cars in the BRDC International Trophy race on 2nd May at Silverstone.

In-between these events came Aintree where again Schell and Bonnier were to drive. Aintree was always a depressing place to go. The garage accommodation was decidedly grotty in a run-down area of Liverpool, where it was necessary to employ a security guard. That said, we encountered friendliness everywhere, and nowhere was there a greater sense of humour than that found in Liverpool. Entry to the circuit was also difficult due to narrow roads and milling spectators. The pit area left a lot to be desired with the individual pits being small and hangers-on generally obstructing mechanics working under pressure, causing tempers to be sorely tested. On one occasion, whilst I was working on a car in front of the pits, an individual – who happened to be a relative of Raymond Mays – asked if he could help. Under some stress I rather impolitely invited him to get to the other side of the pit counter and keep out of my way. Peter Berthon looked at me with a wry smile and a nod. He, too, disliked hangers-on, but if they happened to be friends of RM,

Phil Ayliff, Jimmy Collins and I prepare to push-start Stirling Moss for a Goodwood test drive.

Stirling Moss test driving the P25 BRM at Goodwood prior to coming to an agreement with Alfred Owen to drive a works car in the International Trophy race at Silverstone.

Stirling Moss spins his P25 BRM at Copse Corner during the International Trophy race at Silverstone due to faulty brakes.

he was probably too polite to ask them to move. After qualifying third and fourth in practice, sadly, our efforts proved fruitless once more. Both cars retired in the race due to the long-standing problem of timing gear failure.

Understandably, Alfred Owen was absolutely delighted at Stirling Moss' wish to drive one of our cars at Silverstone. He was the best driver of his day, very demanding, and his input would be invaluable. Agreement was quickly reached, even down to the car carrying Stirling's favourite number 7. Ron Flockhart was to drive the second car but the move did not meet with the approval of team drivers Jo Bonnier and Harry Schell, both very unhappy with the arrangement. Stirling drove both cars in official practice and, unfortunately for we mechanics, preferred the chassis of Flockhart's car but the engine of his own so requested they be swapped. Once again a bunch of weary mechanics worked through the long night, only for sod's law to rear its ugly head once more. Ron came home third while Stirling failed to finish, retiring on lap four with brake failure whilst leading the race. A brake pipe flare cracked on a front brake calliper, causing loss of hydraulic fluid. Stirling's instinctive feeling for a car had caused him to brake early for Copse Corner and he was able to spin the car harmlessly onto the outside grass verge.

Inevitably, some members of the Moss camp blamed the BRM mechanics for this failure, but I do not accept it was their fault, nor, as was one theory, that the brakes were damaged during the engine change: a very unlikely cause. Neither would I subscribe to the theory that a pipe with a cracked flare had possibly been fitted during assembly at the Dunlop works; if it had, the fault would almost certainly have become evident during the brake bleeding process. I firmly believe the pipe cracked during running due to vibration; always a problem with the P25. Whatever the cause – and by no means disputing Stirling's opinion that his own engine was better than Flockhart's – had he not requested an engine change he might well have won the race in his original car …

There was little time to dwell on the Silverstone failure as we were to depart for the Monaco Grand Prix the following day, due to be held on 10th May. There, we were scheduled to run three cars for our regular drivers with a spare available for any emergency. With the three Austins capable of carrying only one car each, an extra vehicle was necessary to transport the fourth car to Monaco. To overcome this problem, an open Ford Thames Trader lorry was loaned from the Rubery Owen fleet at Darlaston, this vehicle displaying the distinctive bright orange livery of the Owen Organisation. Arthur Ambrose and I had drawn the short straw when it came to choice of drivers for this noisy and totally unsuitable vehicle. However, needs must, so off we went.

Travelling through the dense traffic in the centre of Paris with Arthur driving, I glanced down from the lofty height of the passenger seat in the Ford cab at the most beautiful pair of legs in the passenger seat of a sports car alongside. Still admiring this fine pair of limbs it became apparennt they were getting closer, and closer, until finally there was an ominous metallic clang: the front wheel rim of our vehicle had made serious contact with the sports car. The whistle-blowing gendarme on traffic duty, busy dealing with the dense flow, was not interested in our little coming together and, indeed, had no need to be as the male driver of the car was very apologetic and took full responsibility. He was very eager to be on his way, which made us wonder whether he should have been in the company of the owner of the beautiful legs … We eventually arrived at our destination, saddle-sore and with aching bones. This was definitely not the best vehicle to take to a Grand Prix in terms of comfort and the ribald comments it elicited from opposing team members.

1er GRAND PRIX MONACO JUNIOR
XVIIe GRAND PRIX AUTOMOBILE
CHAMPIONNAT DU MONDE DES CONDUCTEURS
MONACO

When visiting a foreign country it was usual practice among most of the mechanics to buy a gift for their wives, sweethearts, concubines or whoever – in my case definitely my wife! (On BRM pay I could not afford a concubine, had I desired one for, contrary to popular belief, we were relatively low-paid.) Job satisfaction was part of our reward, my gross pay for the year being £892, or £17 a week. On this occasion, accompanied by Roy Foreman, I decided to buy a handbag and, browsing in one of the many rather expensive shops, I selected one, which Roy and I both recognised as pigskin. We played ignorant to this as

Arthur Ambrose and I pictured at Monaco with the Ford Thames Trader after an interesting drive from Bourne.

the lady assistant's impersonation of a pig was very impressive, her grunting noises causing us much amusement; eventually, she was joined by a colleague who joined in the impersonation. The ladies found it as amusing as we did and the four of us enjoyed a good laugh. Much to their relief I did finally buy the handbag!

As was usual at Monte Carlo, one practice session was held at six o'clock in the morning, interrupting the local residents' sleep: many Monegasques took their holidays during Grand Prix week to escape the crowds and the noise. Stirling Moss had been practicing Rob Walker's Cooper with a BRM engine installed, but the car was stillborn and never raced. Instead, Stirling elected to drive Rob's Cooper Climax for the remainder of practice, in which he achieved pole position. The best of the BRMs was Jo Bonnier in a disappointing seventh place. In the race the tough circuit took its toll and, once more, the three BRMs failed to contend with the arduous conditions, Harry Schell – our best performer on the day – unfortunately, running short of road when lying third. Jolly Jack Brabham won in a Cooper.

This disappointment did not prevent post-race celebrations, however, which – win or lose – were always good at Monaco and usually held at Rosie's bar, the Kit-Kat, the Sporting club – or possibly all three! The downside was the dreaded flight of 340 steps to climb back to the hotel; somehow, the later it got the more steps there seemed to be. This year Roy and I were returning to our hotel in the early hours. On the way I noticed a coloured fluorescent sign over a door and, assuming it was a café, asked Roy if he would like a coffee. "Can we get one then?" he asked. "Yes, this place is still open" I replied. Roy went in first to be politely informed we were actually in the studios of Radio Monte Carlo and, no, it did not serve coffee.

The 1959 Monaco Grand Prix was significant for the BRM team in that it was the first time that Mr and Mrs Louis T Stanley put in an appearance at a race meeting. Mrs Stanley, Sir Alfred Owen's sister, was a very smart and well-dressed lady, pleasant to converse with and a joint director of the Owen Organisation, along with her brothers Alfred and Ernest. My first impression of Louis Stanley was that he seemed a rather pompous and extravagant-looking person who, though trying to impress, was treated with suspicion by one and all.

A quite unremarkable and pleasant journey across France and the English Channel saw us back at Folkingham to prepare the cars for Holland and the Dutch Grand Prix at Zandvoort in three weeks' time. In the interim period one car had been sent to Zandvoort for tyre and brake tests, and returned with the news that the track had a very rough surface which could cause tyre wear problems.

Sometimes due to pressure of work the staff at Folkingham preferred to have a packed lunch rather than visit the pub. During these lunchtime breaks we entertained ourselves with a variety of activities such as football, card games, or some other – slightly wackier – pastime, one of which was the manufacture of an air-operated gun. The gun was simplicity itself and consisted of a length of straight metal tube and a high-pressure airline. The tube would be charged with a ball bearing taken from a time-expired ball race. When the air pressure was applied by means of a blowgun, the ball bearing would be discharged at high velocity, similar to the operation of an air rifle. Obviously, it was necessary to be very careful where it was directed, but some members of staff were acquiring quite a skill at operating the thing.

About this time Air Ministry contractors had moved onto the airfield, where a construction company had erected a corrugated iron shed – about 200 yards from BRM premises – for use as a canteen by the mainly Irish workers. One day a challenge was thrown down by one of the mechanics. Could a ball bearing fired from the gun be dropped onto the roof of the shed? By a remarkable piece of luck a direct hit was achieved first time. Try to imagine what a 10mm ball bearing suddenly hitting the corrugated iron roof from an altitude of about two hundred feet must have sounded like to those inside the shed! It certainly caused a hasty evacuation of the hut with the confused lunchbreak occupants looking skyward, probably thinking it was some form of chastisement for missing confession! Little did they realise that about two hundred yards away we mechanics were splitting our sides with laughter!

At last we were ready to travel to Holland, full of hope after our second and third places there in 1958. Could we equal that

result this year? Our hotel accommodation was again at the hotel in Haarlem, a few miles from Zandvoort. George Brooks, the humorous Dunlop brakes representative, was also staying there. Continental quilts, or duvets, were becoming popular about now and George always referred to them as Dutch widows.

On our previous visit we had become friendly with the proprietor of a nearby bar, Henk van der Linden, a former Dutch international footballer. Unfortunately for him and other members of the Dutch team, they had been caught smuggling and banned from playing international football.

In view of the findings during the previous week of tests, it was obvious that tyre wear was going to be a concern due to the rough surface of the Zandvoort track. Fortunately, if tyre changes were necessary we had an advantage over opposing teams insofar as we had quick-fit knock-off wheels, enabling much quicker wheel changes compared with other teams which had wheels secured by four or more nuts. Although information gathered during official practice was telling us we would get through the race on the original tyres, we made a great show of performing rather public wheel changes, if only to suggest

Jo Bonnier's BRM leads Masten Gregory's Cooper during the Monaco Grand Prix. Jo retired on lap 46 with brake problems.

to opposing teams that tyre stops were expected in the race.

Practice concluded and we were delighted to have Jo Bonnier on pole position, with Harry sixth; for once we had two happy and contented drivers. Even more unusually was that the mechanics were contented, too, an early night beckoning with only the standard pre-race checks to occupy us.

Come race day morning the excitement mounted. I was mechanic to Harry's car, who arrived at Zandvoort in a beautiful red Alfa Romeo Guillietta and asked if I would drive it to the circuit whilst he took his race car. On arrival at the circuit I told Harry how much I liked the car, it really was a delight to drive. He said "If I win the race I will give you the car"! How I hoped he would win but on reflection, knowing Harry, it probably was not his car to give away anyway! Jo's mechanic Pat Carvath was nearby and, hearing what Harry said, immediately got his brain in to gear and asked Jo "Did you hear that, Jo; if Harry wins he is going to give Dick his Alfa. If you win, do I get your Porsche?" Now, Jo was a very pleasant man, albeit a bit careful with money, and he did not say yes to this, but nor did he say no. Pat, seeing his hesitation, reasoned he might get something, so suggested "I'll tell you what I'll do, Jo. I've worn out so many pairs pushing your car, I'll settle for a new pair of shoes," to which Jo agreed.

So to the race and at the fall of the flag Jo made an excellent start, taking the lead to be immediately challenged by Masten Gregory and Jack Brabham in their works Coopers, Stirling Moss – who had made a poor start – working his way through the field in Rob Walker's Cooper-Climax. The lead was to interchange throughout the race between Bonnier, Brabham and Moss, Gregory having dropped down the field with gearbox problems. Seven laps short of the scheduled seventy-five, Moss – who had driven a demonic race so far – came through in the lead, both he and Bonnier having lapped Jean Behra's Ferrari. On the next lap Stirling did not appear, it was Bonnier leading. Moss had stopped, his epic drive eventually taking its toll on the gearbox of the Cooper-Climax. Whilst not wishing anyone ill fortune, to say we were sorry for Stirling would be far from the truth! Jo then gradually increased his lead over Jack Brabham who had now moved into second place.

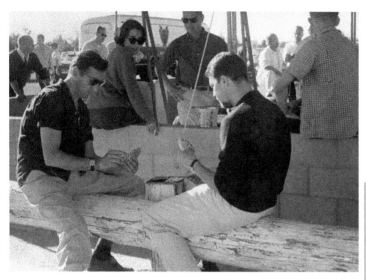

Improvisation to the fore in the form of a table as Roy Salvadori and Jo Bonnier pass their waiting time with a game of cards.

The BRM team relaxes before what was going to be its first Grand Prix win. The team is (left to right): Jimmy Collins, George Brooks (Dunlop), Maurice Dove and Phil Ayliff seated by doors, Dennis Perkins and I seated on bricks and Willie Southcott standing.

A glorious sight for the BRM team and supporters alike. Jo Bonnier leads in the Dutch Grand Prix.

Can it be true? Victory at last! Jo Bonnier takes the chequered flag to win the Dutch Grand Prix, the first Formula 1 World Championship win for BRM.

The anxiety in the BRM pit was unbearable with Raymond Mays displaying all the characteristics of both an ill-sitting hen and a cat on hot bricks, whereas Peter Berthon, who rarely showed any signs of emotion, patiently watched, wearing the slightest smile of satisfaction. Mechanics could be seen with unwittingly crossed fingers, unable to stand still through a combination of excitement and apprehension. The last few laps seemed to take an eternity. Could it be true? Were we going to win a World Championship race at last? The seventy lap marker passed and on and on went Jo, mechanics wringing hands, biting nails, pacing up and down and looking at watches. Was he slowing down? No, the laps just seemed to take longer! Seventy-four laps gone; the next ninety seconds seemed more like ninety minutes, and then the dark green car appeared entering the long straight and at last the chequered flag fell!

What a wonderful sight: people cheering and waving, and there were even tears as Jo continued on his lap of honour, to be mobbed on his return to the pit area. Mechanics pinched each other in case it was a dream but, no, it was real, at long last we had won a World Championship Grand Prix. May 31st, 1959 was a landmark in BRM history. The Duke of Kent was there to congratulate us as well as members and mechanics of opposing teams – Ferrari, Cooper and Lotus – who had watched us suffer through the years. The press, officials, Uncle Tom Cobley, they all came to our pit. Hardened mechanics hugged each other and not a few tears were shed as we rejoiced. It made us feel very proud standing to attention and listening to the British national anthem, this time knowing it was for us! What a day to remember, which was followed by a celebration dinner at The Bouwes Hotel, arranged and paid for by Mr and Mrs Stanley, and then a long night with Gregor Grant (*Autosport*'s editor) doing his stuff on the piano. I recall Jean Behra, our ex-driver who had suffered a dismal race in his Ferrari, putting a note in my hand to pay for drinks for his old mechanics, and saying how he wished it had been him driving the winning car. One sad thought crossed my mind: after all the hours he had spent working on BRM cars, Gordon Newman was missing their first moment of glory, though I have little doubt he would have a drink in our honour.

Alas, all was not a bed of roses. Harry had retired with gearbox trouble and investigations showed the gearbox oil feed and return pipes had been fitted the wrong way round. This should not have been allowed to happen and to prevent a re-occurrence two different-sized unions were specified on future assemblies, which surely should have been in the original specification. I did not get my Alfa-Romeo; Pat did get his shoes although it took him until the Italian Grand Prix four months later and after he had worn out yet another pair.

Celebrations over, we returned home to more congratulations and good wishes, able to hold our heads high as we visited local hostelries. Even the British customs seemed to join in as I had bought a child's tricycle for my small son on which was waived any duty due as we had won the race!

There was no time to rest on our laurels. Back home preparations were commencing for the next race on 5th July, the French Grand Prix on the ultra-fast circuit at Reims. Two cars were entered for Bonnier and Schell with a third as a spare, or to be raced by Ron Flockhart if an entry could be arranged. A further P25 had been loaned to the British Racing Partnership, a collaboration between Stirling's father Alfred and Ken Gregory, Stirling's manager. The car was to be driven by Stirling. This

The BRM workshops on Folkingham airfield. The rocket site under construction can be seen in the background, the building of which meant that BRM lost its test track on the airfield.

arrangement was not very well received by BRM staff at Bourne and Folkingham, who considered it a slur on their ability. As was usual at Reims, one hundred bottles of champagne were awarded to the driver of the fastest lap during practice on the first day, and this year were won by Stirling. It was said some of these bottles came the way of the BRM mechanics; now, I'm not usually one to miss that sort of thing, but certainly none of the champers came my way …

The three BRMs of Harry Schell, Jo Bonnier and Ron Flockhart in the paddock at Reims ready to take part in the French Grand Prix.

We knew it was unlikely BRM would repeat its Zandvoort success, where superior roadholding had played such an important part in the victory. At Reims it was a different matter altogether: we simply did not have the power for the long straights and, despite the car's handsome appearance, the large frontal area created substantial drag. The previous year we had invariably suffered due to the Vanwall's superior 'tear drop' shape on the faster circuits.

The race was run in torrid temperatures, the still-to-be-harvested landscape blurring into a heat haze in temperatures of 100° Fahrenheit (37° Centigrade). Track temperature was 130° Fahrenheit (54° Centigrade).

We came down to earth with a mighty thud, the works cars finishing Flockhart sixth and Schell seventh, Bonnier retiring on lap six with head gasket failure. The power of the Ferrari prevailed and Tony Brooks led from start to finish. Stirling spun his BRM at Thillois on molten tar on lap forty-two whilst challenging for second place, having already set fastest lap of the race. Despite

One of the many light-hearted moments enjoyed by BRM staff, with Jimmy Collins at the rear amused by the comical antics of Pat Carvath and Maurice Dove.

his best efforts he could not push-start the car and collapsed on the grass verge, totally exhausted.

The race was also memorable for the rough conditions of the circuit, which was littered with loose stone chippings, the reason for a number of smashed goggles and, in some cases, eye injuries, including our own Ron Flockhart who nevertheless soldiered on. The heat was almost unbearable, especially for the drivers, many on the verge of collapse. Harry Schell, driving his Cooper in the Formula 2 race which followed, was so disorientated he was coming into the BRM pit instead of his own. Seeing him coming I held out a bottle of water and, wheels still turning, he grabbed it and carried on, the crowd cheering and shouting "Tour de France," which I suppose his flying pit stop resembled.

Next, back to Aintree on 18th July for the second time that year, this time for the British Grand Prix with three cars, again for Bonnier, Schell and Flockhart, and Moss in the rather sickly-coloured light green BRM for BRP. The race being only thirteen days after the Reims event meant there was little time to overhaul the cars. Schell qualified third fastest with Moss a surprising seventh, Bonnier tenth and Flockhart eleventh. During the race

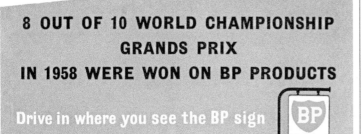

Moss made a pit stop to replace a rear wheel due to tyre wear, the stop taking thirty-one seconds. Noting the condition of the Moss tyre, Dunlop advised us to bring Harry in for a similar tyre change shortly afterwards. Much to his disgust we flagged Harry in, completing the manoeuvre in eighteen seconds, thirteen seconds faster than the BRP stop, a fact that was brought to their attention with quiet satisfaction. Harry showed his displeasure in no small way after the race. He thought the wheel change unnecessary, and maybe it was for, had we let him keep going, it is likely he would have finished higher than the fourth place finally achieved. Stirling made up ground and finished second to Jack Brabham's Cooper.

Two weeks later we were in Berlin for the German Grand Prix on the Avus circuit, a completely different location and type of circuit to the traditional venue of the German Grand Prix at the Nürburgring. The East and West zones were then still divided by barbed wire, replaced by the infamous wall two years later. Avus was part of West Berlin, the race track, in everyday life, a dual carriageway with a hairpin bend at the south end, and what looked like a mountainous brick wall forming the north curve banking at the other. A lap consisted of travelling down one carriageway and up the other side to negotiate the high banking at the north end to complete the lap. A lap was 5 miles (8.3km), a unique circuit.

Arthur Hill and Jimmy Collins, recently out of the army, had gone ahead by road, taking one car through the Berlin corridor to carry out pre-race tests. The remainder of the team with two cars travelled from Blackbushe airport in a British Eagle C54, together with the car loaned to BRP, this time for German driver Hans Hermann. Stirling Moss had elected to drive Rob Walker's Cooper here and BRP would have preferred Ron Flockhart to drive the P25, but pressure from the race organisers caused them to opt for the German to take part in his home Grand Prix. Tony Blankley – a recent addition to the team – and I were to transport one car to Blackbushe in the old Dodge lorry. I drove to Oxford where we stopped for a refreshment break. I asked Tony if he would like to drive the next leg and he agreed but, after a short while, said "When we come to any traffic lights, tell me what colour they are, I'm colour blind"... very reassuring!

We flew into Tempelhof airport, one of Adolf Hitler's famous legacies, and a very impressive structure. Berlin was an extraordinary city with Russian soldiers on guard at the Brandenburg Gate which, later became the main crossing point between East and West once the East Germans built the Berlin Wall in 1961. It made one appreciate which side of the line was preferable! Another famous landmark was the ruin of the Kaiser Wilhelm church in central Berlin, preserved as a stark reminder of World War II.

GROSSER PREIS VON DEUTSCHLAND 1959

The reputed German efficiency was not evident in the pit and paddock facilities. The primitive and filthy pits were too far away from the paddock area, and the organisers insisting that all pit crews be tagged with a lead-sealed wristband to be worn throughout our stay aggravated the situation. It made you feel as if on remand! To add to this, the police were arrogant beyond belief in sharp contrast with those encountered the previous year at the Nürburgring. It was easy to imagine what jackbooted SS police would have been like … did we really win the war? Such arrogance did not deter the 5 feet 4 inch tall 'Sheriff' from threatening one officer with a 2lb copper-headed wheel knocker, however. To add to the chaos, several times the police changed their minds about allowing the racing cars to be driven through the streets to the circuit, though did finally give permission.

Saturday practice was interspersed with a sports car race. In wet conditions the Dutch driver, Carel Godin de Beaufort, spun his Porsche on the slippery brick North Turn banking, went over the top and landed in the paddock on the other side with a crumpled but still driveable car. To everyone's amazement, probably not least his, he drove through the paddock and rejoined the race, only to be black-flagged later and disqualified! Sadly, Jean Behra, also driving a Porsche, was not so fortunate. Spinning on the same wet banking, he careered to the top, hit a concrete structure which ejected him high into the air and into a flagpole standing on the edge of the banking, killing him instantly. It was a tragic loss to motor racing and the BRM team in particular, where he had been a great favourite. He had frequently indicated that

The daunting banked section of the Avus circuit at Berlin. Sadly, Jean Behra was killed here when he lost control of his Porsche and went over the top. Jean was thrown from the car into a flagpole, and died instantly. His was the third Porsche car to go out of control on the banking during the weekend.

he hoped one day to rejoin the team, a hope reciprocated by BRM mechanics.

Unusually, the Grand Prix was to be run in two heats, the fastest aggregate time completing both heats to determine the winner. BRM was not optimistic; again, our engines did not have the power of the Ferraris and our superior roadholding was of no benefit here. Our doubts proved correct with Schell fifth and Bonnier seventh in heat one. In addition to a lack of power, Harry's car was plagued by clutch problems. In an attempt to overcome these by adjustment ready for the second heat,

The paddock at Avus, with Jo Bonnier's car under wraps.

A windswept Willie, choosing to travel second class through Berlin.

Jean Behra in the Porsche RSK in which he lost his life.

it was necessary for a mechanic (guess who!) to go head first into the cockpit. The cockpit was extremely hot, as the car had just completed the first heat at racing speed. With head way down in the cockpit attempting the adjustment, I was conscious of someone peering down at me. Thinking it was a colleague, I rather *BRM cars in the process of being loaded at Berlin's Tempelhof airport for the return flight to Blackbushe.*

colourfully and briefly conveyed how hot it was down there; to my horror, I heard the voice of Mrs Stanley agree with me. I kept a low profile for a few moments after that to hide my embarrassment.

A photograph taken by the 'Sheriff' of Tony Blankley taking a photograph of the 'Sheriff'!

An impressive picture of the Avus circuit taken by Dennis Perkins shortly after take-off from Tempelhof airport. The picture gives the impression that the circuit goes under the road.

In heat two our two cars finished in the same positions as in heat one but swopped around; unsurprisingly, that was the finishing order on aggregate times. The third BRM of Hermann was involved in a most spectacular crash. Entering the South Curve his front brakes allegedly failed and he hit the straw bales marking the curve, which overturned the car, luckily throwing him clear before it landed as a total write-off. This time no hint of blame could be attached to BRM mechanics as the car had been prepared solely by BRP. Post-race the BRP team refused to offer any help to retrieve the crashed car, behaving rather like a schoolboy who has kicked his mate's ball through a window, saying "It's your ball, you go and fetch it." Eventually,the car was loaded onto the Austin transporter and taken back to Bourne by road, the three works cars returning with Eagle Airlines. Whilst relationships between mechanics of BRM

Checking an early P48 rear engine type chassis for torsional stiffness. A load was applied to a secured chassis, and deflection was then established by measuring the movement on the tubes seen clamped at various points along the top of the chassis. This was followed by calculations on Tony Rudd's slide rule which, as only he could understand them, no-one could dispute.

and BRP were normally amicable, the association was never a success and was finally terminated after Avus, about which all at Bourne rejoiced. So we left Berlin after a sad and disappointing weekend with most teams pledging never to race at Avus again, the death of Jean Behra hanging over us.

One of the lighter sides of the meeting was having the Dunlop brake rep, George Brooks, there. George was a very popular and likeable, ruddy-faced man with a droll sense of humour who spoke with a pronounced Midlands dialect and who, at the most tense and exciting moment of a race, was likely to ask in his laconic style "'ere, eh yo erd the test scower?" or "I see the Villa wun agin." It was his job to record brake information, disc and pad wear and the number of laps completed, and take this information back to the Dunlop works for analysis. At Avus I drove two laps of the circuit in Harry's car. George later told me that, in his report to his superiors, he gave the number of laps Harry had driven plus Dick, two. Summoned by his boss, Mr Hodgkinson, he was asked to explain. He told him "Ahr, Dick did two laps, yo shud a sin im, roight up the top o the bankin, jus clippin the bushes, he wus fantastic." Typical of George, but had his description of my journey round that gigantic wall been correct I might have needed some clean laundry.

On my return to Bourne I became involved in building the prototype rear engine BRM that was nearing completion and scheduled to make its appearance at the Italian Grand Prix at Monza on 13th September. Simultaneously, three cars were on their way to compete in the Portuguese Grand Prix at Lisbon on 23rd August. It was whilst on their journey through Spain that Roy Foreman allegedly informed some elderly English lady tourists, which they met during a refreshment stop, that they were transporting bulls to a Spanish bull-fighting arena, and that they had even transported the Little White Bull in the song of that name! It was typical of Roy's sense of humour and I am sure he was absolutely convincing!

The race was not a success from a BRM point of view with only Schell in the points, fifth, Flockhart seventh and Bonnier retiring. As with the previous year, the cars were then reloaded and set off on the three day journey to Monza. A fourth P25 was sent

from Bourne in the hands of Willie Southcott and Arthur Hill. They decided to make their overnight stop at an hotel in the small town of Belley near Lyon. Suitably refreshed and rested, they packed their bags to leave the next morning only to find a one day market had been built around their vehicle. Understandably no amount of persuasion could make the market traders move their stalls, the added attraction of a racing car probably increasing their daily takings, so Willie and Arthur enjoyed half a day's sightseeing instead. Willie probably opened the transporter to show off his racing car and would be mentally redesigning a few things, as was his wont.

The rear engine prototype was allocated the project number 48, thus becoming known as the type P48. We spent long hours completing the car and, to accelerate production, it was decided to dismantle the ex-Behra P25. The front chassis section, complete with front suspension, would now form the front section of the new car. A new rear chassis section was designed, built by Stan Hope and welded to the front section, and an existing 2.5-litre engine installed. Eventually, it was deemed insufficiently developed to race but was completed in time to be transported independently to Monza to make its first public appearance in practice for the Grand Prix. The car was finished after only a minimal amount of testing which meant that performance prospects for Monza were uncertain.

Tony Rudd, Maurice Dove, Alan Ellison and I left Bourne on Sunday 6th September with the new car loaded on a trailer, which had been manufactured from a Rubery Owen caravan chassis and was towed by a Standard Vanguard estate car, a very practical-looking outfit. We had a pleasant journey through France and Switzerland, one of the advantages of travelling with Tony being his talent for finding a good place to eat. Our route took us via the Simplon tunnel to Domodossola, there to join the

The first P48 rear engine BRM, with a large air duct to direct cool air to the engine and the 'bacon slicer' rear brake.

Me, Maurice Dove and Tony Rudd prepare to leave Tony's house in Mill Drove, Bourne, for Monza with the Standard Vanguard and trailer carrying the first P48 car.

Stopped in France to give right of way to French railway traffic.

Enjoying the alpine air are Alan Ellison, me and Maurice Dove before our descent into Italy and Monza.

autostrada toll road to Milan and thence to Monza. It was my turn to drive the autostrada section; a piece of cake, I thought, and so it proved for many miles, with speeds of 80 to 90mph easily attainable. However, all good things come to an end, as the saying goes, and in this case it was true! Seeing the tollbooths in the distance, I decided it was time to think about reducing speed only to find that the trailer brakes were not functioning! The dreaded BRM gremlins were now having a go at the trailer! As I eased off the throttle the trailer let me know who was in charge, beginning to swing side-to-side. Slowing from 80mph with a loaded and brakeless trailer pushing on the overrun was not a pleasant experience, the swinging trailer with its precious cargo causing the outfit to take up more than one lane of the motorway, in very real danger of being deposited in an Italian ditch. I realised then that my passengers had joined me in a period of silence, but by patience, good luck and not a little skill, I managed to regain control; very relieved that I had decided to slow down early. I recall Tony asking quite calmly "Have you got it, Richard"? It was with relief that I was able to reply "I think so," thankful that the traffic had been light. On reaching Monza, with Tony's approval the trailer brakes received attention before the racing cars and were fixed pretty quickly.

Again, we stayed at the Albergo Marchesi, where the traditional business of twosomes calling for nourishment and nooky seemed as popular as ever. 'Oilio' was again in attendance around the workshop, laughing and waving his finger as he recollected his episode with the oil can spout, but what happened next was quite unbelievable. Phil Ayliff, while demonstrating to someone what 'Oilio' had done, proceeded to do the very same thing, but with no brandy to sooth the pain and not a lot of sympathy from his colleagues!

The performance of the new car was noted by contrasting opinion from BRM drivers and a great deal of interest from the other teams. Jo Bonnier's first impression was that it was quick and had great potential, but Schell thought it slower than the P25. After these practice sessions the car was clearly not developed enough to race and the decision was taken to stay on at Monza after the race to carry out further testing.

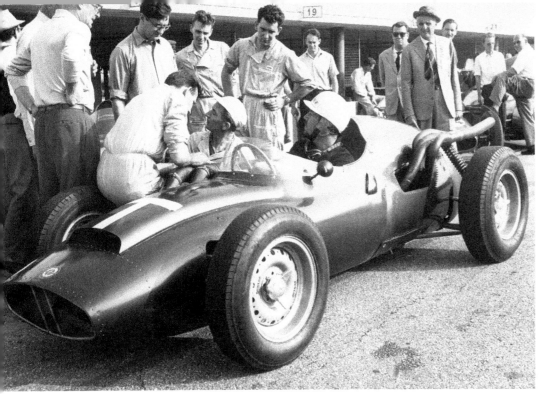

Prior to the race Jack Brabham – who was to drive his works-entered Cooper – was the leading contender for the World Driver's Championship. Time was approaching for the first practice session and I was fortunate to witness John Cooper, a fun-loving practical joker himself, looking absolutely horrified to see his driver walking down the pit lane with his arm in a sling appearing, by a series of gesticulations, to show others what had happened, they, in turn, commiserating with him on his bad luck. Jack, though desperate to win his first world title, could still find time to joke and wind-up John Cooper who, realising the truth, voiced doubt about whether Jack's parents had been married when he was born …

Shortly after, Jack watched as Dunlop tyre technician Vic Barlow carefully checked all tyre pressures on his Cooper. Jack then went out to do more practice laps and stopped on the far side of the circuit to let some air out of his rear tyres, coming in at the end of the lap complaining of poor roadholding and asking Vic if he would check the pressures again. He looked on as Vic, a dedicated professional, studied the readings on the tyre pressure gauge and checked them again in disbelief. Vic looked at Jack, scratched his head, rechecked them with a second gauge and scratched his head again. He was at a loss to explain what could have happened. He looked at Jack, then at the car, then at Jack again, this time detecting a slight grin on Jack's face. Only then did the penny drop, his resultant comment reiterating what John Cooper had already suggested about the timing of Jack's birth!

Jo Bonnier gives his opinion of the P48 to Peter Berthon, Tony Rudd and mechanics, watched by an interested Luigi Villoresi, the Italian former Grand Prix driver.

Sadly, Vic – a nice man and a great professional who loved motor racing – was killed some years later in a road accident.

As usual the Italian police were over-officious, ordering Raymond Mays from the pit road to the other side of the pit counter. Remonstrating that he was doing a job of work – a debateable claim – RM refused to go and a posse of police pounced and attempted to manhandle him. Mrs Stanley, who stood nearby, came to his rescue by knocking the helmet off one of the police officers, diverting attention away from RM. On seeing that the assailant was a lady, no further action was taken!

The race was anything but a success for BRM with Harry Schell finishing seventh, Jo Bonnier eighth, and Ron Flockhart thirteenth. Jack Brabham gained four valuable points towards the title by finishing third to winner Stirling Moss.

On Monday morning, whilst most teams had packed up and departed, we continued testing the P48. One problem encountered was fuel evaporation and, in an effort to temporarily overcome this, Alan Ellison, at Tony Rudd's suggestion, made a spiral aluminium fuel feed pipe to hang out in the cool airstream, which PB amusingly referred to as a snail trail. It was effective, however,, in reducing fuel temperature. After a few days' intensive testing we left Monza for Bourne, driver opinion about the new car's performance still divided.

A minor race – the 25 lap Silver City Trophy at Snetterton on 10th October – brought the 1959 season to a close. Two P25s were entered, one to be driven by Ron Flockhart, the second by a new face at BRM, Bruce Halford. Ron won easily after early

Cars and transport vehicles at the rear of the notorious Marchesi hotel, the Italian base for the BRM team when at Monza.

A cheerful-looking BRM team enjoying a pastime its members were very good at; wining and dining at the Marchesi, a favourite port of call.

A happy pair of mechanics. Colin Atkin and Pat Carvath enjoy an amusing moment in the Commer mobile workshop vehicle at Monza during preparations for the 1959 Italian Grand Prix.

intervention from the Lotus of Graham Hill, a driver shortly to become so much a part of BRM's future. Ron's average speed was over 100mph, faster than the previous lap record. In the gathering dusk of an autumn afternoon, Bruce came home third behind Jack Brabham's Cooper.

And so the racing season in Europe ended in victory. There was to be no let-up in the work rate, however, with modifications to, and testing of, the P48, and also preparation of two front engined P25s to compete in races in Argentina in February 1960. The management – of whom Peter Spear, director of research and development at Darlaston, now appeared to be a permanent member (and who some regarded as Alfred Owen's spy) – was also negotiating with new drivers for the following season. Jo Bonnier had obviously done a good job for us and would be retained. Other drivers under consideration were Dan Gurney, Graham Hill and Mike McKee. Dan Gurney, a tall, 28-year-old Californian, was a Ferrari Grand Prix driver of great promise, whilst Londoner Graham Hill was well known to us and making a name for himself at Lotus. He had become disillusioned by that company's lack of success and repeated failures and, his ability having been noticed by RM, had been persuaded to join BRM. As reliability was not BRM's greatest virtue, it was a brave and somewhat strange decision on the part of Hill.

The winter of 1959/60 was one of the busiest ever seen at BRM with testing at Goodwood continuing into November, building of the new cars, and move of the racing shop from Folkingham to Bourne. If variety is the spice of life, we had had our share in 1959. At last we had achieved our first Grand Prix victory, but the bare fact was that there were still far too many failures. These continuing problems were causing rumblings in the backwaters about changes in management …

Cars and transporters in the paddock at Snetterton, there to take part in the Silver City Trophy race. Bruce Halford, in his first drive for BRM, drove car number 3.

ZANDVOORT ULTIMATUM

Jack Brabham's 1959 World Championship win in the Cooper convinced manufacturers that the rear engine configuration for racing cars was the way forward. To say that the dawning of 1960 at BRM was hectic would be a gross understatement as, shortly before Christmas 1959, Alfred Owen had issued instructions to Bourne that all P25 cars, with the exception of the winning Bonnier Dutch Grand Prix car which was to be preserved as was, were to be converted to the P48 rear engine type, with two cars to be ready to race at the Easter Goodwood meeting on 18th April. These instructions, together with relocation of the Folkingham works to Bourne, meant there were not enough hours in a day as everything was needed yesterday, As always, however, all shopfloor staff rallied to the cause.

The new workshop at Bourne was under construction and scheduled to be ready for occupation towards the end of March. Meanwhile, five P25s were in various stages of conversion, which meant a thousand-and-one components on the parts racks, a rack allocated to each car. By some miracle of forward planning, the new workshop had been completed early and one weekend towards the end of March, with all hands to the pumps, the equipment, benches, jigs, tools, chassis and kettle, etc, were transported from Folkingham to Bourne. By Monday morning it was even possible for work to resume on the cars; rarely had such a wonderfully disorganised operation been more successful!

Total rehabilitation took a few weeks, but the advantages of being at Bourne were very soon apparent. Administration, stores, drawing office and machine shop were all more convenient, and Phyllis Fawcett's tea tasted much better than Jock's, served with a smile and the friendly invitation "Come on you boys."

The long-suffering Ron Flockhart had declined the offer of remaining with BRM as our test driver, so it was Graham Hill and Dan Gurney who subjected the two rear engine cars scheduled to race at Goodwood to intensive testing at Snetterton,

Oh dear! We knew Tony had been under a lot of pressure, but didn't realise the job was really getting him down ...

... it's okay, he's only taking a photograph of suspension angles on the P48.

"Everything's Wanted Yesterday in this Bloody Place"

Goodwood and Silverstone. Both drivers had mixed feelings regarding performance, the anticipated and expected advantages compared to the P25s being negligible.

Jo Bonnier opted to drive his front engine Dutch Grand Prix-winning car in the Easter race and, as it turned out, this was the P25's last works race appearance. Practice times for the three cars were disappointing; Dan and Graham could manage just seventh and ninth fastest respectively in the P48s, with Jo tenth in the P25. The Coopers and the new Lotus proved unmatchable. Dan's race was shortlived; he failed to complete two laps after colliding with Roy Salvadori's Cooper, but worse was to follow. Graham and Jo, although finishing fifth and sixth, were both lapped by winner Innes Ireland in the new Lotus 18, and by Moss in the Cooper. As a disconsolate Graham left Goodwood, he must have been reflecting on what might have been had he stayed at Lotus …

Once more a disappointed Alfred Owen threatened PB and RM he would close down the BRM project, the success he yearned for as far away as ever, it seemed. He issued instructions for an intensive testing programme at Snetterton with one of Peter Spear's staff, Ian Hankinson, delegated to attend as observer. It was a lonely exercise for Ian as we were discouraged from fraternising with him, the admonition "Don't let Hankinson see what you are doing" often heard. This made for quite a difficult situation for we mechanics as Ian was a pleasant man with whom we had no axe to grind, who often travelled with the team.

During these tests a rear anti-roll bar was manufactured and fitted, a decision made by Tony Rudd and unbeknown to Peter Berthon who disliked the idea. However, it did improve roadholding and thus became a permanent feature on the cars, although it was some time before PB would accept the advantage it gave. Why he was so opposed to this one can only speculate, but maybe he considered it detracted from the sleek looks of the car, a consideration he appeared to prioritise.

The P25 had now run its last race as a works entry, so three P48s were entered for the BRDC International Trophy race at Silverstone on 14th May. A new team – the David Brown Aston Martins – had entered cars for the race as a prelude to competing in the Formula 1 Championship with, surprisingly, two front engine models in direct contrast to the latest rear engine trend adopted by established racing teams. Fate decreed the team received a less than auspicious welcome. Whilst a mechanic was warming up one of the brand new stationary Astons in the pit lane during practice on a wet and dismal afternoon, exiting the pits in his Cooper, Stirling Moss hit a puddle and skidded into the Aston, removing its front wheel and immediately reducing the new two-car team to one. A very embarrassed Stirling had to drive Rob Walker's older car.

The ever-popular Harry Schell was entered to race a Yeoman-Credit Cooper. During official practice on Friday 13th, in wet conditions Harry got into an horrendous skid at Abbey Curve, losing control of his car and crashing. His neck was broken and he died instantly. A great character, and popular driver for BRM, had been lost to motor racing. His jocular approach to life, cavalier attitude and playboy manner would be sorely missed by all, none more so than his beautiful girlfriend Monique. After this horrific incident, an air of sadness hung over everything.

Bonnier and Gurney had performed well in practice, achieving second and third places on the starting grid with Hill a disappointing eighth. Race day, and from the fall of the flag Bonnier and Gurney made electrifying starts, to the delight of the large home crowd rocketing into shortlived first and second places, soon overtaken by Moss in Rob Walker's Cooper and Innes Ireland's Lotus. Also in amongst the leading group was a new boy to Formula 1 racing, John Surtees, the former World Motorcycle Champion driving in his first race. Gurney retired after only seven laps with fuel problems; Bonnier later succumbed to what had now become a too-frequent problem, a broken brake pipe; Graham Hill eventually finishing a distant third. Only a very slight improvement in results and not what Alfred Owen was seeking.

There was no time to reflect on what might have been, or to hear Alfred Owen's comments, as the cars were due to depart for Monaco the following Monday. Once more the three Austins and the Commer left Bourne, this time on what would be their

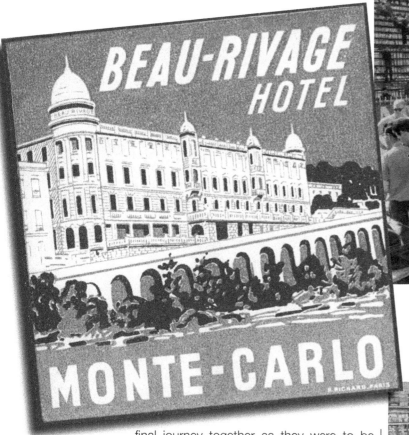

BEAU-RIVAGE HOTEL
MONTE-CARLO

Graham Hill sits on the pit counter while mechanics make adjustments to his car at Monaco. The sparkplug box on the pit counter is a relic from V16 days, made to accommodate 3 sets of 16 plugs.

final journey together as they were to be replaced by a Leyland Royal Tiger chassis fitted with bodywork by Marshall's of Cambridge. This had been designed to carry three cars plus spares, and the single diesel engine-powered vehicle would prove a far more economical unit, both financially and in travelling time when compared with the four petrol-driven vehicles. It was also much quicker to refuel and to get customs clearance on one vehicle than on four. Those most disappointed at the phasing out of our fleet would be the continental filling station proprietors!

First practice at Monaco was declared void, the official timing equipment giving errors of up to six seconds per lap! Once the timing clocks were repaired, Jo Bonnier achieved fifth place on the grid, with Graham Hill sixth and Dan Gurney a lowly fourteenth. At the fall of the flag Jo Bonnier immediately took a shortlived lead, soon to be overtaken by Moss driving Rob Walker's new Lotus 18. Jo remained in second place for seventy-seven of the 100 lap race when he suffered a rear hub failure. He pulled into the pits intending to retire but when it was realised that only four other cars were still running, Jo was sent out to limp round, credited with fifth place and gaining two valuable championship points (he number of points gained during a season decided the amount of starting money paid the following year). Dan Gurney had retired earlier, also with rear hub failure, completing too few

Raymond Mays explains something to Dick Jeffries of Dunlop, whilst gendarmes watch mechanics at work on Graham Hill's BRM.

laps to qualify as a finisher. Graham Hill crashed at the Gazometre hairpin, honest Graham holding his hand up and admitting to his mistake on return to the pits; he'd skidded on a wet patch and crashed into the timekeeper's box, leaving Moss the winner in the Lotus. To see the Lotus 18 win the Grand Prix

Jo Bonnier's P48 BRM leads Jack Brabham's Cooper and Stirling Moss' Rob Walker Lotus out of the Station hairpin in the Monaco Grand Prix. Moss went on to win the race.

Inset: Roy Foreman kindly passes Willie a lighted cigarette: be wary, Willie, it might explode. Arthur Hill has to light his own.

chroniclers to 'Big Loo' which was felt more appropriate). The race also saw a young Scottish driver making his Formula 1 debut in a works Lotus 18, one Jim Clark.

Final practice placed Bonnier, Hill and Gurney fourth, fifth and sixth respectively on the grid. After ten laps of the race, with Hill running a creditable third, disaster struck. Approaching the Tarzan Loop Dan Gurney completely lost his rear brakes due to brake hose failure and careered straight into the wire fencing, the out-of-control car somersaulting and killing a young Dutch boy who had unfortunately strayed into a prohibited area. Roy Salvadori, who was spectating following withdrawal of his Aston Martin, happened to be at the spot and helped release the driver trapped beneath his overturned car, Dan escaping with relatively minor injuries. It was the first fatal accident a BRM had been

once more added to Graham's dismay, causing him to ponder once again his decision to change teams.

The weekend's events had been closely observed by Ian Hankinson, who duly submitted a report to Peter Spear.

The convoy left Monaco on Monday, once again bound direct for Zandvoort where the Dutch Grand Prix was due to take place in just a week on Whit Monday, 6th June. The Commer workshop, its feelings hurt, no doubt, by its impending redundancy, decided to revolt, shedding all but two of its forward gears, and so it was that a decrepit old vehicle eventually limped into the Dutch town. Back at Bourne a new car had been completed for Hill, strengthened new rear hubs replacing the old type that had failed at Monaco, and was despatched to Zandvoort to be ready for when the Monaco contingent arrived. As the race was being held on a Monday, this allowed Alfred Owen to put in a rare appearance at a continental meeting as it did not interfere with his Sunday commitments as a lay preacher. Mr and Mrs Louis Stanley were making regular appearances at race meetings (the latter now dubbed 'Big Lou' by Dan Gurney but modified slightly by some

Graham Hill holds a very secure lead over Dan Gurney at Zandvoort.

135

Dan Gurney and Alfred Owen in conversation before the Dutch Grand Prix.

Dan Gurney and Alfred Owen watch BRM mechanics at work in the Zandvoort paddock.

involved in. Meanwhile, Jo's oil filter sprayed lubricant onto the rear tyres of his car, causing him to spin out of the race. Graham soldiered on to finish third behind Jack Brabham's Cooper and, dare I say it, Innes Ireland's Lotus 18.

In line with normal practice the Dutch police immediately impounded Dan's wrecked car, and subjected Dan to interrogation, after which he was exonerated of any blame. The repeated failings of the cars – frequently due to minor and inexcusable faults – were again resulting in a lack of confidence amongst the drivers, not in the ability of mechanics or an individual, but the entire team organisation. Graham Hill's personal disappointments were magnified by the obvious superiority and success of the Lotus team from which he had recently departed.

It was a dejected trio of drivers that conferred post-race and an impromptu meeting was quickly arranged for that evening at the Bouwes Hotel in Zandvoort, the drivers cleverly seizing the opportunity to air their grievances on this rare occasion when Chairman Alfred Owen, as well as Jean Stanley, Raymond Mays, Peter Berthon and Tony Rudd, were all available. Though not privy to this meeting, I understand that the atmosphere could be described as lively, and it continued into the early hours of the morning. The drivers implied that management and race strategy had not progressed from pre-war ERA days, and Graham Hill cited particular examples where trivial decisions had first to be cleared with Peter Berthon, delaying progress and frustrating drivers and

Dan Gurney before his unfortunate involvement in a fatal accident during the Dutch Grand Prix, when a young spectator strayed into a prohibited area and was killed.

Graham Hill leads Jim Clark's Lotus in the Dutch Grand Prix at Zandvoort.

Below: In June 1960 BRM took delivery of this purpose-built Leyland Royal Tiger three-car transporter. This single vehicle replaced the three faithful Austins and the Commer mobile workshop.

Bottom: The part-loaded rear interior of the Leyland Royal Tiger. With spare wheels stowed on both sides, and one car on the upper deck, two more cars could be accommodated on the lower deck. Additional tools and spare parts were carried in side lockers.

mechanics alike. Famously, Graham is said to have given as an example of this that permission had first to be obtained from PB even to increase air pressure in the tyres – not at all what he had been used to at Team Lotus! Small aggravations like this culminated in the drivers stating they would not drive for BRM again under the present management. One suggestion put forward was that David Yorke of Vanwall fame be recruited as team manager; this was never acted upon or, if it was, then unsuccessfully.

As a result of the meeting Alfred Owen issued the directive that Raymond Mays would remain Race Director, responsible for negotiating starting money, drivers' fees and suppliers' contracts, Peter Berthon would be Chief Engineer responsible for engine design, and Tony Rudd would be in charge of car design, race preparation and strategy. Owen's specific instructions were to build a car to his own design, the most important element of which was to incorporate the drivers' request for a brake at each corner; namely foregoing the infamous 'bacon slicer' disc brake on the back of the gearbox, inherited from the P25. It was a deflated RM and PB, and a rather embarrassed but delighted Tony Rudd who left the meeting. The necessary revolution had begun …

The new Leyland transporter – which was to become a showpiece at the racing circuits of Europe – arrived on schedule, a most handsome-looking vehicle painted in the same dark green livery as BRM cars and decorated with the Owen Organisation's logo. Unfortunately, at the time it was questionable whether the cars were performing well enough to justify such an impressive conveyance, but even if we couldn't win races then at least we

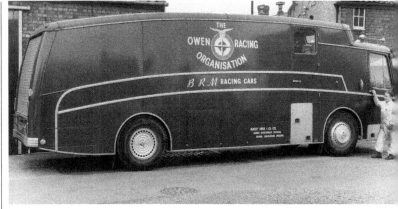

The 'Sheriff,' alias Dennis Perkins in happy mood. Dennis would invariably travel shotgun as second driver to Len Reedman in the new Leyland.

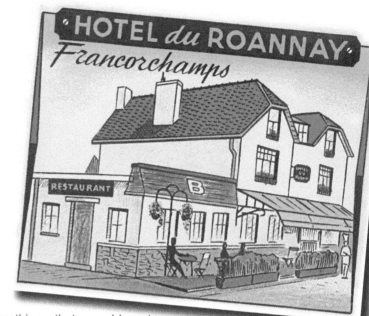

would arrive in style! Meanwhile, the changes ordered by Alfred Owen were becoming effective. Unlike Peter Berthon, who had a tendency to implement his own ideas, frequently against the wishes of the drivers, Tony Rudd appeared to be listening to Graham Hill's suggestions, the latter becoming a regular visitor to Bourne where he and Tony were often seen in deep and earnest conversation around the cars. These visits resulted in a number of short-term suspension modifications in order to improve the roadholding qualities of the car.

The brake hose failure on Gurney's car at Zandvoort was also under intense joint investigation by BRM and Dunlop brake technicians. Subsequent tests showed evidence that the extreme heat generated in the area of the single disc rear brake of rear engine cars was reducing hose bursting pressure to 1500psi, considerably less than the original 5000psi. The temperature in this area of the rear engine car was now much higher than on the P25 front engine model, substantiating the drivers' request to fit a four-wheel braking system. To counteract this in the short term Dunlop recommended steel braided flexible pipes, but specified that responsibility for failure be laid strictly at the door of BRM.

With the Belgian Grand Prix at Spa on 19th June only ten days away, long hours were worked to restore the existing cars to racing condition in the new racing shop; quite a task after their two-race excursion. A nightshift was necessary during that period for which I was one of the unlucky ones selected. Our objective was achieved, however, and the three repaired and much modified cars were loaded into the Royal Tiger, which departed on its maiden journey in the hands of driver Len Reedman and two mechanics. Len was also responsible for the stores and equipment carried. A Ford Zephyr Estate car had been purchased to transport the remaining members of the racing team.

At Spa the drivers appeared in a much happier frame of mind, little doubt due to the organisational changes largely instigated by them and introduced post-Zandvoort. Dan Gurney was still suffering from a damaged wrist, but insisted on driving,

something that would not be allowed in modern-day Formula 1. During final practice both Stirling Moss and Michael Taylor crashed badly in their Lotus 18s, the two accidents allegedly due to construction failure.

The starting grid saw Graham in fifth position, Jo sixth and Dan, under the circumstances, a creditable eleventh. A noticeable feature of practice was the line taken by John Surtees on the downhill approach to Eau Rouge. Whereas the traditional line taken by drivers was toward the centre of the track, Surtees was taking what I assume was his motorcycle line which almost encroached on the pit lane, causing occupants of the lower section of the pit lane to be wary when Surtees was due.

The race was to be run over 36 laps of the 9 mile circuit and the weather was fine. At completion of the first lap Hill was fourth, Bonnier sixth and Gurney twelfth. On lap five Dan retired, soon to be followed by Jo; meanwhile, Graham had moved up into second place behind Jack Brabham and closing, only to drive into the pits on his penultimate lap with a broken crankshaft. Unfortunately, the BRM pit was beyond the start and finish line: had it been before the line, or had Graham thought to stop before the line, he could have pushed his car over after the winner had received the chequered flag and qualified as a finisher, probably in second place.

Although the performance of Graham's car was encouraging, the day was saddened by the death of two promising young British drivers, Chris Bristow and Alan Stacey. Stacey had been Graham's team-mate at Lotus, so his death probably gave Graham further food for thought, perhaps finally convincing him that he had, after all, made the right decision in leaving Lotus.

Although the performance of Graham's car at Spa had been encouraging, we were in for a big disappointment come

138

Graham Hill's P48 BRM in the paddock area at Spa.

The first race meeting for the new Leyland was Spa, here pictured outside the Hotel du Roannay at Francorchamps.

the French Grand Prix at Reims two weeks later, where all three cars failed to finish: indeed, Graham even failed to start the race! After a very good lap in practice, which put him on the front row, he stalled his engine on the starting grid and was immediately shunted up the rear by Maurice Trintignant, damaging the rear suspension sufficiently to cause the car to be wheeled away. Both of the two remaining cars retired with broken valve springs before half distance. It was later discovered that Graham had been doing practice starts on his warm-up lap, thus damaging the clutch, which caused him to stall the engine; a simple mistake – or was it over-enthusiasm on Graham's part? – led to one car being eliminated before the race began.

Jack Brabham clocked up another win in the Cooper-Climax. John Cooper was once again seen performing his now-famous victory roll in front of the pits as the victorious car completed the final lap: it had become his custom to turn head-over-heels as the winning Cooper received the chequered flag, and he had plenty of opportunity to practice that year!

Could we improve in the next race, our home Grand Prix at Silverstone on 16th July where, once again, Alfred Owen would attend? (Although terribly disappointed at the lack of success, he was always encouraging and polite to we lowly workers.) The event did not get off to a good start as Dan Gurney's car was a late arrival, transported in one of the Austin Lodestars. The winch mechanism broke when unloading, allowing the car to run out of control down the ramp, hitting a parked vehicle. This – fortunately – resulted in only cosmetic damage to the car, but

red faces for the personnel involved! Final practice saw Graham second alongside Jack Brabham's Cooper, with Jo fourth and Dan Gurney sixth in a brand new car.

The old assurance that lightning does not strike the same place twice was soon disproved when Graham again stalled his engine on the start line, this time to be hit by Tony Brooks now driving a Cooper. Fortunately, after a hasty check for damage, which proved negative, he was push-started and set about entertaining everyone with the drive of his life. The 30 second deficit between him and leader Brabham was gradually reduced and, by lap 40 of the scheduled 77, he had moved up to second place behind Brabham with now only a six second gap separating them. On lap 54 Graham took the lead after breaking the Silverstone lap record, slowly but surely increasing his lead.

An acrobatic John Cooper performs a somersault as Jack Brabham crosses the finishing line to win the French Grand Prix, a tradition whenever his car crossed a finishing line to win.

Main picture: Jack Brabham completing his lap of honour following his victory at Reims.

With five laps to go he had a two second advantage.

By this time the BRM's brakes were beginning to suffer from the severe hammering to which they had been subjected. Entering Copse Corner Graham was confronted by two back-markers immediately in front of him. In a desperate manoeuvre to overtake them and gain ground on the pursuing Brabham, he did not allow enough time for his failing brakes and spun the car, damaging the suspension and having to retire; a sad end to an heroic drive. Any doubts about whether Graham was a serious Grand Prix contender were now dispelled as he walked back to the pits to tumultuous applause from the large crowd. His reputation grew, too, in the eyes of the BRM team when he apologised for making a mistake. In the excitement it would have been easy to forget the other two cars, but, for the record, Jo retired with broken rear suspension and Dan finished tenth.

Graham had been a member of the London Rowing Club, the colours of which he proudly displayed on his helmet. During a conversation one day he told me that he applied a rowing principle to his race driving: if he saw an opponent make a mistake, or 'catch a crab' in rowing jargon, he would make extra effort to exaggerate the opponent's error. I believe we had just witnessed something similar.

Alfred Owen was a happier man after he had seen Graham's gallant performance, and began to talk enthusiastically about the new Formula 1 specification due for introduction in 1961. Most manufacturers were reluctant to make the change of engine capacity from 2.5-litres to 1.5-litres. Although Peter Berthon and his team were designing a V8 engine to comply with the new regulations, this would not be ready for the start of the 1961

Here I am with apprentice Alan Challis assembling a new car in the Bourne workshops.

season. Therefore, after post-race discussions at Silverstone, and in order to continue racing, it was decided to purchase Coventry Climax engines to use in the interim period.

On 1st August BRM made a token appearance at Brands Hatch with one car driven by Graham Hill. The previous day Hill had driven a Porsche at the Nürburgring. Whether through fatigue or a case of it just being a bad day, both Jim Clark and Jack Brabham outdrove him and, after Clark retired, Graham settled for a distant second place.

The remaining cars were being prepared for the Portuguese Grand Prix on 14th August but, meanwhile, I had become heavily involved in building the new four-wheel brake cars being designed by Tony Rudd, and therefore missed the race where all three of our cars retired. Stan Hope was building the chassis and, when completed, I was supervising assembly of the cars with the assistance of Arthur 'Snip' Chambers, John Sismey, and an apprentice. ('Snip' was so-called because of his continual snipping of the metal necessary in the fabrication of suspension wishbones, the manufacture of which he had become something of a specialist in.) The turnover in labour at the BRM racing section was fairly high. Many employees seemed to think that the job was all glamour and glory, but when they discovered the long hours involved and that better remuneration was available elsewhere, quite often they would move on. Diehards like Maurice Dove, Roy Foreman, Pat Carvath, Willie Southcott and myself were inclined to put job satisfaction as their number one priority.

The Monza circuit had been modified in 1958 to include a banked section, in order to accommodate the Indianapolis boys who were racing their specialist cars at Monza for the first time. The organisers proposed to include the separate banked section in the Grand Prix, but drivers considered this dangerous for Formula 1 cars and British teams boycotted the Italian Grand Prix that year in protest. The race was run and resulted in a hollow triumph for Ferrari, which had no doubt been put under pressure by the Italian government to compete.

Now settled in the new workshops at Bourne, management frequently brought visitors to look around, often providing the opportunity for a little clean mischief, of which sheet metal

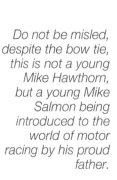

Do not be misled, despite the bow tie, this is not a young Mike Hawthorn, but a young Mike Salmon being introduced to the world of motor racing by his proud father.

worker Danny Woodward was one of the chief instigators. A favourite trick of his, should he be gas welding when a suitable victim was nearby, was to fill a matchbox with acetylene gas. Choosing an opportune moment when the unsuspecting visitor was close, he would ignite the matchbox with the welding torch, the resultant noise similar to the discharge of a powerful shotgun, and quite alarming for the nearby visitor. Dan would nonchalantly carry on working as if nothing unusual had occurred! Another quite amusing exercise was to wire a magneto to a workbench, all of which had metal-clad surfaces with vices attached. It was not uncommon for the visitor to lean on a bench and receive a mild but effective shock at the turn of the magneto. He would then enquire of his escort – invariably Raymond Mays – what had happened, whereupon Mays would gingerly touch the bench and, when nothing untoward occurred, have no explanation to offer.

The revised car, designated the P48 Mark II, was progressing satisfactorily and we took the unpainted version to Snetterton in late August where it was given its initial track test. One test was airflow monitoring around the car, achieved by taping tufts of wool to the skin of the car and observing their movements during running; a primitive but nevertheless effective method. Although plagued by throttle and fuel injection problems, the car showed promise and Graham Hill, who had conducted the tests, left Snetterton in a happy frame of mind.

In early autumn it became known that both Dan Gurney and Jo Bonnier would be leaving BRM, having accepted an offer to drive for Porsche in 1961. Graham was as yet undecided about his future.

There were two 'home' events in September on successive weekends prior to the final championship race of the current

formula in America in November. Neither of these races was particularly memorable for BRM, except that the P48 Mk II made its debut in the Gold Cup at Oulton Park and finished third in the hands of Graham Hill. In the Lombank Trophy at Snetterton the previous weekend three BRMs were entered but we had only one finish – Jo in third place. Lotus 18s won both events. At least Snetterton yielded one notable result in that Graham achieved his first ever pole position for a Formula 1 race.

So to the American Grand Prix at Riverside, California, from where the cars would be shipped to New Zealand for the Tasman tour starting in January 1961. Three cars were raced in America with little success, Bonnier finishing fifth and both Hill and Gurney retiring. Meanwhile, I was busy with 'Snip' Chambers and John Sismey in the construction of new cars being built to Tony Rudd's design ready for the 1500cc formula, the objections of British manufacturers to this specification having been overruled. Until BRM's own power unit was ready the cars were to be fitted with the 4-cylinder, 1500cc Coventry Climax engine, similar to that of our main rivals Cooper and Lotus.

Phil Ayliff suffered rather badly from athlete's foot, as related earlier, and this resulted in an unpleasant odour accompanying him on his travels. Earlier in the season he had been tactfully persuaded to discard his favourite old but smelly shoes in favour of something more suitable and ventilated. He went along with the suggestion and discarded the odour carriers but, unbeknown to him, Roy Foreman had retrieved them. At the annual BRM Christmas dinner held at the Angel Hotel in Bourne, Roy was to be rewarded for his efforts throughout the year by his fellow mechanics. Receiving his present with gratitude and not a little surprise he opened it to find his old pair of smelly shoes!

Another year had passed, progress had been made but we were not yet up among the big boys where Alfred Owen wanted to see us and where we all longed to be. For the time being the harsh reality was that this year we had scored a paltry eight points in the Constructor's Championship, whereas we had gained eighteen points in each of the previous two years since the championship began, On the plus side, Graham Hill pledged his allegiance to BRM and this proved be a long-term alliance that was beneficial to both parties.

The traditional BRM knock-on wheel nut, a distinct advantage over rivals' four-nut fixing when wheel changes were necessary.

INTERCONTINENTAL FARCE

The cars that had raced in America were on their way to New Zealand by sea for the now traditional Tasman Series, Dan Gurney staying on to do the four races alongside Graham Hill. Meantime, I was still heavily involved – along with 'Snip' Chambers and John Sismey – in building the new car being designed by Tony Rudd, designated the P57. This car was to comply with the 1500cc Formula 1 specification, British manufacturers having lost their fight to continue with the present specification. As mentioned in the last chapter, the Coventry Climax engine would be used to power the cars until such time as the V8 designed by Peter Berthon and Aubrey Woods became available. In tandem with this project was the preparation of existing P48 cars, which were to be raced in the Intercontinental Formula. The introduction of such a formula was largely done to appease British teams reluctant to accept the 1.5-litre Formula 1; as it turned out, scant enthusiasm meant that the formula quickly faded away once it was realised that the 1.5-litre formula was here to stay.

Tony Brooks had rejoined the BRM team to drive alongside Graham Hill, and we were led to believe he had been instrumental in persuading Alfred Owen to engage 'Wilkie' Wilkinson as Team Manager and Chief Mechanic, solely responsible for car preparation and race strategy. It was an appointment greeted with suspicion and not a little derision by BRM personnel, from top management to the shop floor, the majority of whom had known this bustling little man for some years and considered him over-endowed with ego. 'Wilkie' was a man who revelled in publicity, always willing to talk with representatives of the press. His directive that mechanics should address him as Mr Wilkinson rather than 'Wilkie' got short shrift and he was quickly nicknamed 'Piccolo Bill' by members of the racing team. Graham Hill was non-committal, his body language indicating he was not impressed with the new arrangement. The appointment had been made when Tony Rudd was otherwise engaged in the Tasman Series and most probably without his knowledge which did not augur well for whatever relationship there might be between the two.

The first BRM to comply with the new Formula 1 specification introduced for 1961. Powered by the Coventry Climax engine as a stopgap until the BRM V8 engine was available.

"Open wide, please." Dan Gurney pictured in New Zealand enjoying a light snack.

"Who're you calling greedy?"

The Coventry Climax-engined P57 BRM first ran on 13th February at the disused airfield at North Witham, fourteen miles west of Bourne, with Tony Rudd driving. His initial opinion was that the car showed promise, and subsequent tests at Silverstone and Goodwood by Tony Brooks and Graham Hill endorsed that. Unfortunately, the car was grossly underpowered compared with the more powerful Ferraris and new German Porsches, a situation BRM would have to endure until its own V8 engine was available. It was obvious the team would not be competitive that season and that, once again, Alfred Owen would be less than pleased. Our main British rivals were in much the same position, also reliant on the same 4-cylinder engine until the new Coventry Climax V8 came on stream later in the season.

The first home event of 1961 was the Easter Goodwood meeting in which four cars were entered: two P48s and two P57s for Graham Hill and Tony Brooks. The P48s were to contest the Lavant Cup run to the 3-litre Intercontinental formula, whilst the P57s made their debut in the 100 mile Glover Trophy for the new Formula 1, in which they qualified fourth and sixth respectively. In the Lavant Cup Graham finished third to Stirling Moss and Bruce McLaren with Tony Brooks fourth. All the entrants were Coventry Climax powered in the Trophy race, run in miserable weather conditions, and Tony Brooks slid off at Woodcote, Graham finishing a creditable second to John Surtees in a Cooper-Climax. One observation made at the meeting was the obvious differences of opinion between Tony Rudd and Graham Hill on the one hand, and 'Wilkie' on the other, Tony and Graham always seeking to improve and 'Wilkie' preferring to leave well alone. The seeds of disagreement had been sown and the team was waiting with some curiosity for them to germinate.

April was a busy month with two further events both run to the new Formula 1. In the first of these Graham claimed pole position for the 150 mile race (curiously named the Aintree '200') with Tony Brooks back in tenth position after a bout of misfiring had interrupted his practice laps. In atrocious weather Graham finished third to the works Coopers of Brabham and McClaren with Tony Brooks a distant seventeenth. The race concluded, the cars were hastily transported to Gatwick airport to be flown to Sicily for the non-championship Syracuse Grand Prix on 25th April, only three days hence. It was at this circuit that Tony Brooks won the race in 1955 at the wheel of a Connaught, the first all-British success in a Grand Prix since the 1920s. He was out of luck this time, though, retiring with a blown engine whilst Graham missed a gear and wrecked his engine as well, limping to the finish but unclassified. The race was best forgotten as far as BRM was concerned! The winner was previously unknown to Formula 1, a young Giancarlo Baghetti driving the new Ferrari 156 (sharknose) in its first race, underlining the fact that a tough season lay ahead of us.

Back at Bourne staff were now stretched to the limit racing the P57 Climax engined cars and the P48 Intercontinental cars. All this in addition to construction of the new P57/8 chassis and development of the V8 engine in readiness for the following year, or, ideally, before. Weary workers became irritable and arguments ensued.

The next scheduled event was the International Trophy at Silverstone on 6th May for the Intercontinental cars. These races were something of a hindrance and, in my opinion, we competed in them solely to keep the drivers happy and fulfil our obligations to the organisers who had invested in the series and expected us to support their races. Qualifying the P48s in fourth and eighth places respectively, Graham and Tony took their positions on the starting grid in the most atrocious conditions, wind and rain sweeping across the circuit. Cars were sliding and spinning in a most bizarre race, pit stops to inspect for damage caused by going off-road were frequent, drivers and pit crews alike relieved to see the chequered flag. Tony Brooks finished in sixth place and Graham Hill ninth after spinning twice.

It was something of a relief when the World Championship at last got under way at Monaco on 14th May. The appointment of 'Wilkie' as Team Manager and Chief Mechanic meant that Tony Rudd was no longer required at races. Like the majority of mechanics, Tony really enjoyed the visits to Monte Carlo, but with the new team management configuration it seemed he would be missing out this year. However, he had different ideas! Graham Hill approached Peter Berthon and requested Tony's presence at Monaco, which was granted. I have little doubt that Tony had been instrumental in encouraging Graham to make this representation to PB (the feeling among the workers was that Graham was distinctly unimpressed with Mr Wilkinson). Tony attending at Monaco did nothing to improve the lack of concord between the pair and it was a subdued Tony who had to be content with the role of observer on race day, while the effervescent new Team Manager revelled in his surroundings.

Since arrival of the Leyland transporter, a new Ford Zephyr estate car had been acquired to transport the mechanics, and this year Roy Foreman and I were passengers with 'Wilkie' our chauffer. The second overnight stop was made at Avignon, where a very tired 'Wilkie' retired early to bed after the long drive (he had declined our offer to share the driving). I awoke early to a wonderful sunny morning, breakfasted, and enjoyed

The paddock at Zandvoort;
but who's the lucky man in a barrel of Heineken?

Leyland Royal Tiger by the BRM
garages at Zandvoort.

the sunshine with Roy with no sign of 'Wilkie.' Realising he had probably overslept, I suggested to Roy we go and wake him. Roy's response was a mischievous smile and suggestion we "let the poor old bugger sleep." As I could see no reason to disagree we continued to enjoy the sunshine. About 10am a bleary-eyed and panicky 'Wilkie' surfaced, bemoaning the fact that he had no time for breakfast, we had not woken him, and we needed to get on the road!

Eventually, we arrived at Monte Carlo where Graham qualified fourth with Tony Brooks eighth after practice was disrupted in order to recover various crashed cars. A disappointing race saw Graham retire on lap 12, with Tony struggling and eventually colliding with Dan Gurney's Porsche, thereafter retiring but classified in thirteenth place. Even the usual post-race celebrations were subdued.

In his memoirs 'Wilkie' claims that though it was usual BRM practice to leave Monte Carlo on the Wednesday or Thursday after the race, he insisted on departure immediately following race day. This is not true as the team usually left race venues the next day, the exception being, for example, Monza, where we stayed on for testing. On this occasion 'Wilkie' was mistaken again. We carried out some repairs to the cars in the Palace garage prior to leaving Monte Carlo on the Wednesday morning, travelling direct to Zandvoort in readiness for the Dutch Grand Prix there five days later on Whit Monday, 22nd May. Necessary replacement engines and spares were transported to Holland to await our arrival.

On this more open circuit (compared to Monaco), the Climax-powered BRMs were no match for the powerful Ferraris, whose three works machines occupied the front row of the grid

after final practice, with Graham a creditable fifth behind Stirling, and Tony a disappointing eighth. The relationship between Tony Rudd and 'Wilkie was deteriorating, Tony banished from the pits by 'Wilkie' which was detrimental to the smooth working of the team and increasingly frustrating Graham Hill. He had become noticeably friendly to Tony Rudd, with Tony Brooks probably asking himself whether he had put the cat among the pigeons by suggesting the recruitment of Mr Wilkinson in the first place. Clearly, it was a situation that could not continue …

Although the roadholding of the BRMs on this twisty and undulating circuit was quite impressive, the lack of power was very obvious; Graham could manage no better than eighth place and Tony ninth. During the weekend Louis and Jean Stanley had observed the friction in team management and were instrumental in changes being made. It was agreed that Tony Rudd would be present and contribute to car set-up and tuning during practice, with 'Wilkie' taking charge on race days. The mechanics were rather surprised at this arrangement, murmuring to each other that it could not last.

Back at Bourne the normal post-race inspections and rebuilds were made with further tests carried out at Snetterton in preparation for the Silver City Trophy at Brands Hatch on 3rd June. It was a minor Formula 1 event in which Tony Brooks finished third with Graham a distant thirteenth after he was dogged by ignition problems, his misfiring car sounding like the proverbial bag of nails!

During this period I was fully occupied in the construction of the new cars in readiness to accept the V8 BRM engine. It was a time-consuming and sometimes frustrating task, the necessary components frequently being in short supply. It was not unknown

to borrow a crankcase or gearbox casting from the machine shop, use it to make engine mountings and various brackets throughout the night, and then return the loaned component to the machine shop the following morning.

The new workshop had a hardboard partition to divide the racing shop from the panel and build shop, which one of the shop cleaners had been detailed to paint white. While he carried out the task, one of the team on the other side would estimate where he was working and give the hardboard a thump, 'accidentally,' of course, but much to the cleaner's annoyance. Also at about this time a Day-Glo orange band was painted on the nose of the racing cars to make them easier to identify when approaching the pits during a race, and it was not uncommon to see people walking about with the heels of their shoes painted this bright orange, the work of some mischief-maker. I recall one man foolishly claiming that no-one would be smart enough to paint his shoes; in less than five minutes he was displaying a pair of Day-Glo heels! Members of the local constabulary often visited us and it was obvious that one of them would soon become a target, which is what happened. A member of staff, Ben Casey, laughingly approached a particular constable two days later in Bourne town centre, claiming that it was he who had had his heels painted. The officer denied it, but close examination showed some paint still visible on his shoes!

The staff was delighted to learn during June that HM Queen Elizabeth had honoured Alfred Owen in her Birthday Honours list. Receiving a knighthood he was now Sir Alfred Owen in recognition of his civic services to Staffordshire.

At the next two races, both World Championship Grands Prix, we were simply putting in an appearance for the sake of the drivers, the underpowered Climax-engined cars being uncompetitive on the fast circuits of Spa Francorchamps and Reims. In the former, after a variety of annoying minor problems, Graham retired with oil loss and Tony finished thirteenth. It was inevitably a Ferrari walkover, the type 156s in a class of their own and filling the first four places. It was at Spa, whilst Willie and I were working late into the night in the garage at the Hotel du Roannay, that one of the many onlookers, who never seemed to require sleep, was interested to know when the new car would appear. He asked in an upperclass English accent if I could tell him how long the V8 engine would be? Willie found it difficult to contain his laughter when, donning my best deadpan look, I told him we were hoping about 24 inches. The enquirer went on his way looking bemused!

Reims witnessed another mediocre performance by the BRM team. In intense heat Graham qualified in sixth place with Tony eleventh, once again no match for the Ferraris. In the race Graham finished a creditable sixth, but Tony retired with cooling problems after only four laps. The race turned out to be history in the making with Giancarlo Baghetti competing in and winning his first World Championship race, again in a Ferrari 156, the first driver to win a World Championship Grand Prix at the first attempt.

The first of the new chassis designated P578 (to denote the V8 engine as opposed to the Coventry Climax) had been released to the final build department by Stan Hope's fabrication section.

The British Empire Trophy at Silverstone on 8th July was considered another 'nuisance' race by shopfloor workers, a further outing for the Intercontinental P48s and, hopefully, something for the British supporters to cheer about. In addition to ourselves, Cooper and Lotus teams made up the other major entries. A disappointing practice resulted in Tony in sixth place on the grid with Graham eighth. Graham, never one to shirk a scrap, drove a magnificent race in poor conditions to finish third, Tony having retired with a broken crankshaft.

Late in the evening of Wednesday 12th July, the 1.5-litre BRM V8 engine first ran on the test bed at Folkingham, an event which signalled the start of the most successful period in the history of British Racing Motors. Though not without its teething problems – principally oil and water leaks – the initial run showed great promise. If the engine had not been run at that time, it would have been delayed until the Friday as, being a suspicious lot, none of us wanted such an important event to take place on the 13th! The test house was a haze of oil smoke but the sound of those multi cylinders in action was music to our ears!

At the British Grand Prix at Aintree on Saturday 15th July, both practice and the race itself were run in dreadful conditions, Tony qualifying sixth with Graham a lowly eleventh. Both cars suffered misfiring problems in the race with 'Wilkie' calling them in for a plug change. This failed to rectify the problem with Graham's car and he retired with a broken valve spring, but it did appear to be the solution to Tony's difficulties. As the track dried he drove magnificently and recorded the fastest lap of the race to finish ninth, although two laps down on the winning Ferrari; 'Taffy' von Trips, Phil Hill and Richie Ginther making it another Ferrari 1-2-3. Tony Brooks expressed his dissatisfaction at racing an uncompetitive car despite a creditable drive given the conditions.

The loss of the test track at Folkingham meant much precious time was spent travelling to Snetterton or Silverstone for all our serious testing. Fortunately, Lincolnshire – proudly known as 'Bomber County' – had a number of redundant wartime airfields, and the former American base at North Witham twelve miles west of Bourne was proving very useful. Running alongside the A1 trunk road, the disused runway on this base was used to carry out minor proving tests. Here, 'Wilkie' carried out shakedown runs on the cars now being prepared for the German Grand Prix, to be run at the Nürburgring on 6th August.

As these cars departed for Germany, Arthur Chambers, John Sismey and I worked flat-out to complete the build of the first V8-powered car, with instructions that it was to make its first race appearance at the Italian Grand Prix at Monza on 10th September. It was a very interesting and exciting time but, combined with tiredness and frustration, there were many problems to overcome. With several different draughtsmen designing the various components it was quite common for parts to conflict and, as we were in the build shop at the end of the line, it was invariably down to us to find a solution. Many expletives were heard in conjunction with comments such as "No need to ask which prat designed this," at the same time knowing full well it was likely we would have made the same mistakes ourselves. It was generally great fun and, apart from some derogatory inter-personnel comments, most of it was jocular with good camaraderie. Raymond Mays became a daily visitor to the build shop to witness progress, which was often not fast enough for his satisfaction. He would ask questions: "Why is this not done"? or "Have you got so-and-so yet"? or "When will you have that finished"? He also became something of a progress chaser. I recall on one occasion wanting some standard small bore rubber hose, RM enquiring why it had not been fitted yet. I told him that Clarrie Brinkley was out of stock. "Bloody ridiculous" he replied as he strode out of the workshop to give 'Brink' a rocket. Remarkably, the hose was obtained from an outside supplier within a few hours! This sort of incident was very frustrating. Some of the stores personnel did not appreciate the number of components needed in building a new car and often, when requesting small items such as nuts and bolts, we would be greeted with the words "Christ, what are you doing with them, eating them? You had some of them yesterday."

Meanwhile, over in Germany the team was experiencing the usual problems at this daunting venue with its varying characteristics; so hard to achieve good roadholding on such a long, twisty and undulating circuit: it was very difficult to find a suitable compromise. Graham took sixth place on the starting grid with Tony ninth but Graham's race was shortlived, as he crashed out at the start of the second lap while engaged in an overtaking manoeuvre with Hans Herrmann at the South Curve. Tony retired with a broken valve. Stirling Moss drove one of his finest races in the wet and took the chequered flag in Rob Walker's Lotus 18/21 using the underpowered 4-cylinder Coventry Climax engine similar to our own. It was his second victory of the season against the dominant Ferraris.

The following day saw the final race for the 2.5-litre BRM P48s as works entries. Both drivers had flown back from Germany to compete in the Guards Trophy at Brands Hatch on August Bank Holiday Monday. It was stretching the team and resources to the limit with our cars in two different countries over the same weekend! In addition to the feverish activity on the P578s in readiness for Monza, we also had the non-championship Formula 1 Modena Grand Prix the week before in which we were entered. It was getting ridiculous: men were

A determined-looking Graham Hill before the Italian Grand Prix at Monza, despite the knowledge that a lack of power from the Coventry Climax engine would mean he had little chance of victory.

Taffy von Tripp's Ferrari receives the chequered flag for finishing in second place in a rain-soaked German Grand Prix at the Nürburgring.

The Leyland on its way to the Nürburgring.

tiring with tempers becoming frayed. As things turned out, the Guards Trophy at Brands Hatch was the last race of the shortlived and unloved Intercontinental formula, Graham finishing third in the race and Tony Brooks retiring with a broken throttle. With the P48s now redundant we could at last concentrate our energies on the new cars in order to make an assault on the World Championship in 1962.

In the build shop we had now obtained a suitable mock-up engine which enabled the pipework, control fittings, linkage wiring, etc, to be finalised and make ready the chassis to accept a working engine. It arrived in the build shop in early August and, once assembled, had a warm-up run at Bourne before the unpainted car was taken to North Witham airfield for its initial track test. Driven by Tony Rudd, much to everyone's relief, initial signs were good: we had gears and the wheels turned! A second car was nearing completion and it was confirmed that evening that two cars would definitely go to Monza for high-speed test runs, prior to official

Totally against the advice of his mates, Pat would insist on having the curry!

"Cor, that's better ..."

practice, with a remote possibility of running them in the Grand Prix on 10th September. Toby Swain, a native of Bourne employed by Carlton's in Abbey Road, Bourne, and a highly experienced coach painter, was now making an excellent job of the paintwork on the racing cars, often working long into the night in order to meet departure deadlines.

Meanwhile, the two Climax-powered cars left for the Modena Grand Prix with 'Wilkie' in charge. Graham lined up fourth on the grid, Tony eleventh on row five. Tony finished in sixth place in the race with Graham seventh after running with the leaders and holding fourth place for much of the race. He lost time, unfortunately, when a wheel had to be changed following a puncture caused by hitting debris from a 'blown' engine. The following morning the cars went direct to Monza.

Peter Berthon had, by this time, separated from his wife Lorna, arriving at Monza with his new girlfriend Anthea Butcher, a charming South African lady who was soon to become his second wife. The time came to load the new P578/1 into one of the remaining Austin Lodestars and point it in the direction of Monza. Over my ten years at BRM I had become accustomed to being 'on the road,' we mechanics living a day at a time on our wits, and was something of a relief to be heading south once more after the long weeks spent at Bourne and Folkingham building the new cars.

We arrived at the well-known Hotel Marchesi at Villasanta on Sunday 3rd September, one week prior to the Italian Grand Prix. This was still one of our favourite hotels and it soon became apparent that the oldest business in the world was as brisk as ever here. Testing planned for the following day on the Monza circuit was delayed until Tuesday due to a police investigation following an incident on the track during the previous day's motorcycle racing. Our team from Modena duly arrived to join us on Monday afternoon, followed by the second new P578/2 from England on the Tuesday evening; a total of four cars now garaged at the rear of the hotel.

Despite the track being temporarily unavailable we still had much to do, checking and rechecking or, in Raymond

Mays terminology: "leaving no stone unturned." There were seats to be tailored to suit the drivers, pedals to adjust and, last but not least, the not unpleasant task of awarding marks out of ten for the ladies being escorted to and from the hotel chambers.

Once again, the race that year was to include the use of the full circuit, including the high-speed banked section. The British teams had overcome their objections of the previous year and turned up in force. The cars would cover a lap of the old track, at the end of which they were routed onto the banked section, a lap of this and they would return to the old track, making a lap distance of 6.2 miles (10.00km). For testing purposes we were permitted to use either one of the single circuits or a combination of the two. On the banked section centrifugal force caused the suspensions to bottom, thus with no suspension movement the drivers decided it was too bumpy and protested, complaining of being thrown about which could result in neck injury. Their complaints

Graham Hill driving the P57 Coventry Climax-engined BRM at Monza.

To Dick With my Best Wishes Graham Hill

In the new P57 BRM V8 at Monza. The car so impressed the press it was quickly dubbed 'Little Miss Elegance.'

Rear view of 'Little Miss Elegance' outside the garage at the Marchesi Hotel, Villasanta.

fell on deaf ears, however, and the race went ahead on the combined circuits – for the last time, as it turned out.

Satisfactory testing conditions were at a premium with the Grand Prix taking place the following Sunday, and many wanted to make use of the track, including our own drivers in their Climax-engined cars. Although we had not been told when testing began, I believe that BRM management had already decided that the new cars (the P578s) would not take part in the race. It was a wise decision considering past failures suffered through running under-developed cars.

Lined up in the pit lane our new car looked magnificent and attracted a great deal of interest from the press and other teams. There was a real sense of pride as the engine was fired up and the strident din of the V8 reverberated around the pits, in complete contrast to the flat tones of the 4-cylinder Climax engines. On Tuesday 5th September Graham Hill drove the first laps on the full circuit, complaining of heat in the cockpit and the engine blowing oil out of the breather at speed. Otherwise first impressions were positive and so back to the hotel garage for modifications, ready to return the following day. This process continued for the rest of the week until official practice for the race began. We would have a few laps followed by a plug check to assess fuel mixture, sometimes with the driver cutting the engine while flat-out, and then back for minor modifications before going out to test again. We were joined at the track by the second V8-engined car and the process continued with both cars into the official practice sessions for the Grand Prix, at which time it was announced that the new cars would not race.

Arthur Hill had been sent to the airport by 'Wilkie' to collect a package, using the Ford Zephyr as transport. Whether Arthur was distracted by the local crumpet I don't know, but he somehow lost concentration en route: 'Wilkie,' sitting on the hotel balcony when Arthur returned, was not amused to see him drive straight into the gatepost of the Marchesi, considerably modifying the front of the Zephyr.

Whilst our testing had been going on, 'Wilkie' and his men had been preparing the Climax-engined cars (P57s) for the race. The Grand Prix was of vital importance to Ferrari drivers Phil Hill and

'Taffy' von Trips, the only two contenders still able to win the title, one of whom would become the 1961 World Champion. However, the race became one of the most tragic events of Formula 1 motor racing when the von Trips Ferrari and the Lotus 21 driven by Jim Clark were involved in a high-speed collision approaching the Curva Parabolica: Graham Hill, following close behind, was extremely lucky to miss the gyrating cars. Sadly, 'Taffy' von Trips was killed, along with fourteen spectators, when his car careered into the crowd, leaving a sad and dejected Phil Hill to become 1961 World Champion. Fearful of being detained by the officious Italian police authorities, Jim Clark and Colin Chapman of Lotus made a hasty exit from Italy by air. They became the subjects of a lengthy enquiry into the accident and were advised not to return to that country in the near future. As for the BRMs' race, Graham Hill retired with a broken engine, still distressed from witnessing such an horrific accident. Tony Brooks was denied fourth position on the line from Jack Lewis in a Cooper by the width of a tyre tread, but finished a commendable fifth.

As on the previous Monday the Monza circuit was closed to allow the authorities to complete their investigations into the von Trips/Jim Clark accident. This delayed continuation of our testing programme but at least provided our personnel with the opportunity for some leisure time. Dan Woodward and I decided to visit Milan, and Vic Barlow of Dunlop kindly offered to drive us there and collect us at a pre-arranged time. We looked around the magnificent Gothic cathedral and the colourful shops displaying exotic clothes, with prices far beyond the reach of humble race mechanics. We could, however, sample and enjoy the delicious 'gelati'! We returned to our pick-up point in a car park to wait for Vic to drive us back to the hotel … and we waited and waited! Eventually, we wandered towards the bus station, luckily to meet Peter Berthon who told us he was deputising for Vic who had been summoned back to England where his mother had been taken ill. Unfortunately, PB had gone to a different car park so we were lucky to meet up with him.

It was back to testing for the remainder of the week, modifying and repairing cars and often reinforcing cracked frames that had suffered under the stress of the banked circuit. This was certainly finding the weak spots which could only stand us in good stead for the future: if the cars could withstand the harsh treatment of the banking, they would have a good chance of surviving on most other circuits. On the Wednesday our work was interrupted by the Italian police once again, their investigations into Sunday's accident still ongoing. Eventually, they allowed us use of the banked section only, which did not affect their enquiries.

Peter Berthon, always seeking improvement, would frequently ask for some adjustments to be made to his Ford Zephyr, which was fitted with a Raymond Mays Engine Conversion. It was invariably Phil Ayliff's lot to make these adjustments and, looking out of my hotel window one day, I spotted Phil finishing the job and walking away, toolbox in hand. Cupping my hands I shouted "Ayliff!" It had the desired effect because he turned round and went back to the car. PB looked up and said "Yes?" Phil asked "Did you call me?" to which PB replied, of course, "No." At that moment Phil looked up and saw me and exclaimed "I bet it's that bloody Salmon again." It left them both smiling and me laughing.

On Thursday 14th we had a near disaster. While negotiating the banked circuit Graham Hill's car caught fire, although he managed to keep it under control and bring it to a halt, eventually extinguishing the flames with his overalls. Graham complained that we had taken a long time to reach his car; even though it was normal procedure always to set out immediately a car was overdue. What was inexcusable was the fact that, on this occasion, the rescue vehicle did not carry a fire extinguisher, which was immediately remedied. There was no positive evidence of what had caused the fire, but a leaking fuel metering unit connection was suspected. It was certainly an incident of grave concern to both driver and mechanics.

After more tests on Friday, the cars were loaded ready for our return to England. Almost 500 running miles had been achieved and results overall were encouraging, although many working and testing hours were still to be spent before the cars were considered raceworthy. The aim now was to achieve that

More mischief; what are Willie and Dick up to now? Looks like they're skiving off to a "bring a bottle of Chianti" party.

Surprising what effect Chianti has on some people; it's sent Dan Woodward right up the pole, claiming he has captured Posto Due.

state ready for a race at Brussels on 1st April 1962: only BRM could choose April Fools' Day for the race debut of its new car!

At Monza the car had generated a lot of interest from would-be purchasers of cars and engines, which was something Sir Alfred Owen was keen to achieve, having already spent over £1,000,000 on the BRM project. Although he hoped to see some return on his money, in fact only a small number of sales were made, the small machine shop at Bourne finding most of its time occupied by producing parts for the team cars. I feel the management at Bourne did little to cultivate a successful commercial enterprise despite enquiries from the likes of Lotus, Yeoman-Credit, and even Facel Vega in Paris, who were interested in developing a roadgoing 2-litre version.

Tony Marsh had purchased a P48, which he ran at Zeltweg in Austria without success, retiring with engine failure. On 23rd September Graham Hill and Tony Brooks raced P57s in the BARC International Gold Cup at Oulton Park under the supervision of 'Wilkie' Wilkinson, in turn supervised by Raymond Mays. On a wet track Graham briefly led the race, only to retire with engine failure after completing 38 of the 60 lap race; Tony Brooks finished in fourth place. Stirling Moss won the event in the Ferguson P99 four-wheel drive car, a singular success for this innovative design.

The final race of the World Championship series was the United States Grand Prix on 8th October, to be held at Watkins Glen in New York State where two P57 Coventry Climax-engined cars were to represent BRM. A skeleton crew of 'Wilkie,' Roy Foreman and Dennis 'The Sheriff' Perkins accompanied the cars; not really the way to compete in a World Championship race! In fact, it turned into something of a comedy of errors, with a certain amount of friction between 'Wilkie' and Graham during the expedition. It would seem that Graham did not appreciate that just two mechanics could accomplish only so much work, and he ended up making his own adjustments to the car one test day whilst alone at the circuit. Despite the unease between the two senior members of the contingent, Tony Brooks took a commendable third place with Graham fifth after a pit stop to rectify an ignition fault.

Roy, unfortunately, trapped and badly cut the tendon on his finger the following morning whilst loading the cars and spares for shipment back to England. It incapacitated him to some extent but, as they were on their homeward leg, they would somehow manage with two men and an invalid, little knowing that Graham had spoken to Raymond Mays and wanted his car to be rerouted to a race in Mexico! It was a seemingly infinitesimal request when sitting in an office in far away Bourne, to which RM readily consented. However, the situation in America was vastly different with more arguments between 'Wilkie' and Graham, a frustrated 'Wilkie' trying to arrange workshop accommodation

Sales in a local hardware shop in Bourne increased when someone at BRM came up with the novel idea for these induction trumpet plugs to prevent debris entering.

in New York and transport to Mexico, but encountering problems with trades unions and spare parts lost in transit. All of this was to no avail, however, as the Mexican race was cancelled.

Following his return from America, Tony Brooks wrote to Sir Alfred Owen to tender his resignation as a BRM driver. He had not been happy during this second spell with the company, believing that Graham Hill had received obvious priority over him against the terms of his contract which stipulated equality of treatment between drivers. Probably as a result of this he appeared to have become disillusioned with motor racing and intended to spend more time with his family, soon to be increased, at the same time developing his garage business near the old pre-war Brooklands racing track.

The most important objective during the winter months was to fine-tune and build reliability into the new cars. Problems with the fuel system metering unit during Monza tests had prompted Lucas to introduce a smaller unit, necessitating many hours' development on both test bed and track. At this early stage the Lucas transistorised electronic ignition system was in the development stage. Many other modifications were also necessary, particularly chassis reinforcement and improvements for driver comfort, and we anticipated long days testing on cold, wet and windy racetracks throughout a busy winter.

Meanwhile, at Bourne Tony Rudd was taking a much more active part in decision making, often – it seemed – regardless of Peter Berthon. Peter Spear was making ever-increasing visits from Darlaston and, as in most industries, various rumours circulated regarding management changes and relocation to the Midlands. With Christmas imminent we would have to wait and see what 1962 would bring although two things were increasingly obvious: Sir Alfred Owen and his brother Ernest were losing patience and demanding some success whilst their sister Jean seemed content to sit on the fence, and the pontifical Louis T Stanley was revelling in the company of the many celebrities who frequented the world's motor racing circuits.

JUST CHAMPION, CHAPS!

Early in 1962 the Owen Organisation announced the names of the two BRM drivers for that year: Graham Hill would be retained and joined by diminutive American driver and Korean war veteran, Richie Ginther, who had been persuaded to leave Ferrari for Bourne. Whilst not in the top echelon of Grand Prix drivers, Richie was recognised as an excellent test driver. Innes Ireland had been offered a drive and would have liked to have joined but would not renege on his promise to Colin Chapman that he would drive for Lotus.

January and February were spent building more cars, modifying the original ones and developing engines, with the occasional day's testing at North Witham or Snetterton. Serious track testing began in March, only one month before the first race of the year.

On 18th March at North Witham airfield Richie Ginther tested one of the new cars, which almost ended in disaster. Entering the straight approaching the makeshift pit the car was seen to be on fire. It transpired that a fuel connection on the high-pressure outlet of the fuel pump had worked loose and burning fuel was being pumped onto the driver's neck! When the car stopped, a quick-thinking Arthur Hill grabbed Richie and smothered him with his body to extinguish the flames. Dennis Perkins – who, by chance, had just arrived in his car – rushed a badly burned Richie the thirteen miles to Stamford Hospital. Richie was detained and eventually made a full recovery, although his injuries necessitated a long spell off work, with members of staff taking it in turns to make bedside visits. He was able to drive again by mid-April; he jokingly remarked it was fortunate that English mechanics were at the scene of the fire for, had it been the Ferrari boys, they would have run away! I prefer to think that this was not true.

On 27th March we tested at Snetterton with Graham Hill driving, a final session before the first race five days hence. During these tests Tony Rudd was summoned to take a telephone call. Tony was famous for his witty remarks and, on this occasion, said he had

Alan Ellison and a colleague put the final touches to the bodyshell on a new P57 car in the panel section of the Bourne racing shop. All body panels were now made at Bourne.

been summoned to see Sir Alf at the Kremlin, adding "probably to give me the chop"! Tony attended as instructed. What was discussed was not revealed at that stage but we later learned that, as Sir Alfred was totally dissatisfied with the progress and performance of BRM, Tony had been issued with an ultimatum, a second meeting comprising Tony Rudd, Raymond Mays and Peter Berthon, together with Peter Spear and the Rubery Owen company secretary, Mr J A Glover, scheduled at Darlaston for Tuesday 3rd April.

On Thursday 29th March the new car left Bourne for its race debut in Brussels. The race was to be run to an unusual format in that it would consist of three separate heats, the idea being that three separate starts and finishes would add to spectator excitement. On a very wet track with rain pouring down, practice did not allow for a comparison to be made between the new BRM and the Lotus cars of Stirling Moss and Jim Clark. Graham achieved third place on the grid behind Jim Clark on pole and Stirling second.

In the first heat of the race on April Fools' Day, both Moss and Clark experienced problems, Moss having to use an escape road after a misjudgement and Clark suffering mechanical difficulties. This allowed Graham to go on to win the first heat; a promising debut for the new BRM. That promise, however, was shortlived. When the starter's flag fell for the start of the second heat, Graham's car sat motionless on the grid, his arm held high to signal that his engine had stopped. After the remainder of the field had left the grid, Graham was push-started by mechanics only to be black-flagged, the official signal from Race Control for a car to come into the pits as push-starting was not allowed. He was therefore disqualified from the race. Apparently, interpretation of the regulations regarding push-starting was open to debate, depending on which language was being read. Remember, it *was* April Fools' Day …

Back at Bourne speculation was rife as to the agenda of the meeting to be held at Darlaston. One absentee from the meeting was Raymond Mays who, probably suspecting that drastic reform was on the cards, had conveniently found himself otherwise engaged. On arrival at work the following morning,

Wednesday 4th April, Tony Rudd had been to the works early and posted notices signed by Sir Alfred Owen informing staff that, with immediate effect, Tony Rudd was to become Chief Engineer and Team Manager of BRM. Peter Berthon was to become consultant to the Rubery Owen Group under Peter Spear. In addition to his promotion Tony had been informed he must win two Grand Prix races in 1962 – or else!

Obviously, this move initiated lengthy discussions of varying opinion amongst personnel. Supporters of Peter Berthon were dismayed, whilst many others – myself included – welcomed the move. Although certain of PB's sincerity, we believed that Tony Rudd had the more futuristic outlook on motor racing and was willing to get his hands dirty in the process.

'Wilkie' was removed from the racing team management to concentrate on racing car and engine sales. Though Sir Alfred was keen to promote such sales, this move, I suspect, had been prompted by Graham Hill. The atmosphere between

Graham and 'Wilkie' had never been good, and in America the previous October it had reached an all-time low. To add to this, in contrast to the Hill/Wilkinson situation, a very cordial relationship had developed between Graham Hill and Tony Rudd which blossomed further under the managerial changes.

In addition to Graham and Richie, a third driver arrived on the scene, Bruce Johnstone, a relatively unknown South African whose mother was a friend of PB's lady friend. Despite a slight whiff of cronyism, Bruce was a friendly young man whose primary job was as test driver, and he received every encouragement from RM.

One of Tony Rudd's first structural changes was to recruit Cyril Atkins as Chief Mechanic. Cyril had held this position at Vanwall, which had now ceased racing. He was welcomed with mixed feelings for, although more popular than 'Wilkie,' it was felt that Phil Ayliff was doing a good job and was being badly treated. In fact, the change was too much for Phil, who eventually left to take up a post with Dunlop Brakes, becoming a successful businessman in the anti-lock brake field in the process. Cyril was a good organiser and some considered his organisational skills superior to his mechanical skills. For reasons which escape me, Tony Rudd nicknamed him 'Tonto,' which he was to endure throughout his BRM career.

Ten days after Tony's elevation to Chief Engineer one car was entered to race in the Lombank Trophy at Snetterton, Graham Hill to drive. (Richie was not yet sufficiently recovered from his burns to drive the second car.) After the first practice session, in which Graham had achieved third place to Clark and Moss, a crack was discovered on the engine mounting. The car was returned to Bourne and fitted with a replacement engine.

Back at Snetterton, Graham Hill made an electrifying start, which was most encouraging. Unfortunately, his engine developed a misfire and he was overtaken by both Clark and Moss, regaining second place when Moss retired. He held this position until the end of the race. It was a very pleasing performance and a satisfying start for Tony Rudd and his staff. 'Wilkie' Wilkinson also had some success in his capacity as salesman, having sold two of the earlier versions of the P57 to Tony Marsh and Jack Lewis,

both cars modified to accept the V8 engine. Both were entered in the Pau Grand Prix in France scheduled for 23rd April.

On the same date the works cars were entered in the 100 mile Glover Trophy Race at the Easter Monday meeting at Goodwood. Richie Ginther tested both cars at North Witham and declared himself sufficiently recovered to take part. Once again the practice session was dogged by bad weather, with Graham making second fastest time and Richie sixth. The start was a mini disaster for the BRMs, Graham almost stalling his engine; he recovered and was relegated to mid-field. Richie's engine failed to start because he had switched off the fuel pump due to a misunderstanding. The car had to be pushed to the pits to comply with regulations and eventually started three laps late. Graham recovered magnificently from his poor start to win the race, whilst Richie pressed on to finish in tenth place. Graham's victorious drive was his first actual race win for BRM and for himself.

The day was marred by the serious injuries sustained by Stirling Moss when he was involved in a devastating crash at St Mary's Corner. Having made a pit stop for throttle adjustment, Stirling found himself two laps behind Graham but was rapidly making up ground. Whether he had mechanical failure or it was a simple case of driver error was never established; at the time he was attempting to pass Graham and so unlap himself, but veered off at undiminished speed and hit the protective earth bank. Stirling was cut free from the wreckage and rushed to hospital in a coma, where he remained for almost three weeks before being taken elsewhere for more specialist treatment. Happily, he did recover although, sadly, the accident brought to an end the racing career of this great British driver.

The next race for the works entries was the Aintree 200, as usual a race of 150 miles. During practice Richie's engine started to make noises not normally associated with those of a racing car, and so an engine change was made. Graham had run off the road in practice and damaged the front of his car and, to rectify this, two panel beaters had travelled from Bourne. The garage used at Aintree was far from ideal for the task and necessitated working most of the night. Eventually, both cars were rebuilt and race-prepared. It was a futile effort, though, as both cars failed to complete the race: Richie had crankshaft bearings fail, whilst Graham's car was retired with a broken oil pipe. The Aintree bogey had struck again! While the failures were disappointing, we were still on a learning curve with the cars and remained hopeful that the modifications made as a result of information gathered during those minor races would stand us in good stead for the World Championship events.

Two cars were sent to Zandvoort for testing at the beginning of May in preparation for the first of the championship races, the Dutch Grand Prix on 20th May. Prior to that, there was the usual BRDC International Trophy at Silverstone on 12th May, the most important of the early season non-championship races. After qualifying, with Graham on pole position and Richie fourth, the race had contrasting fortunes in store for the two drivers.

Poor Richie was having a fraught introduction to BRM in his first race at the circuit. On lap five he lost control at Club Corner in the wet conditions, hit the bank and seriously damaged the car, fortunately without personal injury. Both cars were fitted with megaphone-type exhaust systems, four exhausts emerging from each side of the engine in stack pipe formation. It gave the cars a very impressive appearance! Graham made a poor start, once more having to play catch-up. After being forced to make an excursion onto the grass when overtaking a slower car, he found himself thirty seconds behind race leader Jim Clark in the Lotus. To add to his woes he was shedding exhaust megaphones at regular intervals but, undeterred, gallantly pressed on at undiminished speed. Rain began to fall and, on the wet track, Graham started to close the gap between himself and Clark, snatching victory in the last few yards having demolished a deficit of seventeen seconds in the last six laps. It was a very exciting and rewarding race for both Graham and the Bourne contingent, and probably a memorable day, too, for four spectators who could each possibly have returned home with a BRM exhaust pipe as a souvenir.

Back at Bourne two cars were hastily prepared for the Dutch Grand Prix. Unfortunately, it was not possible to repair Richie's

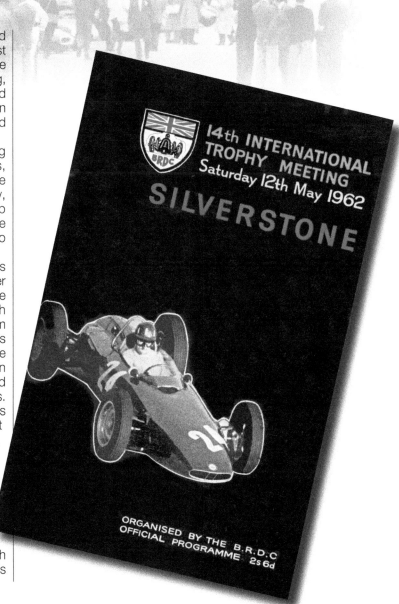

Graham Hill winning the BRDC International Trophy race at Silverstone after shedding a number of exhaust stack pipes.

The clearance between brake pad and disc was critical; here, Dick Salmon checks brake pad clearance on a P57 car watched by Roy Foreman, Jimmy Collins and Pat Carvath at the rear.

Preparing a P57 car in the Bourne racing shop. Roy Foreman and I discuss a brake calliper problem. Also working on the car are Cyril Atkins, Jimmy Collins and Pat Carvath.

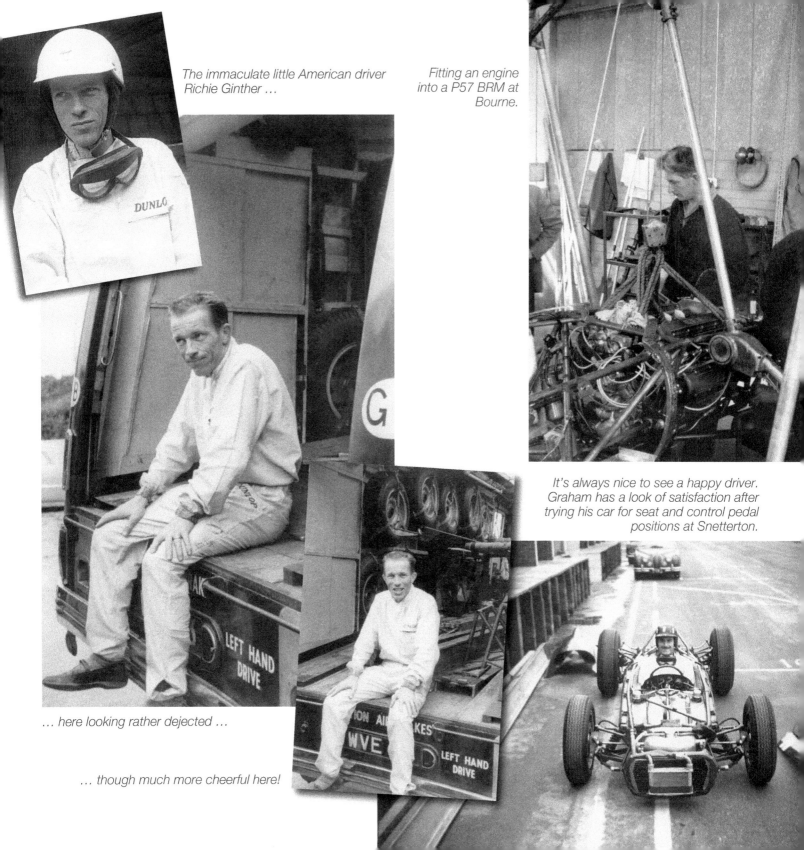

The immaculate little American driver Richie Ginther …

Fitting an engine into a P57 BRM at Bourne.

It's always nice to see a happy driver. Graham has a look of satisfaction after trying his car for seat and control pedal positions at Snetterton.

… here looking rather dejected …

… though much more cheerful here!

The instrument panel on a P57 BRM in racing trim. Left to right: rev counter, oil pressure, water temperature and fuel pressure gauges.

The look of concentration and determination for which Graham became well known.

Silverstone car in time after his accident, so a 1961 chassis was updated as close to 1962 specification as possible. On Thursday 17th May we departed from Bourne for Zandvoort via Harwich and the Hook of Holland ready for the first practice session on Friday.

As so often was the case at this seaside circuit a strong, cold wind was blowing in off the North Sea. This invariably brought sand with it, which lessened tyre adhesion on the twisty track and also detrimentally affected external working

parts, throttle controls in particular. This did not deter Graham, however, who made fastest time on the first day's practice. Conditions were even worse for the second day's practice and generally times were not improved on, with the exception of John Surtees in a Lola Climax V8 who took pole position. His fastest time was treated with some

Graham Hill and wife Bette following Graham's win in the Dutch Grand Prix, his first World Championship victory.

suspicion, general opinion being that the official timekeepers had made an error. We did, however, have Graham in second place on the front and Richie on the third row in seventh place.

Race day – thankfully – saw improved weather conditions as the cars lined up on the starting grid. As was becoming a regular occurrence with Graham, he did not make a particularly good start, which allowed Jim Clark in the new Lotus type 25 to take the lead. Richie made an even worse start and found himself down in tenth place. Clark continued to lead from Graham until lap eleven when he slowed with gear selection problems. It was wonderful to see the BRM in the lead, the Ferraris and remainder of the field trailing behind. Richie, meanwhile, had problems, suffering from an intermittent misfire. He was accidentally shunted by Trevor Taylor's Lotus and retired. Graham pressed on and, by lap sixty of the eighty lap race, had a thirty second lead, which he maintained until he saw the chequered flag.

A delighted BRM crew congratulated Graham on his first World Championship victory. A tearful Raymond Mays, unable to watch the last few laps, emerged from his hiding place: celebrations went on long into the night. Furthermore, and not least importantly, Tony Rudd was halfway to meeting the demands of Sir Alfred Owen to win two championship races. Although only one race had been staged, we were actually leading the World Championship table! If nothing else, this was good for morale.

Roy Foreman being tow-started at Bourne after rebuild: cars were taken to the eastern outskirts of Bourne, away from the residential area, and towed along a dirt track to fire them up.

How our fortunes had changed; victorious in three of the last four races we had entered. Nevertheless, we knew we could not be complacent: the new Coventry Climax V8 engine was, by this time, in general supply, which meant that all teams were on a much more even footing, unlike the previous year. Not only were Lotus and Cooper thus equipped but also the major private teams such as Bowmaker-Yeoman, with Lolas for John Surtees and Roy Salvadori and the UDT Laystall Racing Team. Lotus had unveiled the sensational type 25 'monocoque' at Zandvoort, in addition to the first appearance of the flat 8 air-cooled Porsches. With Ferrari bound to be strong, we knew we had very tough opposition.

In contrast to previous years the Dutch and Monaco races were the opposite way round, and we had two weeks in which to prepare the cars and travel to Monte Carlo for the second race of the series. This time a third car had been made ready and was taken as a spare. We again travelled in the Ford Zephyr, Roy Foreman, Dennis 'Sheriff' Perkins and myself, with Cyril Atkins the chauffeur the 'Sheriff' acting as navigator. (The 'Sheriff' had a remarkable gift of being able to locate those restaurants and hotels with good wine cellars!)

Practice and pre-race preparations were always hectic, the more so with a new type of car, and many hours were spent making the necessary adjustments, particularly to suspension settings necessary to contest this tight road circuit. To avoid overheating here from minor frontal collisions (often unavoidable at Monaco) teams could be seen modifying car bodywork in an effort to improve cooling systems. The pre-race workload was further increased when it was decided that Richie was going to race the third car, especially as he requested that the engine be exchanged for the engine from his original car, necessitating the burning of more midnight oil.

In 1962 the race was still started from the harbourside, which called for a mad dash to the first corner, the Gasometer hairpin. The long hours worked into the night on Richie's car were to no avail as he was involved in a multiple accident there on the first lap. It appears Richie's throttle stuck open, at least partially, and he spearheaded straight into the safety barrier lining the outside of the corner, taking two other cars with him. His car was severely damaged and an errant wheel flew through the air, striking and killing a marshal. Graham was also involved in a minor coming together with Willy Mairesse's Ferrari on that crowded first lap, but fortunately was able to continue in second place, eventually to take the lead from Bruce McLaren. At the halfway stage Graham had built a comfortable lead on McLaren of forty-five seconds and, on lap ninety of the scheduled 100, there was still a thirty-five second gap when Graham became concerned about a low oil pressure reading. On lap ninety-two his concerns became reality when he came to a halt due to engine failure at the Station hairpin; the big end bearing, without an adequate supply of lubricant, had succumbed to the punishment meted out by this demanding circuit.

We were terribly disappointed to come so close to winning our second consecutive Grand Prix but not depressed; we had a good car and our hopes were high for the future. In the circumstances the win by Bruce McLaren was a popular one.

The big question asked on our return to Bourne was: what had happened to the 2½ gallons of engine oil used during the Monaco race? Investigation indicated that the distributor oil seal had been fitted the wrong way round, allowing oil to escape. I do not know whether the verdict was conclusive, but it was another lesson learnt the hard way that would not be allowed to happen again.

Various test exercises took place at Silverstone and North Witham before the next race, the Belgian Grand Prix at Spa-Francorchamps on 17th June. One of the more significant changes was to dispense with the stack pipe type exhaust system and replace it with a more traditional tailpipe layout which, on the test bed, had shown a slight power increase.

On the afternoon of 13th June the team departed for Belgium, again to stay at the Hotel du Roannay. In practice Graham was in top form, qualifying on pole position, but Richie appeared to struggle on this very fast and demanding nine mile circuit where he could do no better than ninth position on the starting grid. Graham initially led the race, but after a few laps was dogged by an intermittent misfire which allowed Jim Clark in the Lotus 25 to overtake and lead the race, Graham dropping back to fifth.

An accident between Trevor Taylor's Lotus and Willy Mairesse's Ferrari enabled Graham eventually to move up to second position and gain six valuable Championship points. (Richie had retired earlier with gearbox failure; the Italian Colotti gearbox was being used as an interim measure until our own new version – being designed by Alec Stokes – went into production.)

The hotel at Francorchamps was one of our favourites, providing good food and an excellent place to stay, family-run and where the friendly staff were always welcoming. During his visit to America the previous year the 'Sheriff' had paid a visit to a joke shop and acquired a number of items of amusement, one of which was put to use there, to the consternation of du Roannay hotel staff. One evening while dining, the 'Sheriff' placed some realistic-looking artificial vomit under an adjacent vacant table, which was pointed out to the waitress, who gave an alarmed gasp and rushed into the kitchen. We could hear the agitated voices of the staff and the rattling of what could only be cleaning equipment. Very soon an embarrassed-looking young lady arrived with a mop and bucket, searching in vain for the beastly deposit which, lo and behold, had disappeared! She returned to the kitchen from where, once again, a cacophony of alarmed voices could be heard. Almost immediately the first waitress and the cleaner together rushed back into the dining room without the cleaning equipment, and mysteriously the vomit had returned. The waitress pointed it out to the bewildered cleaner, saying in her native tongue what I can only guess was "What the bloody hell is that there?" The cleaner returned to the kitchen to retrieve her mop and bucket, once more to find a clean floor. This same scenario was repeated yet again, by which time she began to smell a rat, looked at the floor and then looked towards our table where we were finding it difficult to keep straight faces. A huge smile steadily grew on her face, turning into such a laugh she appeared to be in danger of wetting herself! The penny had dropped and she quickly summoned all the staff to come and look. They were highly amused but no doubt the two members of staff involved were teased for some time to come.

Back at Bourne preparations were under way for the next race, a non-championship event at Reims on 1st July, followed by the French Grand Prix at Rouen a week later. It was another rushed programme, far from ideal for a team chasing the World Championship. Ideally, we could have missed the Reims event but it was always well funded and the minds of management and drivers seemed to be focused on revenue.

Graham qualified second on the long triangular Reims circuit but an out-of-sorts Richie could manage only ninth fastest. In first practice Graham had been quite disturbed to find he was slower than Masten Gregory driving a hybrid Lotus fitted with the BRM V8 engine, which may have inspired Graham to out-drive him in the final session. Bruce McLaren won an exciting race in his Cooper after a three car dice between himself, Graham and Jack Brabham, with Hill having the satisfaction of setting a new lap record. After winning two World Championships with Cooper (1959/1960), Jack Brabham had gone on to form his own team but was temporarily driving a Lotus 24 Climax until his own new car became available.

The folly of competing in the Reims race now became apparent, with engines and gearboxes transported to and fro between Reims, Bourne and Rouen like ping-pong balls, in order to repair cracked castings and carry out general overhaul. It left little time for routine car maintenance. However, achieving the impossible was normal work practice for us and two cars were rebuilt in time to take part in the first practice on Friday 6th July.

Compared with the fast straights encountered at Reims, the sweeping curves and undulations of the bumpy Rouen circuit were better suited to the excellent roadholding qualities of the BRMs, with Graham achieving fastest time on day one and Richie fifth. Saturday's practice saw Graham concede fastest time to Clark, but he was happy to be on the front row as he considered the second grid position more advantageous than pole for getting a good start. A struggling Richie was way back in tenth place on row four. Graham's theory proved correct as he immediately went on to lead the race from Clark. Meanwhile, Richie's engine failed to start and he had to be pushed to the pits for assistance, losing over a minute. Graham continued on his way until, on lap thirty-four, in the process of lapping Jack Lewis's Cooper on the straight for the second time, Lewis tucked

Jim Clark pitted during practice for the non-championship race at Reims.

Charles and John Cooper oversee operations in the Cooper pit at Reims.

A contented-looking Richie and Graham before the Reims Grand Prix, a non-championship event.

Bourne to be rebuilt overnight, Richie, suffering from a severe cold, could not drive to his full potential. With the spare engine fitted ready for Friday's practice, Graham qualified fifth and Richie eighth, neither driver happy and Richie complaining of lack of power. Again, this meant working long hours into the night to fit the engine that had been removed from Graham's car, overhauled and returned from Bourne.

in to pick up the slipstream, misjudged the manoeuvre and hit the rear of Graham's car, causing him to spin off the track. He managed to rejoin the race but at a cost of thirty-five seconds with the lead passing to Jim Clark.

The involvement with Lewis had more serious repurcussions later when Graham stopped at the Nouveau Monde hairpin to investigate the throttle system, which had evidently been damaged in the incident. He was able to limp back to the pits and eventually sent out to be classified as a finisher and claim the prize for fastest lap. Meanwhile, Clark also had problems and retired, leaving a delighted Dan Gurney to claim victory with the Porsche flat 8, a first World Championship win for both car and driver. An inspired Richie, possibly through sheer frustration after his delayed start, drove a magnificent race to finish third. The chagrin of England's football team losing to Brazil in the quarter-finals of the World Cup, together with the disappointment of Graham's failure, was evident on the faces of the BRM team.

Returning to Bourne disappointed but not downhearted, more testing followed at Snetterton in readiness for our home Grand Prix at Aintree on 21st July. Both drivers and all the staff were keen to do everything possible to keep us competitive in the Driver's and Manufacturer's World Championships, both of which we were leading at this stage of the season. Imagined or no, there always seemed to be an air of gloom at Aintree, a place disliked by mechanics and drivers alike. It was no surprise, therefore, when fortune took a downturn.

Graham did not seem at all happy in practice, and even less so when his engine blew up and was removed and returned to

Louis and Jean Stanley were now regular attendees at race meetings, and on rare occasions 'Big Lou' would prove useful. Here, in the early hours of the morning, he used his influence to acquire some liquid refreshment for the nocturnal mechanics by persuading a patrolling police officer to wake the landlord of a nearby public house and supply us with some beers! However, the following morning we would see the more usual side of Louis Stanley when he arrived at the circuit laughingly gloating that a police escort had accompanied him on the fifteen minute journey from his hotel, whilst in his words it had taken "Mays" an hour and a half to negotiate the traffic!

Heavy overnight rain had soaked the track, but it had dried out for the start of the race. Graham – on row two with Richie immediately behind him – were both baulked by Innes Ireland, suffering with gear selection problems, from the start. Clark went into the lead and maintained it throughout the race. Graham began to recover from his unfortunate start and had moved up into fourth place after fifty of the seventy-five laps. At this stage of the race Dunlop technicians were becoming concerned about tyre wear and, not wanting to lose time with a wheel change pit stop, Graham was instructed to slow down and maintain fourth position to ensure collecting three Championship points, this giving him a one point lead over Jim Clark. Richie had a dismal race, both he and his car not feeling well, ironically finishing thirteenth. Pleased that the Liverpool excursion was over, we returned to Bourne, gratified to still be topping the championship table.

How it used to be. Lotus mechanics work on Jim Clark's car in the Aintree paddock.

The three cars were dismantled and rebuilt. Following more test days at Snetterton, on the morning of 1st August we departed from Bourne bound for the Nürburgring, little realising that one of the most incident-packed and eventful weekends lay ahead of us. From Dover we took the ferry to Ostend, thence via Brussels and Liége, passing the circuit at Spa Francorchamps and on into Germany, again to be accommodated at The Wildes Schwein Hotel in the pleasant little town of Adenau.

The first appearance of a new car at the Nürburgring invariably made for a difficult time. Such a long circuit, with its numerous twists and turns and varying gradients, took up a great deal of time in making suspension adjustments and selecting optimum gear ratios. Graham was getting to grips with the track during the first practice session when he was involved in a most frightening incident. Carel Godin de Beaufort, driving his own privately-entered Porsche, had a television camera mounted high on his car behind the driver's head, probably the first time a camera had been used for the purpose of filming from a racing car whilst travelling at speed. Unfortunately – particularly for Graham – the camera was not satisfactorily secured, and during the fast downhill descent known as the Foxhole near Adenau it fell off and was left lying in the centre of the road. The first driver to arrive was Graham, to be confronted by this large black object. Unable to take avoiding action at an approximate speed of 130mph, he had no option but to run over the thing, rupturing the oil tank in the process and allowing oil to escape onto his rear tyres, causing him to spin on his own oil. He lost control and crashed, finishing up in a ditch behind the trackside hedge, hidden from view. (See pictures on folloowing page.) He was able to get out of the car in time to see Tony Maggs in a Cooper also spin off and, realising that a multiple accident was imminent, rushed down the track with arms waving to warn his fellow drivers, even though obviously badly bruised and shaken. The car was recovered with difficulty, the rescue crew unable to locate it so well was it concealed behind the

It was very difficult to pass the Hotel du Roannay without calling. Here, the team prepares to leave, having enjoyed lunch there on the way to the Nürburgring.

One of the many fun-filled happy moments shared by me and Willie: what a pair of pricks.

What is teetotaller John up to here – must have won them in a raffle?

Graham Hill's BRM as found at the Nürburgring following his incident with the camera.

Graham's crashed car hidden in the bushes at the Nürbugring. Mechanics had difficulty finding it to retrieve.

The wreck of Graham Hill's BRM after removal from the undergrowth, Richie Ginther displaying the evidence with the film from the guilty camera. Mechanics Dennis Perkins, Dick Salmon and Roy Foreman gaze at the wreck in disbelief.

Tony Maggs wearing a slightly manufactured look of dismay following his crash at the Nürburgring.

hedge. Eventually, it was returned to the garage, quite obviously not repairable in time to take part in the race so Graham had to contest the race in the spare car. Meanwhile, two furious team managers, Raymond Mays and John Cooper, were pursuing the television company for compensation for two wrecked cars.

Bravely, a bruised and stiff Graham arrived the following day for practice. Fortunately, he had made a satisfactory time before the previous day's incident and, as rain was falling on the second day, his time was good enough to put him in second place on the starting grid. Richie, unfamiliar with this demanding circuit, achieved seventh place. (Unfamiliar or no, he nevertheless gave me a frightening ride round the Nürburgring in a souped-up VW Beetle.)

On race day morning Graham arrived at the track still stiff and bruised, but looking very determined. Last minute adjustments were made as necessary, and the cars were about to be wheeled from the garages to the pit area when the heavens opened to such an extent that the start was delayed. Drivers were allowed a reconnaissance lap to judge if the circuit was fit to race, with positive findings.

For some reason Cyril Atkins had removed his trousers from beneath his overalls, perhaps because of the inclement weather, and placed them on a dry bench in the pit area. Roy Foreman noticed a tiny mouse trying to seek shelter from the rain and immediately took pity on the wretched creature, picking it up and placing it in the comfort of Cyril's trousers. What he had

Richie was almost forgotten, though finishing in a worthy eighth place. Jim Clark recovered somewhat from his delayed start to finish fourth. The World Championship was still wide open with Graham leading Jim by eight points.

not realised was that the mouse was also hungry. When Cyril came to put on his trousers after the race he discovered the mouse had been dining on them, and obviously had a good appetite, resulting in the exposure of a large area of his right buttock. Needless to say everyone was highly amused – with the exception of Cyril!

The race was eventually started an hour late and Graham, despite his Friday excursion, looked confident. After witnessing a few races mechanics can pretty well judge the mood of a driver, so it was reassuring to see Graham give us his familiar wink, indicating that all was well. From the start Dan Gurney took the lead in the flat 8 Porsche 804, much to the delight of the home crowd, with Graham in close attendance in second place. Clark, having made a poor start, was some way down the field. When the cars appeared in the distance towards the end of the first lap some nine minutes later, Gurney was still in the lead, and the crowd in the huge, packed grandstand opposite the pits roared its encouragement and approval. Then, as if a switch had been thrown, there was suddenly silence from the massive stand as Graham overtook Dan right in front of them; it could not have been arranged better by design and is a moment I will never forget. Graham continued in his impeccable style to record a momentous victory, his car never missing a beat in atrocious weather on a rain-soaked track. Following his awful accident in practice this ranked, in my opinion, as his greatest drive for BRM. He received congratulations from many people, and his wife Bette was delighted. In the excitement

This joyous occasion was marred by an incident involving Louis Stanley and Raymond Mays, who had been reduced to tears by Stanley who had, for some inexplicable reason, chosen this moment to confront and ridicule Raymond Mays about his sexual proclivities. This was certainly neither the time nor the place to embarrass a man who had done so much to help BRM reach the heights it was now enjoying in the motor racing world – far more than Louis Stanley would ever achieve.

Sir Alfred Owen's instructions to Tony Rudd to win two Grand Prix races had been complied with and our future now seemed assured, at least for the time being. In addition, the win would give the team a larger amount of starting money in forthcoming races. Although the Nürburgring was not the best place to celebrate a victory due to the widespread location of the various hotels, we BRM boys adequately improvised by holding a jubilant evening in Adenau. Friendly banter between the locals and ourselves helped create a convivial atmosphere, and it was a happy and contented bunch of mechanics that eventually retired to bed that night.

Unusually, there was a gap of six weeks before the next World Championship race in Italy, but this did not mean we had time on our hands. We knew that BRM winning both the Driver's and Manufacturer's World Championships was a distinct possibility but, after so many years of struggle, we could not relax the momentum for a moment if we were to pull off the greatest prize in motor racing. In an endeavour to achieve this aim, improvements and testing were never-ending.

Team Lotus mechanics working on the cars of Jimmy Clark and Trevor Taylor in the very basic facilities of Oulton Park.

The Stanley family at Oulton Park; daughters Bobbie and Catherine, son Edward and Mrs Jean Stanley talking to Bette Hill and Pam Rudd, with Louis Stanley and Tony Rudd at the back.

In the meantime there were other racing engagements to fulfil. On 1st September we were due to contest the International Gold Cup at Oulton Park, and a fortnight beforehand two cars were taken there for testing. This allowed Richie to familiarise himself with the circuit and also allow a frustrated Bruce Johnstone to at last drive a car. Peter Berthon and Raymond Mays had given Bruce various undertakings but these remained unfulfilled because of the changes in administration. Furthermore, maybe with some pressure from Graham, Tony had become somewhat disinterested in Bruce's racing career. However, Bruce had somehow enlisted the assistance of Sir Alfred and was to drive a car at Oulton Park. In the event the test day was not beneficial because of bad weather, a wet track preventing the drivers achieving any significant times. Knowledge was gained however, should the foul weather be repeated for the race two weeks ahead.

Once official practice got under way, Graham Hill put in the first 100mph (161kph) lap of the circuit. However, this did not give him pole position as unusually Richie out-drove him on this occasion to give him his first pole for BRM, with Graham third fastest behind Jim Clark, and Bruce Johnstone ninth. The race developed into another battle for the lead between Graham and Jim Clark, this time Clark coming out the winner with Graham having to content himself with second place. Richie retired with engine failure while Bruce drove a sensible race,

John Sismey, Roy Foreman and Cyril Atkins preparing one of the P57 V8 cars in the Bourne workshop in readiness for the Italian Grand Prix.

picking up places as others retired, resulting in his finishing a creditable fourth.

With three cars prepared as close to perfection as we knew how, we left Bourne for Monza on Monday 10th September on what was undoubtedly the most important assignment in the history of BRM, sitting on top of the World Championship table with only three events to go. We needed to win in Italy to consolidate our position ahead of Jim Clark's unrelenting pursuit in what was now looking increasingly like a two horse race for the title.

Len Reedman was, as usual, driving the Leyland Royal Tiger containing the three cars, accompanied by the 'Sheriff' and Pat Carvath riding shotgun. Roy Foreman, John Sismey and I had the doubtful privilege of again being chauffeured by Cyril 'Tonto' Atkins in the Ford Zephyr Estate. Travelling through Switzerland on the second day of our journey we were overtaking a loaded hay cart on a narrow mountain road. Roy reached out and grabbed a handful of hay. At our next stop he put the hay on the roof rack, convincing Cyril he had been too close to the loaded cart! Cyril said "I knew I was close, but I didn't think I was that close, but I must have been to collect that lot." Later, like happy schoolboys, during a roadside break we were shouting and listening to the echo of our voices from the mountains, attracting the attention of a local herdsman leisurely driving his animals down the mountainside, cowbells jingling merrily.

We arrived at Monza on the Wednesday in anticipation of being allowed to complete some laps on Thursday ahead of Friday's first official session. It was imperative some mileage be recorded with full tanks ahead of official practice as all three cars had been modified to carry a greater fuel load to meet the demands of a 300 mile race on such a high-speed circuit. These tests satisfactorily carried out, the cars were checked over and put to bed. Like us, they deserved an early night!

Over the preceding weeks a great deal of work had been carried out on the engines in conjunction with Shell in an effort to increase power. The result was immediately evident from the beginning of practice on this ultra high-speed circuit, this time

thankfully without the inclusion of the banking. The morning dawned bright and clear, Graham's frame of mind replicating the weather and Richie in similar mood – so far so good. The cars performed well, Graham getting fastest lap on that first day and winning the 200,000 lire prize for this, which sounds an awful lot of money though was, in fact, only about £200 sterling; to us, though, the lap time was worth more than the money. Richie – who was familiar with the circuit from his Ferrari days – was in sixth place. Graham was alternating practice laps between his own car and the spare and, at close of practice, was of the opinion that the spare car had more power but that his own handled better. He therefore asked for the engines to be swapped. Tony Rudd agreed to his request and whereas in the past this might have been done grudgingly, this time willing hands hastily carried out the task. Richie was happy with his car and was doing everything possible to help Graham.

Final practice saw Graham overtaken by Jim Clark for the fastest lap to gain pole position, but only by the narrowest of margins – 0.3 of a second – but he was happy to be on the front row. Meanwhile, Richie was complaining of overheating and it was decided to let him take the spare car. As this had been set up for Graham, considerable adjustment was necessary due to the size difference between the diminutive Richie and the somewhat larger Graham. The change seemed to inspire Richie who moved into third fastest place, putting both BRMs on the front row of the grid, alongside Clark.

We were grateful to see that weather conditions were set fair with both drivers looking calm and content. With fifteen minutes to go Graham was lying on the seat in the pits casually reading a book; as he approached his car he gave us his now-familiar wink. We nudged one another; he was up for it today! Fuel consumption versus capacity was of some concern and, after the warm-up lap, both cars were topped up with fuel, the cars shaken to allow the flexible tanks to be filled to the very limit. Once again Graham did not get the best of starts: this was becoming something of an enigma with him. He soon made amends, though, and drove in hot pursuit of Clark, overtaking him on the first lap, while Richie

An impressive shot of the Leyland Royal Tiger taken by John Sismey against an Alpine background on the return journey from Monza, with Len Reedman, Dennis Perkins and John Sismey.

maintained his third place with instructions to shepherd Graham and, if the situation allowed, protect him from predators coming up behind. Clark had to stop on the third lap, which allowed Richie into second place, the ideal position from which to control the pursuing field and allow Graham to gain a good lead.

After the threat posed by third-placed John Surtees had evaporated due to engine failure, these positions were maintained until the chequered flag: we had just witnessed the finest team achievement in the history of BRM. I cannot recall seeing two drivers looking so happy, Graham slightly bemused at how easily the race had been won. In the euphoria of winning it was easy to forget the important part Richie had played, not only by his back-up tactics and finishing second in that particular race, but also the important development work in which he had been involved. Tony Rudd always rated very highly Richie's development knowledge and ability as a test driver. Raymond Mays, to whom this victory meant so much, was again on the verge of tears, this time, though, genuine tears of joy. An overjoyed Bette Hill, who had appeared quite composed as she sat on the pit counter throughout the race keeping the lap chart for Graham, kissed and hugged her husband on his return to the pits. An excited Jean Stanley, representing her brother Sir Alfred, together with husband Louis, was at the forefront of the celebrations, no doubt delighted that the money invested by The Owen Organisation in the BRM project was at long last beginning to bear fruit. So many people – not least Colin Chapman of Lotus and John Cooper of Cooper Cars – congratulated us. Even the Italians, many of whom had become our friends over the years, were so delighted they seemed to have forgotten about their beloved red Ferraris, which finished fourth and fifth. After their success of the previous year they were without a win all season, now that the British cars had achieved significant improvement in performance.

It was a proud and happy group of people which stood to attention to listen to the British national anthem played as a tribute to the victor. The figmental title 'Ambassadors to Britain' tag, given to us all those years ago by Jim Sandercombe, had now become a reality. Consistent with usual practice the cars were impounded until the scrutineers had completed their obligatory check for irregularities – always an anxious time for drivers and mechanics – to be released later with a clean bill of health. When the fuel tanks were drained it was found that Richie's car contained a mere pint of petrol and Graham's a gallon, which meant that, at the consumption rate of approximately one gallon per lap, Graham might not have been able to complete another lap and Richie certainly would not have done so. Either Tony had worked his famous slide rule to perfection or he had had an enormous piece of luck, but who cared? That evening Jean and Louis Stanley invited us all to dinner at their hotel in Milan.

We were now in the lead in both Driver's and Manufacturer's Championships. Never before had the team faced the prospect of two races of such vital importance as the two remaining. The first was the American Grand Prix at Watkins Glen in New York State on 7th October, a race I did not attend. Following track tests at Snetterton, three cars were air freighted to America. Richie was marginally faster than Graham in practice, achieving second fastest to Jim Clark in pole position, with Graham third. An exciting race saw the two title contenders alternating for the lead in the early stages. Richie backed up his team-mate in third place but retired with a blown engine at one-third distance after performing so well in front of his home crowd. At lap twenty of the 100 lap race Clark went into the lead to stay, eventually winning from Graham by nine seconds.

The points total for the drivers now became a mathematical equation. In 1962, the points system was such that only the best five results from the nine events counted towards the Championship. As Graham had gained points in more than five races, he would hereafter lose the points awarded for his lowest finishing position. The situation before the final race in South Africa was that Hill had thirty-nine points compared with Clark's thirty points. If Clark won he would collect a further nine points which would give him the Championship because he had won four Grand Prix races to Graham's three. If Clark failed to win, Graham would be champion. The possibility of neither of them winning the race was not even considered: in simple terms, Clark had to win to be World Champion. Instead

Cyril Atkins preparing a car, Dennis Perkins working on Graham Hill's car no 3, and John Sismey at the bench in the immaculate-looking Bourne racing shop.

of being able to maintain the momentum and get on with the job in hand, we faced an agonising wait of two-and-a-half months before the championship would be resolved in South Africa on 29th December. Rarely can teams have been placed under such intolerable pressure!

Prior to the Grand Prix two races were to be contested in South Africa: the first at the Kyalami circuit at Johannesburg on 15th December, followed by one at Westmead in Durban. Combined with the third major event at East London at the end of the year, the three races were collectively known as the Springbok Series. We faced a logistical nightmare with three races on successive weekends many thousands of miles away. Three cars were shipped to Durban in large wooden crates, spares and toolboxes packed around the cars like sardines in a tin. A big worry was what condition would they be in on arrival at Durban after being craned on and off ship and a three week sea voyage? A spare engine was flown out later.

On the morning of Sunday 9th December I visited my mother who was recovering from a heart attack at the Butterfield Hospital in Bourne. In 1962, Bourne had two wonderful small hospitals but now, in 2006, with double the population, the nearest hospital is eleven miles distant and it can take as long as ten days to see a doctor. So much for progress.

Later that foggy day, John Sismey and I flew out of Heathrow, our destination the Jan Smuts airport at Johannesburg, calling at Amsterdam, Rome, Nairobi and Salisbury en route. It was goodbye to England until the new year; there was no question of our returning for Christmas since the South African Grand Prix took place on 29th December. Roy Foreman, Cyril Atkins and the 'Sheriff' had left a few days earlier. Pat Carvath, whose wife was expecting their first child, unfortunately missed this important trip.

The warm air at Johannesburg was a welcome change from the cold, damp weather we had so recently left behind. Johannesburg was a vibrant city, colourful rickshaws plying their trade and happy street urchins making pleasant music with a variety of homemade instruments. The downside came at nightfall when many beggars could be seen sleeping in doorways, with only cardboard boxes for beds. It looked more like London in the 21st century.

In addition to the main reason for our visit, it was intended we be used as a publicity vehicle for the Owen Organisation's companies in South Africa. We were accommodated in the Carlton Hotel, with use of the Grosvenor Motors garage premises for car maintenance.

The Kyalami circuit was situated a few miles outside the city in the windswept Witwatersrand foothills, 7500 feet above sea level, notable for gold mining. The thin air at this altitude necessitated significant carburation adjustment; in practice, Graham's car suffered from overheating. In what proved a futile attempt to increase cooling, Cyril Atkins' tin snips destroyed the beautiful lines of 'Little Miss Elegance' by enlarging the air intake aperture of the nose cone.

Following troublesome practice sessions, Graham qualified third and Richie fifth. Much against the wishes of Tony Rudd, at the behest of Raymond Mays a third BRM had been entered as a private entry to be driven by Bruce Johnstone. Strict instructions were given that this entry should not interfere with the works cars in any way and, in fact, it did not take part in the first race. The BRMs were beset by troubles in that initial race of the series, the first of which was when Graham once again made a poor

Cyril timekeeping and Dennis giving signals during practice in Johannesburg. The stopwatch clipboard held three watches: depressing a flap at the top of the clipboard would start one watch, stop one and zero the third.

start. Eventually, both cars retired having succumbed to failures exacerbated by overheating; in Graham's case ignition failure, whilst Richie suffered gear selection problems and complained his car would not handle well on left-hand corners.

It was a very disappointing start to our South African campaign, a fact that did not go unnoticed in the local press. The immediate response to the overheating problem was to have larger radiators flown out from Bourne, but time was of the essence with the race at Durban only one week away and the most important race in the history of BRM two weeks away. The cars were transported to Durban by road, the mechanics flying in a Viscount aircraft of South African Airways. Once established in our hotel I had the opportunity to visit my Aunt Emily who had left England in the 1920s to spend her working life in South Africa. The cars eventually arrived in those giant boxes, to be unloaded by local black labourers, one of whom, unusually, had striking ginger hair and bright blue eyes, leaving us to laughingly contemplate which ship his dad had been on! Compared with the dry heat of Johannesburg, Durban was very humid, the circuit in the barren and sandy suburbs of the city. Safety considerations were at a minimum with poor facilities and a bumpy track.

During our pre-race preparations, a worried-looking Cyril Atkins – who had been responsible for ensuring that

John Sismey makes an adjustment to Richie's car at Durban. Roy wipes his hands (he had probably fallen down and got them dirty …), Cyril grimaces and I look on, whilst Graham (behind me) scratches his head and thinks.

Melon-eating contest at Durban. The 'Sheriff' times the event while Cyril removes the pips with a pencil.

More delicious melons being enjoyed by the BRM men, and an unknown gatecrasher.

They certainly like their melons; another supply for the BRM boys.

Cyril appears to be enjoying the comforts of South African transport.

Improvisation was often necessary at race meetings, as Dennis Perkins and John Sismey demonstrate here when topping up the coolant level.

the required wheels had been shipped from England – was seen sucking on his pipe, repeatedly looking through the stock of wheels. Asked what the problem was, Cyril explained that, for some reason, he had two odd wheels; further investigation showed that Richie's car also had two odd wheels. We had discovered the reason for Richie's poor handling in the last race. Being a close-knit team, Richie was never told; like parliament and the "thirty year rule," only now can it be revealed! Fortunately, by juggling wheels and tyres, and the driver's lucky choice of wheels, we overcame the problem.

Our performance at Durban was an improvement on that at Kyalami but still far from World Championship class. Race format was two heats and a final. Practice was blighted by a tragic accident involving a promising young driver, Gary Hocking, from Bulawayo who had recently graduated from motorcycle racing to cars. Careering off the track, his car hit some recently felled tree stumps, which cost him his life. Richie started from second place on the grid to win the first heat after interchanging first and second places with Jim Clark a number of times until a misfiring engine slowed Clark. Graham had claimed pole position for heat

Rhodesian driver Gary Hocking preparing to go out in practice, with him his mechanic Tony Cleverly. Sadly, it was his last drive: his car left the road at speed and crashed into a recently felled tree stump with fatal results.

Waiting for the action at Durban.

Enjoying a little leisure time in East London whilst waiting for the cars to arrive from Durban.

two, but was left in third place from the fall of the flag, his delayed grid departure causing increasing concern. He finally completed the heat in second place behind Trevor Taylor's Lotus. Richie was in pole position for the final with Taylor's Lotus splitting the two BRMs. Clark, after problems in his heat, had to start the final from the back of the grid. Trevor Taylor led from the start, pursued by Graham and Richie. On lap thirteen, Graham again suffered a failed ignition system and coasted into the pits to rejoin the race ten laps later. Clark, meanwhile, had come through the field to take second place with Richie third.

Flying down to East London was a magical experience. Following the shoreline of the Indian Ocean at about 1000 feet, seeing the small shanty settlements with their straw-constructed dwellings to starboard, and the beautiful blue of the Indian Ocean to port, was truly memorable. Arriving at East London we were accommodated in Deals Hotel and again garaged at a branch of Grosvenor Motors with our allocated workshop below ground level, giving us cooler working conditions.

No, not a scene from a Western but a street in East London.

Chauffeuring the 'Sheriff' round East London, with Roy riding shotgun. I never did get paid for the ice cream.

Our South African venture was becoming increasingly frustrating and we weren't looking anything like World Champions. Willie Southcott had now flown out to join us, which could only be good news, and Tony Rudd was also on his way. Sir Alfred Owen had conveniently arranged to visit his companies in South Africa and would be present for the Grand Prix at East London. For the benefit of our most loyal supporter, we just *had* to improve on our last two races! The biggest obstacle in our way was the improving Lotus. In both reliability and speed it was an ever-increasing threat and we needed an immense change of fortune if we were going to overcome its challenge: in the last two events we had been a rather poor second best.

The BRM team arrives in East London for the South African Grand Prix.

Members of a Bourne mafia gang, in South Africa on an important assignment. Note violin case on the floor …

Working conditions in hot climates demanded an adequate amount of fluid was imbibed daily. Here, Roy and I adhere strictly to the rules …

Roy Foreman was always a very health-conscious person; here's his 'medicine chest' to prove it.

The vehicle designated as Graham's race car had been prepared as a super lightweight version, with extra weight-reducing holes drilled wherever possible. Any and every item was fettled for lightness, even the reverse gear – which was compulsory – was replaced with a nylon alternative. The Owen Organisation's publicity representative, Mr A F Rivers-Fletcher ('Rivers' to us), had arrived to film the event and liaise with the company's South African personnel. On the morning following our arrival in East London Willie needed to speak to 'Rivers' and called a telephone number he had been given. Asking if a Mr Rivers-Fletcher was staying there he received the reply: "If he is, he must be having a wonderful time as this is the YWCA," which Willie found highly amusing!

With the cars' arrival from Durban, Christmas Day saw everyone working, continuing through most of the night into Boxing Day. Tony Rudd and Graham Hill spent time in lengthy discussion, low oil pressure on all the engines a cause of great concern. The first unofficial practice took place later on Boxing Day with a gale force wind blowing off the sea. Jim Clark and

Graham shared fastest time with Richie third. Tony Rudd was most displeased to see the Lotus fitted with the same Lucas fuel injection system as that fitted to the BRMs; a system we had spent most of the season helping Lucas to develop. Tony thought it most unfair of Lucas to supply Lotus at this late and critical stage of the season. However, business is business and Lucas was only ensuring that, whatever the result, it would be able to advertise its equipment as that used on the World Championship-winning car!

Following final practice Graham was to share the front row of the grid with Jim Clark, albeit almost one second a lap slower, with Richie down in seventh place. Graham had run a near-race distance in practice which, coupled with the running completed in the previous two races, meant that the engines on the three cars were, like the mechanics, looking decidedly tired! The stark reality was that if Clark had a trouble-free race he would almost certainly win the championship. All we could do was to build as much reliability as possible into Graham's car.

At 10pm on the evening prior to the race, a shop floor discussion took place in the garage where stood three chassis minus engines, the floor littered with various car and engine parts, nuts and bolts, Coca Cola tins and other paraphernalia. With his racing team in this distressing state Sir Alfred Owen arrived, a disbelieving look of dismay on his face at the confusion he saw. Although of small consolation, word came through via the grapevine that Lotus was also having problems with gearboxes!

The two cars were eventually rebuilt, pre-race checks carried out – then carried out again – and race day dawned clear and bright, the high wind having subsided; race conditions were near-perfect. The cars were towed to the circuit where huge

Richie Ginther's car being towed by the shore of the Indian Ocean, on its way to the East London circuit.

A confident-looking BRM crew before the South African Grand Prix at East London; and they say the camera never lies ....

crowds were gathering for this unique event. As was normal in that country at the time, black spectators were segregated from white. At 2.15pm the traditional parade of drivers took place in a convoy of MGA sports cars, followed by driver briefing. Graham – understandably, I suppose – appeared less composed than usual but if he had known what was going on behind the pits he would have had even more to worry about! As I was preparing to drive his car to the front of the pits, the clutch failed to operate. John Sismey described my face as ashen, a description I will not dispute! We quickly agreed that I would change the master cylinder, John would change the slave cylinder and both would help to bleed the system, and the job was done in about half the usual time! Graham, passing by during this operation, enquired if everything was OK and was reassured, little knowing how near he had been to the clutch failing on the starting grid. Sir Alfred Owen was making one of his rare appearances in the pits, so some of the more usual language was toned down in front of our Methodist patron. The pit was organised, each person ready to perform his specified duties, and the cars were on the grid: at 3.00pm everything was in the hands of Lady Luck.

A smoke signal from the Lotus camp informs the team that BRM is 1962 World Champion.

The starter's flag fell and they were off! At completion of the first lap, Clark was leading Graham – we really did not have eyes for anyone else. Clark's lead increased each lap, Graham could only sit and play a waiting game and, at three-quarters distance, the Scotsman led by approximately thirty seconds. Then, were my eyes deceiving me or did I see a small trail of smoke from Jimmy's car? A further lap assured me that my eyes were indeed in focus as the smoke trail had become more obvious; we in the pits could not have wished for a better sight. A lap later Jimmy came into the pits to retire and, at that moment, Graham became the new World Champion! Like the true professional he was, Graham eased the pace slightly for the remaining nineteen laps to ensure he finished. Once he took the chequered flag he was not only World Champion but had also won the race.

Once his driver was out of the race, Colin Chapman was the first to visit our pit to offer his congratulations. We were personally congratulated by Sir Alfred, who could only have been amazed at the transformation from the debris he had seen in that garage the previous evening to this race-winning vehicle. Unfortunately, Richie did not have such an event-free race,

A despondent-looking Jim Clark accepts that his Driver's World Championship hopes for 1962 have been dashed after retiring his Lotus with gearbox failure. In the background, excited BRM team members prepare to signal their drivers with the news that Graham Hill is the new World Champion.

having to pit stop for a change of plugs, though nevertheless finishing seventh. Stirling Moss, Mike Hailwood, Paddy Driver and many other drivers and celebrities came to congratulate us; it was a moment to savour! Not surprisingly, Graham was remarkably cool after winning, appearing to treat it as an everyday occurrence. He did, however, wear an enormous grin as he thanked us all for our efforts and was grateful for the congratulations heaped upon him. I am sure he was inwardly thrilled at what he had achieved.

Naturally, although our wives and children back home in England would have preferred their husbands and fathers to be with them at Christmas, it was generally accepted that absence was all part of our vocation, and for us to return as members of the World Championship-winning team was almost as exciting for them as for us.

Graham Hill driving to win for BRM the South African Grand Prix, the 1962 Driver's World Championship and the Constructor's World Championship.

The climax to an exciting and memorable year as the thumbs-up is given by our sometimes frustrated, but always optimistic, chairman Sir Alfred Owen, together with Graham Hill.

Eventually, the cars were returned to the garage premises, the proprietors requesting that the winning car be placed on display in the showroom. I had driven the winning car from the circuit and was in the process of reversing it into the showroom. Selecting reverse gear and easing the clutch, I heard a low-pitched whirring sound and the nylon reverse gear, which had been fitted for lightness and had never been tried, was stripped of all its teeth. Had Graham required the reverse gear it would have been useless. I wonder if he was ever told, or if, in that exciting time, he would even have cared?

That evening, suitably rested and cleaned up, we were invited by the organisers to a barbeque. To our dismay the gatekeeper had not been notified of our arrival, and a rather arrogant 'jobsworth' would not allow us to enter unless signed in by an official. To our relief Innes Ireland arrived and persuaded the human obstacle he had the authority to sign us in. Glancing at the

visitor's book after this little confrontation I noticed – typical of Innes – that he had us all domiciled at the Battersea Dogs' Home. Thereafter, we enjoyed an excellent evening.

Once again the cars were re-crated, both cars and boxes now looking decidedly travel-weary. We saw them transported to the dockside at the mouth of the Buffalo River ready for shipment back to the UK, and at last relaxed. One thing we had come to appreciate in East London was the greater sense of humour of the coloured population compared with that of its white counterpart. For instance, back in England at around this time comedian Harry Worth was seen doing his famous shop window trick, where he would stand at the corner of a window and raise one leg and one arm, the reflection making it appear that both arms and both legs were being raised. When the BRM boys performed this tomfoolery at a suitable shop window in the town, the coloured people found it highly amusing whereas the white population, many of whom were of German descent, seemed to regard us as buffoons!

On New Year's Eve we flew back to Johannesburg. The celebrations there were extraordinary with throngs of people in the streets at the turn of the year, car horns blaring and revellers dancing on the roofs of cars, drivers unable to escape through the dense crowd. The following day we boarded a South African Airways Boeing 707 bound for Heathrow. I was delighted to arrive back at Bourne, to see my wife and son again and enjoy a belated Christmas.

Meanwhile, back in England the BRM team – prior to our arrival from South Africa – had been presented with a further award. At the prestigious BBC Sports Personality of the Year ceremony, at which Anita Lonsbrough had been voted Sports Personality of 1962, BRM had been voted Team of the Year. At the BRM works some members of the racing team, myself included, were photographed for a Shell advertisement. This advertisement, I assume, was shown worldwide, and those taking part were remunerated with the magnificent sum of £2 per person. Hardly an acceptable amount today, I suspect.

Our Christmas break did not last for long. The reality was that the first race of the new season was but three months away and all too soon it was back to work. A fantastic and memorable year had come to an end.

A CIVIC RECEPTION 13

The question on everyone's lips when we returned to work in 1963: could we emulate our performance of the previous year?

A major step in racing car design – and the way ahead – was monocoque construction as used by Lotus in the type 25 in 1962. This type of construction did away with the tubular chassis and, at that stage of the design, was a box-like metal structure with a cradle attached which supported the engine and ended behind the driver. The box sections contained rubberised fuel tanks, making the structure safer but lighter at the same time.

The progressive development undertaken by Colin Chapman had already proved advantageous during the latter part of the previous season and, to this end, Tony Rudd and the drawing office staff had begun to lay down a prototype design and a build programme. However, Sir Alfred Owen made a decision which quickly shattered the plans. In January Tony Rudd and Raymond Mays were summoned to a meeting in London. There, they were informed by Sir Alfred that he had agreed with the Rover Motor Company to jointly build a gas turbine-engined car to compete for the special prize being offered for the first gas turbine-powered car to complete the Le Mans twenty-four hour race to be held in June. Rover would supply the power unit, which it had been developing for some years, the chassis to be designed by Tony Rudd. The car was to be built at Bourne with the assistance of Motor Panels of Coventry, an Owen Organisation company, which would be responsible for the bodywork. Added to Tony's responsibilities for the Formula 1 team, and given the limited labour available on the shop floor, such a venture was not going to help in our quest to consolidate our position as World Champions.

Despite the efforts of Stan Hope, Alan Ellison, Dan Woodward and Bill Wilcox, who were working long hours on the construction of the new monocoques, and those of a small team – including me – manufacturing suspension parts and many other accessories, it soon became clear we would need

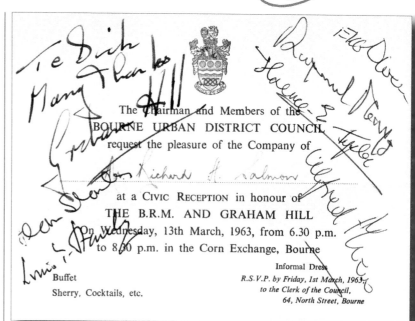

The invitation card to the civic reception hosted by Bourne Urban District Council to honour Graham Hill and the BRM team on their 1962 success.

to continue to use the 1962 cars for the first races of 1963, beginning with the Lombank Trophy at Snetterton on 30th March. Tony Rudd had gone one stage further with our monocoque compared with the Lotus 25, which was open along the top, rather like a bath tub. The BRM was simply a tube with a cockpit opening but carried the engine on a tubular sub-frame bolted onto the rear of the monocoque, similar to the Lotus. Full monocoques, with the engine a stressed member, were still to come.

The Bourne Urban District Council had generously arranged to hold a civic reception on 13th March in honour of Graham Hill and the BRM team winning the World Championships.

Some of the office ladies who worked behind the scenes at BRM enjoying the civic reception. Sybil Ingleby is standing next to Graham Hill, and seated are Gill Parker (nee Wesley), Pat Reeson, Shirley Legge and Phyliss Fawcett, flanked by George Bull and Don Woodward.

Various models of BRM cars had been manoeuvred – with some difficulty – into the Bourne Corn Exchange. The then chairman of the Council, Mrs Florence Tipler, had extended invitations to all BRM staff from Bourne and we were joined by Sir Alfred and Lady Owen, Raymond Mays, Graham Hill, Jean and Louis Stanley and other distinguished guests. The liquid refreshment provided by the Council was a welcome rebate on our rates demands … What a memorable evening it turned out to be!

The two drivers of the previous year – Graham and Richie – had been retained and were to drive in the Lombank Trophy at Snetterton. A noticeable change for the coming season was the new, striking bright orange overalls worn by BRM mechanics, orange being the corporate colour of The Rubery Owen Group. The weekend of the race was a wet and dismal occasion. Graham's car suffered fuel injection pump problems and, unable to achieve a good practice time, he was relegated to the rear of the grid. The fact that he was driving the lightweight championship car from South Africa must have been a good

BRM workers raise their glasses to Graham Hill at the civic reception, standing, left to right, are: Jerry Edwards, Councillor Burchnell, Pat Carvath, Alan Challis, John Speight and Dennis Perkins; front: Jim Collins, Nev Rippin, John Sismey, Arthur Hill, Don Woodward and Arthur Chambers.

omen. Graham's lowly grid position seemed to inspire him as, driving a fine race, he worked his way through the field to win; a good start for the season made all the sweeter by his beating Jim Clark's Lotus 25. Richie qualified second and raced well but eventually dropped back to finish fifth.

Tony Rudd's head must have been in a constant spin during this period, making numerous journeys between Bourne and Coventry to liase with the Rover BRM's body builders, and eventually to observe the car's first test run at MIRA, the Motor Industry Research Association test track at Nuneaton. Designing the new monocoque Formula 1 car at Bourne, and supervising the continuous testing, engine development and racing programme, made him a very busy person. High blood pressure could not have been invented then or surely he would have been a sufferer!

The next race meeting was the ever-popular Easter Monday event at Goodwood on 15th April, which proved a weekend of mixed fortunes, both cars suffering from misfiring engines. However, this did not prevent Graham from securing pole position with Richie fifth. Once again Graham experienced a poor start. (It has always mystified me how such a talented driver was frequently unable to get his car cleanly off the line, although he certainly made up for it once under way; it raises the question: could he have been even more successful had he been able to make better starts?) Graham had led the race for 37 of the scheduled 42 laps when his engine failed and Richie also retired. The weekend's proceedings were observed by Sir Alfred Owen, looking nothing like the chairman of a large organisation, attired, as he was, in crumpled sweater and Wellington boots.

John Sismey 'Snip' Chambers and I were now heavily involved in assembly of the first monocoque. A new feature of this car was flexible fuel bag tanks manufactured by Fireproof Tanks at Portsmouth and installed inside the bodyshell. When I visited the works I was surprised to learn of one test procedure in which a completed tank would be filled with water and thrown off the roof of the building. Heath Robinsonesque, maybe, but effective! The company also produced buoyancy bags as part of the survival equipment for helicopters.

Two more races were contested before World Championship events started: the Aintree 200 on 27th April and the BRDC International Trophy at Silverstone on 11th May. With our massive workload the Syracuse Grand Prix was given a miss but it was good to know that one of our 'customer' V8 engines powered Jo Siffert's Lotus 24 to victory there: 'Wilkie' Wilkinson's department was proving successful! With only minor adjustments necessary Aintree proved a very satisfactory meeting, victory going to Graham Hill ahead of Jim Clark, with Richie Ginther fourth. The meeting was also notable for another unusual occurrence at Aintree – the weather stayed fine; the all-too-familiar Aintree gremlin had been tamed.

Silverstone was a less successful weekend. Apart from our two cars, the third car entered was the original P5781 ('Old Faithful') which had made its debut at Brussels the previous year with Graham driving, and which 'Wilkie' had sold to the Italian Scuderia Centro Sud, so it was smartly painted in Italian racing red. None of the three cars finished the race, rising star Lorenzo Bandini being disqualified in the red BRM for receiving a push-start after a pit stop.

Three cars were taken to Monaco: one each for Graham and Richie, plus a spare (due to the shortage of cars, BRM retrieved the one sold to Scuderia Centro Sud only a few weeks earlier and it was this that was the spare, nicely repainted in BRM's dark shade of green once more). I did not attend the race, a great success for the team, being too busy building the new car. After a terrific duel between the two BRMs and Jim Clarks Lotus 25, the BRMs prevailed to record a win for Graham with Richie second, the Lotus gearbox failing at three-quarter distance.

Graham Hill being congratulated by Pat Carvath, watched by Bette Hill with trophy and Cyril Atkins and Tony Rudd following victory in the Monaco Grand Prix.

The first monocoque now stood on its wheels; alas, too late for the Belgian Grand Prix on 9th June. The team departed for Spa with the 1962 cars to a wet, windy and not very successful weekend, but at least the food was good at the Hotel du Roannay. Graham put his car on pole position; the best Richie could manage was ninth. Race day dawned with violent thunderstorms and torrential rain, delaying the start of the race for half-an-hour. Once the rain stopped the race was started on a still-damp circuit and Clark and Hill showed the rest of the field clean pairs of heels, soon to lead by 30 seconds. Once again the heavens opened and at this point Graham retired out on the circuit with gearbox failure; given the weather conditions he probably considered himself lucky! The weather was so bad that Tony Rudd and other team managers pleaded with the organisers for the race to be stopped but their pleas fell on deaf ears and Clark went on to win. Richie toured round in the dreadful conditions to finish fourth.

Sandwiched between the race at Spa and the Dutch Grand Prix was the Le Mans 24-hour event for which the Rover-BRM had been built. The race was a great success for the car, ably supervised by the effervescent 'Wilkie' with the assistance of Arthur Hill and John Sismey from BRM, plus Rover personnel who looked after the gas turbine engine. The car was driven by Graham Hill and Richie Ginther and completed the target distance in less than twenty-one hours without a hitch. It established a benchmark for the performance of a gas turbine-driven car.

With the new car completed, it was good to be back on the road once more bound for Zandvoort and the Dutch Grand Prix on 23rd June. En route we called at Snetterton for a test run with the monocoque, then, in driving rain, continued to Harwich for the ferry to the Hook of Holland.

In practice on the first day a rather sick-feeling Graham struggled to make an impression, trying both the new car and his 1962 version. After final practice he opted to drive his older car, having qualified second, with the ultra reliable Richie sixth fastest. The BRM starting jinx struck again, this time with both cars failing to make a good start off the line. Despite his hesitant departure Graham was soon pursuing race leader Jim Clark with Richie mixing it with the following pack. However, Graham failed to finish. After a noticeable misfire and a desperate pit stop, his engine finally cried enough, coming to a halt with valve gear failure, Richie continuing to circulate to finish fifth. Following the race Tony decided we would stay at Zandvoort another day to do some comparison tests between the old car and the new model. The general opinion was that the new car was at last nearly raceworthy and, hopefully, would be ready to compete in the next race, the French Grand Prix at Reims on 30th June.

On Wednesday morning, 26th June, we left Bourne for the race the following Sunday, taking one new-type car and the two older models. In addition to our overalls, one obvious change was the 'Day-Glo' orange band painted round the cars' noses to satisfy Ernest Owen who had suggested that the cars also be

Graham Hill in a not very successful Dutch Grand Prix, retiring on lap 69 with engine failure.

painted orange in line with Rubery Owen corporate colours. At this time cars were still painted in their national racing colours and orange just happened to be Holland's! The orange noseband undoubtedly assisted recognition of our cars from a distance, appreciated as much by spectators as by our own pit crew.

We arrived at Reims to be installed once more in the garage close by the now-familiar Lido restaurant and Louis Hadsveld's tyre depot. The new car was showing much improvement during first practice, despite the seemingly ever-present problem of misfiring engines, eventually resolved by changing to another make of sparkplug. The second practice session was a comparative waste of time; heavy rain preventing some of the teams from arriving at the circuit because of muddy conditions at the entrance. Final practice saw Graham put the new car on the front row of the grid in second position, with Richie Ginther a lowly twelfth, but now our problems really began.

The wheels had obviously come off Tony Rudd's faithful slide rule because, when calculating fuel consumption for the new car, tank capacity was something like six gallons short of the amount required to complete this very fast race. Tony, as ever, was not short of an excuse, claiming that the rubberised fuel tanks had shrunk, which was possible but not to the extent of six gallons! In our favour was that sheet metal worker Danny Woodward was a member of the team here on that occasion and what a wonderful job he did in increasing fuel capacity to the required level. Fortunately, a spare auxiliary aluminium tank had been taken to Reims with the intention of fitting it should it be decided to race the new car. Now that the decision had been made, although fitting the tank was a simple task, getting a driver in with the extra

tank fitted was an entirely different proposition, especially with Graham Hill who had the most awkward-shaped legs due to an accident earlier in life. This meant another all-night session, with Danny working miracles to get the required amount of fuel into the car. The spare tank was mutilated and two tanks made from it; one which protruded through an aperture at the lower part of the windscreen above the driver's legs, and the second at the rear above the gearbox, both fed into the main tanks by a Bendix electric fuel pump. It was a major task not completed until 2pm on Sunday with only one hour before the start of the race, and the engine in Richie's car had also to be changed! We were just about making it through that weekend, and the long night before the race was made easier by disposing of the contents of a large bottle of brandy supplied by 'Big Lou.'

Eventually race time arrived, albeit 25 minutes late, and with it something of a fiasco. Horror of horrors, after all our work, Graham Hill's car would not start on the starter motor on the grid!

Willie giving Richie's V8 engine one of his little tweaks.

192

The race organiser instructed it be push-started and wheeled back to its position, totally against the rules. Graham was later penalised one minute for breach of the rules but the all-night session proved worthwhile after all because Graham finished in second place, later relegated to third due to the one minute penalty. Such was the way of things in those days … Richie retired early in the race with a holed radiator but another BRM finished tenth, this being 'Old Faithful' now back in the possession of Centro Sud and driven by Lorenzo Bandini.

On our return from France Tony Rudd, Danny Woodward and I took the monocoque car to the MIRA test establishment near Nuneaton for wind tunnel tests. There, the airflow path over the car was observed by taping wool tufts onto the skin. Four giant propellers created the airflow and, to establish a realistic test, a driver had to be seated in the cockpit. I had drawn the short straw for this task and was soon complaining that I would be adding to the list of flu victims back at Bourne! Fortunately, I was given a let-out when one of the MIRA staff suggested using a dummy, to which I replied "We're already using one." However, the suggestion was taken up and Danny and I went to collect the dummy which stood about six feet tall and allegedly weighed nine stone, though felt more like fourteen stone. It had movable joints, knees, ankles, elbows, etc, and was used for crash tests. Taking it to the car was ridiculously funny with Danny and I telling it what an idiot it had been to go out and get so pissed it could not walk back by itself. The hilarity did not stop there as we then struggled to get it into the car, not easy given the narrow cockpit of a racing car; its leg shape was worse than Graham's! Eventually successful, we put the car into gear to prevent it from being blown back by the force of the air current. When the airflow started, however, the car began to roll; it seemed the dummy was now taking the piss as it had its foot on the clutch! The tests – though interesting – were inconclusive, the various changes to fairings, mirrors, etc, making little significant difference to the readings.

For the next event at Silverstone, the British Grand Prix, a second new car was available for Richie Ginther. It was decided that the team would return to Bourne after each practice, abandoning our previous arrangement of using the garage at Brackley: this would add about two hours to the travelling time but would give us the use of our own workshop facilities, plus the advantage of being able to call in extra labour if necessary. The accounts department also enjoyed not having to pay hotel expenses! Following final practice this strategy proved most beneficial, as the engines in both Hill's and Ginther's cars had to be changed. The British Grand Prix was undoubtedly BRM's most prestigious race of the year, and yet it always seemed to be the team's Achilles heel. We hoped this year was going to be an exception.

The cars lined up on the grid with Graham on the front row having been third fastest, and Richie in ninth position. Fuel capacity was again a major concern and both cars were filled to the brim on the grid. These efforts were in vain, however, because Graham lost second place when the engine cut at Stow on the last lap, allowing John Surtees' Ferrari to take the position with Graham coasting third over the line with a dead engine. Our disappointment was tempered by the fact that Richie finished fourth and Bandini's 'Old Faithful' backed us up in fifth place with the Centro Sud entry. There was even a 'customer' in sixth place, Jim Hall's Lotus 24 with a BRM V8 engine. How times had changed!

Practical jokes were still abundant in the racing shop, 'Snip' Chambers playing a rather disgusting one on George Bull, a member of the inspection team. One of the commodities frequently used in race car preparation was Evostik adhesive, and a dirty-looking dried chunk of this had been left on a bench vice. 'Snip' attracted the attention of George and showed it to him, complaining that some filthy sod had removed a bogey from his nose and wiped it on his vice. George fell for it and immediately fetched Manager Jim Sandercombe to witness this disgusting item, whilst 'Snip' and those of us in the know

One of the pranks that BRM team members played on the visiting public. Inside the kennel, an old kettle is tethered …

found it difficult to hide our laughter. What 'Sandy's' thoughts were I still wonder! Life was never dull and it was remarkable how easy it was to wind up people; it was very soon obvious which ones would bite. For example, I was standing outside the workshop one lunchtime talking to 'Snip' when George Edwards, one of the cleaners, passed by. Knowing of his fiery temperament, I casually remarked to 'Snip' when the poor fellow was within earshot "He's another one." George took the bait, hastily instructing me that if I had anything to say, I should say it to his face!

During 1963 the Owen Racing Motors Organisation decided we should have another open day, to which members of ORMA (Owen Racing Motor Association, which had long since replaced the British Motor Racing Association) were invited, together with family and friends. Whilst distracting a little from the main objective of winning motor races, it was nevertheless a great success and attracted many visitors.

As usual, we had one or two surprises in store for our visitors. A dog kennel was set up, trailing out of which was a chain secured to a post with a notice saying "Please do not feed the water otter." Ninety-nine percent of the visitors must have bent down to peer into the kennel, only to come face-to-face with a very old kettle. And, of course, a few people were walking around with a blue ring round their eyes after looking in a tracking gauge eye-piece marked with mechanics' blue. Overall, it was a very rewarding day for visitors and staff alike.

The next championship race was the German Grand Prix at the Nürburgring on 4th August, which we looked forward to after our eventful and successful race of the previous year. Once again the new car was little better than the 1962 type 578s, since these were a known quantity, drivers and management decided they would be better off using them on this very demanding circuit. It was unfortunate that the monocoque construction on which we had pinned all our hopes for that year was still considered not fast enough, and Tony Rudd was already working on a new car for 1964. BRM

was therefore less competitive than had been hoped, a situation which a tolerant Sir Alfred Owen reluctantly accepted. To rub salt into the wound, Italian Lorenzo Bandini was faster than Graham driving Graham's 1962 'Old Faithful' and qualified in third place on the front row. Graham was fourth and Richie sixth.

The race, however, was a short one for both Bandini and Hill, the excitable Italian crashing on lap one with Graham little better off, retiring on lap two with gearbox failure. Richie saved the day, motoring steadily to third place behind winner John Surtees' Ferrari and Jim Clark's Lotus 25. Our engines were pulling more than 11,000rpm on the long straight but Richie really pushed his luck when the car jumped out of fourth gear early in the race and buzzed the engine to well over 12,000rpm. Our engines were certainly built to last!

Back at Bourne one of Jim Sandercombe's economy drives resulted in the purchase of sickly green-coloured plastic cups for the shop floor workers, although not office staff. The plastic cup idea was abandoned, however, when Roy Foreman drilled a minute hole through the handle of a number of them and we complained that they leaked! Investigations revealed the problem and the hint was taken – crockery cups were reinstated.

Around this time we missed two or three non-championship races but were well represented by a number of private entrants using our 'customer' engines. Then it was off on our enjoyable jaunt to Monza for the Italian Grand Prix on 8th September. However, much to my delight – and probably to the dismay of Sandy who had to pay the bill – I went by air, carrying gearbox spares in my luggage, the only available flight being a first class seat in a Caravelle of Air France. This was luxury indeed with the added pleasure of free champagne during the flight!

The race was to be run on the combined road and banked circuit once again, eventually changed to the road circuit only. The BRM monocoque car was at last shown to be competitive; Graham qualified it in second place and chose to use it for the race whilst Richie was back on the third row. Graham made a very good start (for a change!) and led off the line, becoming involved in a terrific slipstreaming battle with Jim Clark, John Surtees and Jack Brabham in his Brabham BT3 Climax V8, each taking turns

to lead. Graham was eventually forced to retire with clutch failure but Richie drove a magnificent race and finished in second place for the second successive year. These slipstreaming battles were almost inevitable on the fast Monza circuit, and sometimes just who would win was not decided until the last moment. On this occasion Jim Clark was a clear winner, World Champion for the first time with three races still to be run.

"You should not smoke when asleep, Willie. Hope my old sergeant doesn't catch you."

Once again the opportunity was taken to stay for an extra day's testing, following which we returned to England, this time Willie, Colin Atkin and I taking a very pleasant train journey from Milan to London via Switzerland and Paris.

Now my racing days were over for the year, and I was fully occupied with building the first of the 1964 cars. The team, however, had one more race to contest at Oulton Park to complete the British season, plus the Grand Prix of the United States, Mexico and South Africa. For the Gold Cup at Oulton Park two old-type cars were entered and a fairly routine weekend saw an unusual result for BRM with Graham beaten into third by Richie, who took second place to Jim Clark. Two cars were sent to America where another 1-2 result was scored, Graham winning the race and Richie second, with the added bonus of seeing both BRMs lapping Jim Clark's Lotus. The two cars were then sent on to Mexico where, for the second time in five weeks, Richie came home in front of Graham in third to Jim Clark and Jack Brabham with Graham fourth.

The large number of wheels and tyres necessary to maintain a two car Grand Prix team in the 1960s.

In early December the first of the 1964 full monocoque-type cars stood on its wheels at Bourne. Although BRM was renowned for building cars pleasing to the eye, to me this was exceptional, the most beautiful racing car I had ever seen. If it had performance to equal its looks it was certain to be a winner. For BRM Graham and Richie again contested the final race in South Africa on 28th December, but it was a far cry from the situation the previous year as Jim Clark was already World Champion so inevitably the race became something of an anti-climax. However, Graham finishing third and Richie retiring meant that the two BRM drivers finished joint second in the Driver's Championship and the team was also second in the Manufacturer's Championship.

What might have been had the Owen Racing Organisation not become involved in the Rover gas turbine project at Le Mans earlier in the year? At short notice it diverted resources which, with hindsight, might have been better spent defending our hard-won World Championships. Viewing the bigger picture there can be little doubt that the success of the Rover-BRM was of huge importance, and a source of great pride to Sir Alfred Owen, but it took our eye off the ball and the Formula 1 project suffered accordingly. As a team, though disappointed we were not disheartened: the new year – and our exciting new car – beckoned …

"Oi, Pat, remember it's an ebb tide …"

Missing the Point

In early February 1964 the new monocoque car was taken to Silverstone for initial track tests, along with one of the 1962 cars for comparison, both to be driven by Graham Hill. It was a bitterly cold, wet day with gale force winds blowing across the Northamptonshire countryside; hardly the conditions in which to prove a new racing car. Despite the weather, the results of the day's test gave positive signals because the new car was one second a lap faster than the old one.

As usual on our test days at Silverstone we adjourned for lunch to the local pub in the village and, on this particular visit, we were more than pleased to shelter from the biting wind. The fare there never varied: thick slices of bread, a slab of butter, a large chunk of Cheddar cheese and pickled onions, served by a jovial and ruddy-cheeked landlord. On one occasion we arrived to find him with a broken arm which he had sustained one night when, hearing a noise, he had gone to investigate and fallen down the stairs.

Driver continuity is important in any team, especially when developing new cars. Richie had always been extremely good as a test driver, and in 1963 had proved his worth as a race driver, too, achieving some very good results and even beating Graham on occasion.

There were no races 'down under' to distract us so we were able to concentrate on building the new monocoques to be well equipped to go straight into the traditional non-championship races in England, beginning with the first race of

1964, the *Daily Mirror* Trophy at Snetterton on 14th March. As it happened, we were still awaiting 13in diameter wheels from an outside supplier to complete the second monocoque so therefore took along just the first of the new cars for Graham Hill to drive.

As so often at that time of year it was another wet and windy weekend; roll on the sunnier climes of Monaco! After good practice sessions that saw Graham second to Jim Clark, the cars lined up and Graham immediately took the lead, only to fall victim to the torrential overnight rain which had left huge puddles on the circuit. At the

A dismayed Pat Carvath looks at what was a new car, the result of it aquaplaning with Graham Hill on the flooded track at Snetterton.

end of the Norwich Straight the BRM aquaplaned and became airborne, crashing heavily into the safety bank. Our beautiful new car was a complete write-off and Graham sustained a neck injury, which troubled him for months afterwards, when he was often seen wearing a bulky, padded neck support collar. Incidentally, it was at this race that Graham experimented with a curious 'windmill'-type visor, the revolving vanes designed to prevent condensation and throw aside heavy raindrops. However, I do not recall seeing it again!

Our mood after the race was as bitter as the weather as we scooped up the wreckage and made our way back to Bourne. There was much work to do and, with Easter early that year, we were out testing at Goodwood the week before the traditional 100 mile International Trophy, that year sponsored by the *News of the World*. As Richie Ginther was unavailable for the race, British driver Richard Attwood made his Formula 1 debut driving the second BRM, which, incredibly, was the original 1962 'Old Faithful,' temporarily back in our possession once more. After the Snetterton setback we were left with the second of the 1964 monocoques for Graham to drive. Graham was happy with the car and came third fastest in practice behind Jack Brabham and Jim Clark, while Richard Attwood was driving sensibly for his first outing.

Graham made a good start and overtook early leader Clark to gain a sizeable margin when he stopped on the fortieth lap with ignition failure and was out of the race. Failure to finish was disappointing but it was an encouraging start for the new car. Generally, Graham was very impressed but found it required a great deal of concentration to get the best out of it. Richard Attwood drove well on his first outing for BRM to finish fourth in what was absolutely the last works outing for 'Old Faithful.' Arthur Hill was maintaining this Centro Sud BRM at Bourne, helped by a mechanic supplied by the Italian team, a lad called

John. Danny Woodward's liking for handing out nicknames came to the fore again when he referred to John as 'Gobbler,' for what reason I do not know. John's response was "My name is John, not Gobbler" and, with the usual BRM wit, was thereafter known as 'John Not-Gobbler.'

Our two drivers shared mixed fortune at the next event, the Aintree 200 on April 18th, the first outing at which both new 261s were available. Richie was back with us again but crashed badly in practice at the tricky Melling Crossing. He caught the grass verge on leaving the corner, which flipped the car, trapping him in the cockpit as the car slid upside down along the grass for a hundred yards. His small stature probably saved his life because he ducked down into the cockpit and the roll bar did the rest. Richie had some nasty accidents during his time with us and, on this occasion, was very lucky to escape with only two broken ribs. All was not lost, however, Graham taking pole position on the grid but having to be content with second place to Jack Brabham at the fall of the chequered flag.

Only one works BRM was entered for the International Trophy at Silverstone a fortnight later, as Richie was still suffering from his recent accident at Aintree. British spectators loved their motor racing and have always been immensely loyal; a huge crowd in excess of 100,000 people turned up for this non-championship event on what was a bleak and often wet day. The crowded lanes then were no deterrent, despite the hours it took to get home. They were rewarded by an absolutely thrilling race won by Jack Brabham in his own car but with Graham Hill alongside him at the chequered flag. Both were awarded the same race time of 1 hour, 22 minutes, 45.2 seconds although, curiously, the race was not ranked a dead heat.

The next two days were hectic as the cars had to leave on Tuesday at the latest for Monte Carlo and the Monaco Grand Prix scheduled for the following Sunday, May 10th. After the setback at Aintree with Richie's damaged car, a desperate effort was made at Bourne to restore the status quo and ensure the team had two 1964 261s for this important first race of the championship calendar. Once more Graham Hill showed what a master he was of this famous and exciting street circuit. There was

Graham Hill, in the monocoque BRM, speeds along the harbour front at Monaco.

a furious scramble for the leading grid positions, Graham finally relegated to the second row with third fastest time. Graham's forcefulness in practice was mirrored in the race, pushing Jim Clark and Dan Gurney from third place for all he was worth. He took the lead at half distance and held it to the end, backed up by the brave Richie Ginther in second place who must have been feeling the effects of his Aintree injury on this tight circuit in a race lasting 2 hours, 41 minutes. Over the years Graham built up an amazing relationship with the race at Monaco, again winning for BRM in 1965 with further victories in 1968 and 1969 after he had moved on to Lotus.

We made an uneventful journey direct to Zandvoort from Monaco, 'Tonto' our chauffer in the Ford Zephyr estate, accompanied by Roy Foreman, Pat Carvath and myself. As this was a dedicated circuit instead of closed public roads it meant that we had generous practice opportunities, a total of six hours official practice being available over two days. We were using the same cars as at Monaco and Graham was in third place on the grid, beaten by an 'on form' Dan Gurney and also Jim Clark. Jim disappeared into the distance to win easily, but Graham had an eventful race, suffering fuel vaporisation due to unusually hot race conditions at the Dutch circuit. The engine was constantly cutting out and back in again, giving poor Graham a very uncomfortable ride until, in desperation, he came into the pits at half distance where a bucket of cold water was thrown onto the fuel pump mounted on the floor of the cockpit. Graham is reported to have said that it had the effect of cooling his ardour as well as the pump as he accelerated away from the pits, eventually finishing fourth with Richie way back in eleventh position after two stops for coolant.

Three weeks later we were at Spa for the Belgian race on 14th June, once more to enjoy the splendid hospitality of the Hotel du Roannay. Practice had been run in incredibly hot conditions but race day was a little cooler. With a race distance of 280 miles (451km – 32 laps) of this very fast circuit, fuel consumption was critical.

Graham started from the centre of the front row, but pole sitter Dan Gurney in a Brabham raced away into an unchallenged lead leaving Graham and Jim Clark in a slipstreaming battle for second place throughout much of the race. After more than two hours of racing at an average speed of 133mph, the finish was pure pantomime when, two laps from the end, Gurney slowed, out of petrol and out of the race. Graham was suddenly in the lead but, unbelievably, stopped at Stavelot, also out of petrol. Clark and McLaren came through to finish first and second, both with spluttering engines, the drivers throwing the cars from side-to-side in a desperate attempt to pick up the last remaining drops of fuel. The race was a huge disappointment for us, Graham finally classified fifth, a sad result for what was a brilliant drive.

During the race Graham had been given the signal to switch on a fuel pump to transfer fuel from an auxiliary tank into the main tank, the pump to remain on for two laps in order to conserve the battery; he was then signalled to switch off the fuel pump. Unfortunately, the pump had previously been used for an experiment in the test house at Folkingham where a reduced rate spring had been fitted, causing the pump to move less fuel in a given time. Thus, at the end of the two laps, the auxiliary tank still contained almost a gallon of fuel – Graham's own team had robbed him of victory! I am of the firm belief that this mistake cost Graham a second world title and, had a standard factory pump been fitted, am convinced that Graham would have won the race. Whether Sir Alfred Owen and Graham Hill were ever

aware of the facts, I have my doubts. To compound the chaos, the man with the chequered flag was wrong-footed, confusion at the finishing line causing him to show the flag to the wrong driver, and not once but twice! Ironically, a steadily-running Richie finished fourth at Spa to give us valuable manufacturer's points.

For the next two race meetings I was confined to Bourne constructing more new cars but, for the record, the team attended the French Grand Prix at Rouen-les -Essarts on 28th June where Graham unexpectedly found himself on the third row of the grid. During practice he had some misgivings about hurling the car through the sweeping curves leading to the hairpin, but this did not worry him in the race where he had a race-long battle with Jack Brabham in his type BT7, Graham being ahead at the line in second place by less than a second. Richie Ginther picked up fifth place and Dan Gurney ran out a popular winner in the other Brabham BT7, claiming not only his second career Grand Prix but also his second Grand Prix at this challenging circuit, previously accomplished in 1962 with a Porsche.

The British Grand Prix came a fortnight later and was held for the first time on the wonderful extended circuit at Brands Hatch. I really should have been there because the sight of Grand Prix cars rushing through the wooded Kentish countryside must have been truly memorable. More than 100,000 spectators obviously thought the same and, with the likes of Graham, Jim Clark, Dan Gurney, Jack Brabham and John Surtees at the absolute peak of their abilities, race prospects must have been good.

Although Jim Clark led from flag to flag it was a mightily fought race with no quarter given and none expected. Graham hounded Jim all the way and was beaten by less than three seconds. Although it did not take part in the race, it's worth mentioning that BRM's experimental four-wheel drive car – a concept very much occupying the minds of designers at that time – made its first appearance in practice at Brands Hatch driven by Richard Attwood.

At Bourne we were beavering away, and also had back for service and repair various BRM cars that had been sold. It was not unusual for the teams whose cars these were to have their own mechanics working in the Bourne workshop alongside us, and one of these was a young lad to whom RM had apparently taken a liking. RM would often visit the workshop in the evenings when the lad was alone, much to his annoyance. Toby Swain, who was contracted to paint the racing cars, also worked in the evenings for his own convenience, able to proceed with paint preparation when the BRM mechanics had ceased work for the day. RM could be heard approaching on one particular evening when Toby and the lad were working. The young man told Toby of his fears to which Toby replied "Not to worry, I'll get rid of him for you." When RM arrived Toby looked at him and asked "Are you all right, Mr Mays, you don't look very well?" "Really, don't you think so?" RM responded and quickly left. Toby said to the young man "Now watch his bathroom light come on. I'll bet he goes to look at himself in the mirror." Sure enough, it did!

I was to attend the German Grand Prix at the Nürburgring, the next championship event. Before that most of the teams attended the non-championship Solitude Grand Prix, near Stuttgart, a fast circuit formed from public roads. Despite not having a prominent driver, and certainly no Formula 1 car, the Germans had always been hugely enthusiastic about motor racing, going back to the pre-war days of Mercedes-Benz, Auto Union and the great German aces of that time. The Formula 1 race at Solitude was really an add-on to a motorcycle championship event at which over 300,000 spectators attended.

A sole BRM was entered for Graham Hill. He was lucky to return from the race unscathed because it started in torrential rain and Graham went off into the woods on his first lap, taking a telegraph pole with him and wrecking the car.

Once at the Nürburgring we again stayed at the homely Wildes Schwein Hotel in Adenau. The strength of the beer could easily be underestimated, a fact which a young apprentice, making his first trip with us, discovered to his cost.

John Surtees and his Ferrari had found terrific form by this stage of the season and claimed pole position with Graham back

GROSSER PREIS
VON DEUTSCHLAND

2. AUGUST 1964

AUTOMOBIL-WELTMEISTERSCHAFT

NÜRBURGRING

AUTOMOBILCLUB VON DEUTSCHLAND

Unverkäufliches
Freiexemplar

on the second row in fifth place, Richie in eleventh. Graham loved the supreme challenge of this unique circuit with its 174 corners and his aggressive style always seemed to pay dividends. However, there was no stopping John Surtees that weekend and, as in 1963, he came home the winner once again with Graham trailing in second place with a misfiring engine. Richie was out of the points in seventh position with a similar problem. Engines had been our Achilles heel throughout the weekend. First Richie then Graham broke their engines in practice due

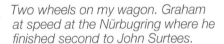

Two wheels on my wagon. Graham at speed at the Nürbugring where he finished second to John Surtees.

to selecting the wrong gear and over-revving. To have experienced two engine failures due to the same cause suggested the chassis was flexing due to the exceptional stresses created by this circuit, the gearbox selectors out of phase with the lever in the cockpit.

A car making its first appearance in Grand Prix racing was the Honda driven by a virtually unknown American, Ronnie Bucknum.

An unusual addition to the event was the inclusion of a cycle race in reverse direction over five laps of the Nürburgring, one of the entrants being British champion, Tommy Simpson.

Ultimately, the weekend was marred by the tragic death of Baron Godin de Beaufort following an accident during practice. The ever-popular Dutch driver took part for fun and was always full of enthusiasm, even though he was never going to win a Grand Prix in his outdated, privately-entered Porsche.

Once more I was required at Bourne to complete construction of a new car for Monza, so did not join the team on its trip to Austria for the championship race there on 24th August. For the first

Main picture: A test day at Snetterton, and ex-World Champion Graham tells future World Champion, son Damon, how it's done.

Above: Graham and his daughter Brigitte watch son Damon take his first step toward becoming the family's second World Champion.

Right: Final starting grid instructions from father to son.

and only time the race was held at Zeltweg on a simple layout using the runways of a military airfield. We were suffering from a shortage of cars at this time, Graham having damaged one of the regular 1964 cars during a test session at Snetterton, and the latest car – which Graham had crashed at Solitude – hastily rebuilt for him to use in Austria. The concrete surface of the circuit had badly broken up and took a tremendous toll on the cars during the race. The event will always be remembered as the occasion when the 'number two' drivers had their moment of fame at the expense of the championship contenders, who all fell by the wayside because of the tremendous hammering the cars received. Lorenzo Bandini won for Ferrari and Richie was second for BRM, followed by a number of private entrants. Graham retired early having started from pole position.

The latest car had been completed with a revised engine. It was expected that we would have had this engine in use much earlier in the season, but numerous setbacks and crashed cars meant that our attention had been diverted to more pressing matters. Jimmy Collins and I left Bourne for Monza on Sunday, 30th August. The car was loaded onto an open-top BMC lorry, universally known as the 'Coal Cart,' the only resemblance to a racing car transporter being its British Racing Green colour. Maximum speed was 50mph, which increased slightly when descending a hill with the benefit of a following wind! The early part of the journey was relatively uneventful as we passed through French countryside with which we were now familiar, albeit in a noisy diesel lorry. Eventually, after we had crossed from France into Switzerland and approached the town of Vallorbe for a second overnight stop, the lorry cried enough; the fuel injector pump had given up. Far below we could see our intended destination and, after walking down the hill and back on a reconnaissance mission, we decided, if we could get the vehicle to the top of the hill we could coast down the other side into the town. We propelled the lorry forward to the brow on the starter motor and then coasted safely down the hill, a nervy experience without a servo to assist the brakes! At the bottom we drove straight into an hotel car park with great relief and booked to stay the night there.

We had no contact numbers other than for Bourne but I remembered that RM usually stayed at the Lausanne Palace Hotel, so hoped we could contact him there. No such luck, but the hotel staff gave me a number where they thought he would be and luckily we found him. He must have commanded a great deal of respect in Lausanne for, as I made the connection, it sounded as though a massive party was taking place. When RM came to the telephone, though, total silence fell. He was able to motivate a rescue, arranging for the lorry to be towed into Lausanne the following morning. We stayed there for two days until a replacement pump had been brought from Zurich, watching the first day's practice at Monza on the hotel television.

Eventually on the road again it was a race against time to reach the St Bernard tunnel before it closed for the night. We just made it and arrived at Villasanta in the early hours of Friday morning, much to the relief of Raymond Mays. Our delayed journey meant that we had no opportunity to try the new car in

Torment at Monza. Graham Hill raises his arm on the starting grid to signify he cannot move, the reason later diagnosed as clutch failure. This failure most probably cost him a second World Driver's Championship.

A pleasant fall street scene in the beautiful town of Watkins Glen, USA.

Glen Motor Court Motel, Watkins Glen, New York State.

pre-practice sessions, and Graham had no alternative but to use it in the race because of engine problems with his older car.

We desperately needed a good result from Graham at Monza to keep him ahead in the World Championship table, but John Surtees in the Ferrari dominated practice on the home circuit, much to the delight of the 'tifosi,' the enthusiastic Italian supporters. Surtees duly obliged by taking pole position, with Dan Gurney second, Graham Hill third and Richie a lowly ninth on the fourth row. On race day our hopes were immediately dashed. As the flag fell for the start and the cars roared away, Graham remained stationary on the grid: the clutch had failed, allowing Surtees his second victory of the season and record maximum points. Richie became embroiled in the usual Monza slipstreaming battle, finishing fourth by less than a whisker behind Bandini's Ferrari.

Despite his start line retirement at Monza, Graham still led the title race with two races remaining, the points table reading 32 for Graham, Jim Clark with 30 and John Surtees on 28. As only the six best results in the season were to count, Graham would lose the two points he had scored in Belgium if he was to score more than two in either of the two remaining races. Should he finish higher than fourth in both remaining races, he would also lose the three points scored in Holland.

In late September we flew out of Heathrow for New York and from there collected a Ford Mustang provided by the Ford Motor Company. We felt pretty good as we made our way through New York State to Watkins Glen. An overnight stop was made at a motel from where we explored the village and the local hostelry. At the time of ordering our drinks the proprietor would not accept immediate payment and we assumed he was applying the French custom of paying on departure. We were in for a pleasant surprise, however, as it turned out that the inn was due to cease trading that very evening, to be demolished to make way for a motorway, as a result of which all drinks were on the house!

Graham and Stirling in earnest conversation prior to the start of the US Grand Prix.

Two views of the crowded starting grid for the US Grand Prix, with John Surtees' blue and white Ferrari in pole position. The purple-jacketed, cowboy-hatted individuals are American officials.

The unusual livery of the works Ferrari of John Surtees, so painted because of a dispute between Enzo Ferrari and the Italian Automobile Federation.

The excellent garage facilities provided for all teams at Watkins Glen.

Tex Hopkins, his striking purple suit displaying individual style, waves the starter's flag to release the field.

Tex retreats from the grid.

The very name Watkins Glen reflected the beauty of the place, situated in the Finger Lake region of New York State with the wonderful spectacle of vivid red maple trees so evident in the fall. The town was named after its founder, Englishman Dr Samuel Watkins, who, in 1828, arrived in an area previously occupied by the Iroquois Indians. Our accommodation at the Glen Motor Court overlooking Seneca Lake and the distant hills, combined with the apparent wealth of the area and the hospitality of the American people, made it the most pleasurable of the Grand Prix venues I had visited. The 2.3 mile circuit was equally grand, located in a pretty undulating wooded area just outside the town. The modern garage accommodation nearby was a mechanic's dream.

Bizarrely, the Ferraris were looking nothing like Ferraris here, wearing the blue and white livery of America. Enzo Ferrari had fallen out with the Italian Automobile Federation over the homologation issue of the 250LM, and this was his personal form of protest, the cars being entered in these two end of season races by Luigi Chinetti's North American Racing Team. For all practical purposes they were factory cars being looked after by factory mechanics.

Graham had the latest car and the engine which had failed at Monza, whilst Richie had a new engine in an adapted, older monocoque since there was insufficient time to build another completely new car. Jim Clark in the Lotus took pole position, Surtees second, Gurney third and Graham a rather disappointing fourth whilst Richie, in his home Grand Prix, was very disappointed to be a lowly thirteenth on the two-by-two grid in front of his home crowd. Graham was not happy, fidgeting and requesting numerous adjustments to anti-roll bars, and even, finally,

requesting that the rear anti-roll bar be changed. Unbeknown to him this could not be achieved in time.

Huge crowds poured into the circuit, camping overnight and all of them in party mode, enjoying barbeques and plenty of beer. It was a glorious, sunny autumn day. It's a fact that Americans very often have to be different and grandiose, a trait applied to the race start procedure. Firstly, a miniature cannon was fired, the loud explosion scaring those not expecting it, followed by the flag to start the race, a spectacular procedure performed by Tex Hopkins in a flashy purple suit leaping high into the air and simultaneously waving the flag to release the field. Surtees

John Surtees' Ferrari leads Jim Clark's Lotus and Graham Hill's BRM away from the start and out of the first corner of the US Grand Prix.

Graham Hill is interviewed by the press following victory in the US Grand Prix.

took an immediate lead with Graham fourth but, by lap five, he had moved into second place with Clark the leader. Lap forty-five and Clark retired his car to the pits, eventually taking over team-mate Mike Spence's car with the intention of pushing the other title contenders down the field even though he could not score points himself. Surtees, Hill and Gurney had been involved in a tremendous battle behind Clark, but eventually Hill pulled well ahead after Surtees spun and Gurney retired with loss of oil pressure. To our intense relief Hill went on to score a remarkable victory with Surtees now trailing thirty seconds behind in second position. Ginther was lapped three times but nevertheless finished fourth and, again, gained valuable manufacturer's points. Just to show that our customers were enjoying success, too, Jo Siffert came home third in Rob Walker's Brabham-BRM V8. After the race I asked Graham how the car had handled and he said it was perfect. I feel sure he never knew I had not changed his rear anti-roll bar!

Following our victory, Mrs Stanley and her husband treated us to a T-bone steak, after which 'Big Lou' asked if we had enjoyed it. Alan Challis, a recently qualified BRM apprentice nicknamed Dobbin, said, tongue-in-cheek, that he had and could eat another. Big Lou said "Then you shall have one" and delighted in watching him attempt to eat it all!

The final race of the season was the Mexican Grand Prix three

The fruits of victory. Tony Rudd, Cyril Atkins and me share a memorable moment with winner Graham Hill after the US Grand Prix.

Jimmy and I with one of the Ford Mustangs provided by Ford of America: we bought the champagne.

Jimmy Collins fishing at Acapulco.

"The next one's on you, Neddy." Giving the donkey a bottle of beer at Acapulco. Apparently, this was a regular part of his morning diet supplied by tourists. I imagine he would then sleep all afternoon.

weeks away, which left us with time to relax and enjoy ourselves for a while, as we were not returning to England in the interim. With our race cars thankfully intact after the American event, our workload was considerably eased, and I even had time to play my first game of golf at the Watkins Glen course, a pleasant 9-hole course frequented by chipmunks and snakes! Meanwhile, all of the team's cars were sent on to Mexico City in huge hired open-deck transporters, each car individually wrapped in polythene. This left us with free time to visit Niagara Falls, the sensation of being below and behind that torrent of water an awesome experience. Also on our itinerary was the Corning Museum of glass making.

At last we left for New York, to spend a day there before taking a flight to Mexico City. The Mexican authorities were offering free return flights to Acapulco from Mexico City to anyone with a return ticket from New York. As the cars would be another seven days getting to Mexico, some of the team, myself included, took advantage of the offer. We enjoyed boat trips, one to an island where an attraction was the donkey that drank beer. He would quickly swallow two or three bottles-full but what he was like at the end of the day in the busy season I cannot imagine! I detest rats but Acapulco was the one place I have been pleased to see one! Sitting in a bar one evening a huge rat appeared from a hole in the floorboards, I said "Christ, look at that" whereupon the rat disappeared, leaving my colleagues believing I had had too much to drink. I was quite pleased when it showed its face again to convince them otherwise! Back in Mexico City the different lifestyles of its population were very apparent. The extreme poverty in suburban areas – tin shacks for dwellings, undernourished children and dogs running about in the dusty roads – starkly contrasted with the city

This is the life; relaxing on a boat trip at Acapulco.

Graham turns tin basher. With mechanics reluctant to damage the body panels, Graham takes it upon himself to modify the cockpit of the brand new car.

centre and its prestigious hotels, restaurants and shops just like any other major capital.

The cars eventually arrived from America so we were once more kept busy preparing them for this make-or-break event, which was to be witnessed by HRH the Duke of Edinburgh. The points situation now was such that if Graham Hill finished no lower than third he would be World Champion, regardless of where Jim Clark or John Surtees finished. If Graham was lower than third either Clark or Surtees could be the new champion.

Similar to Kyalami, this was a high-altitude circuit, some 5000 feet above sea level, the rarefied atmosphere causing unusual problems for fuel injection systems. It was an artificial circuit in a sports park on the outskirts of the sprawling, stifling city, where crowd control was completely inadequate by any standards. Our engines seemed to suffer from the thin atmosphere more than the Coventry Climax because Jim Clark was easily fastest with Graham back on the third row, behind John Surtees, in sixth place almost two-and-a-half seconds slower. Richie, not in a position to be of help to Graham, was back in eleventh place.

Arriving at the circuit on race day, the 'Sheriff' discovered that someone had nicked his overalls. Now, bearing in mind he was only just over five feet tall, I can only surmise what a shock the thief would have had if he happened to be a six-footer! The cars were on the grid an hour before the start while the drivers were introduced to the President of Mexico. Then, thousands of balloons were released straight into the flight path of the airport as two small planes popped them with their wings and propellers!

Right from the start the odds were stacked against Graham. The elastic on his goggles broke just as the starter was about to drop the flag and Graham was not even in gear! That set the tone for his race and, approaching half distance, he was spun round by a pursuing Lorenzo Bandini as he attempted an impossible passing manoeuvre at the hairpin. Hill's exhaust pipes were damaged and after two pit stops he limped home in a lonely eleventh place behind winner Dan Gurney in the works Brabham-Climax. Eight laps from the chequered flag race leader Jim Clark's engine had been suffering from loss of oil (shades of East

London 1962) and he trailed home fifth, a lap behind. That put paid to his championship chances. At the last moment, Lorenzo Bandini in the 12-cylinder Ferrari, allowed his team leader, John Surtees, to take second place ahead of him by less than one second, giving John his first and only World Championship on four wheels!

For us, seldom had a race promised so much and delivered so little; the entire team – not least poor Graham – was simply devastated. We had lost the Driver's Championship by one point, the narrowest of margins. Three points lost the Manufacturer's Championship, even more important for the industry. Was Bandini's coming-together with Graham deliberate? Does oil float on water …?

So, a disappointing end to what had been an exciting season, leaving us with a trio of 'if onlys': if only the fuel pump fitted for Spa had not been experimented with; if only Graham's clutch had not failed at Monza; if only Bandini had looked where he was going (but, then again, *I* believe he did …)

We returned to England. The Mexican trip – despite the result – was the most enjoyable I had experienced with BRM. Richie Ginther had driven his last race for us. He had been a good test and development driver, but not quite in the top flight. Graham was to continue in 1965 and was to be joined by Jackie Stewart, a young, up-and-coming Scottish driver.

An unexpected and unique honour to crown a momentous year occurred on a cold November day when Jim Clark, Graham Hill, Bruce McLaren (Cooper), and Jack Brabham drove their Formula 1 cars through the City of London as part of the Lord Mayor's Show, and as a tribute to the British Motor Industry. It was just a shame that in the convoy Graham was second to our greatest rival!

THE WRITING ON
THE WALL

Incredibly, the new Championship trail of 1965 began on 1st January, which meant we had less than two months in which to draw breath and prepare for the new season. In no time at all I was on my travels again, this time to South Africa, my colleagues on this excursion sounding something like characters in a Western, bearing the nicknames Tonto, Dobbin and the Sheriff!

The South African Grand Prix was Jackie Stewart's first World Championship race. He had really been thrown in at the deep end by BRM as he had very little time for testing before our departure. A new car had to be built up for him, similar to Graham's Mexico car, and we went to great lengths to make it fit him (later, Tony Rudd even specifying seat covers in Stewart tartan!) Fortunately, the cars went to South Africa by airfreight, giving us more time to prepare them in the Bourne workshops.

After an abbreviated Christmas we flew to Johannesburg, there to take the internal flight to East London via Durban. The diversion gave me a second opportunity to meet my aunt, the last time she saw any of her family. The event was an easy victory for Jim Clark, who took pole position in practice, with the two BRMs of Graham and Jackie fifth and eleventh respectively. Race day was dry and cloudy as Jim Clark shot into an immediate lead at the fall of the flag, which he maintained for the entire 85 lap race with a winning margin of thirty seconds over John Surtees, Graham three seconds adrift in third position. Jackie Stewart finished in a creditable sixth place to gain one point in his first World Championship race. His comment on getting out of the car: "Christ, I didn't realise these cars were so bloody heavy."

On 13th March, a bitterly cold day, the first Race of Champions was held at Brands Hatch with Graham and Jackie entered for BRM. The race was run in two heats, the aggregate times of the two to decide the winner, who turned out to be Mike Spence, after team leader Jim Clark crashed in the second heat. Once again Jackie showed what a sound investment BRM had made by coming second, whilst Graham retired.

The sleek-looking 1965 P57 BRM. Note how the side induction trumpets compare with those in the centre of the V on earlier engines, now replaced by the inboard exhaust system.

Jackie Stewart's BRM being taken for weighing at East London.

Little did I know then but this was to be the last race I attended as a racing mechanic. Shortly after our return to Bourne I made what I now consider to be a big mistake, which was to change my life. Tony Rudd offered me the position of assistant to Les Bryden, the Production Manager which, after discussion with my wife, I accepted. After fourteen years of travelling it would allow me to spend more time with my family. Things did not work out quite as anticipated, however,

Right: The slim lines of the 1965 P57 BRM, shown to good effect in this picture.

Jackie Stewart prepares to go out to practise for his first Formula 1 Grand Prix drive at East London. A sixth place finish was the start of a fantastic Formula 1 career for him.

and, after the excitement of racing I quickly became bored; there was so little to do and I soon realised that the workload of the Production Manager did not warrant an assistant. I had become something of a progress chaser, often travelling to suppliers to collect urgent parts, often for a white elephant known as the H16 engine! On reflection I should have asked to return to the racing team as I feel I would still have had something to offer.

INDIANAPOLIS

RECORD SPEED OVER 150 M.P.H.

MAGNIFICENT
BRITISH VICTORY FOR LOTUS-FORD
1ST JIM CLARK

SECOND—LOTUS-FORD, PARNELLI JONES
THIRD—BRABHAM-FORD, MARIO ANDRETTI

ALL CARS EQUIPPED WITH
GIRLING
DISC BRAKES
THE BEST BRAKES IN THE WORLD

Thrilling the crowd. Graham Hill driving the new BRM to third place in the 1965 South African Grand Prix.

Graham Hill at speed in the South African Grand Prix.

I failed to do so, however, and, in November 1967, together with the Production Manager and other personnel, I was made redundant.

In actual fact, had I returned to the racing team my time there would have been shortlived. By the early '70s the BRM's gradual demise had begun and, when speaking to former colleagues, it became apparent that, under the direction of Louis Stanley, the team which he had renamed Stanley BRM was being run under farcical conditions and could not survive.

Had it not been for two important factors, it is my opinion that BRM would not only have survived but would have prospered.

First was the folly of attempting to build the complicated H16 engine, the simplicity-of-design lesson is one that should have been learned from experience with the V16. BRM had won the World Championship with a V8 engine in 1962, and in 1966 and 1967 (the first year of the 3-litre formula) Brabham drivers won both the Driver's and Manufacturer's titles with a straightforward Australian Repco V8 engine. The other significant factor in BRM's downfall was the influence of Louis T Stanley, a man inexperienced in the finer points of Grand Prix racing with a lifestyle which the BRM budget could ill afford. (Stanley had a reputation for being an expert in spending other people's money.) Had the sponsors been shown the respect they deserved, and seen a more positive attempt to achieve a return for their money, in my opinion Bourne could still be a major contributor to the Formula 1 motor racing world.

To further substantiate the last statement, on 12th April 2006, I and ten of my former BRM colleagues, as members of that wonderful organisation the Grand Prix Mechanics Charitable Trust, were privileged to visit the headquarters of the Williams Grand Prix team, the venue for the annual luncheon and get-together. We were all impressed with the magnitude of the Williams establishment, and the unanimous opinion of the ex-BRM staff was, that, but for the folly of deciding on an H16 format engine, and incompetent management under Louis Stanley, similar success could have been achieved at Bourne …

To Lotus – AND BEYOND

Life had to go on and, though reluctant to uproot my family and move from Bourne, I took the job of quality engineer at Lotus Cars at Hethel in Norfolk. Initially, I commuted weekly, travelling to work early on Monday mornings and returning on Friday evenings, but eventually I moved my family to a bungalow in the village of Wicklewood, close to the Lotus factory. I had spent many hours looking at properties and, finding one I liked, my next move was to visit the local inn, The Cherry Tree. Here, I was made most welcome; so much so that the decision to purchase the bungalow was an easy one …

I thoroughly enjoyed my days at Lotus Cars. The work was interesting, testing cars, visiting dealerships and carrying out investigations into various defects. One of the most pleasant tasks was the proving run of the Lotus Elite undertaken by selected drivers round the Norfolk countryside in six hour shifts, the aim being to cover 1000 miles every 24 hours until the car had recorded 50,000 miles.

Alas, the turnover in labour at Hethel was extremely high with frequent redundancies in line with car sales. If car sales were good, redundancies were low and vice versa. After dodging the axe twice, I eventually fell victim. Seeking advice in the local Job Centre, the assistant there said: "I bet you're from Lotus." One day I met up with Ken Brown, a former colleague and good friend who was in a similar situation to my own. Ken told me he had an interview for work at Perkins Engines in Peterborough the following week, and would I care to travel there with him? I agreed to this and, whilst there, enquired about job opportunities for myself, and was engaged that day as an engine tester in the experimental department. Ironically, Ken was not offered a job that day but was taken on at a later date. Conditions at Perkins Engines were in stark contrast to what I had become used to, largely due to the influence of trades union, about which I had mixed feelings. Many people were of the opinion that if your ambition was to become a foreman, you had only to become

The H16 BRM, something of a white elephant. In the author's opinion, it played a major part in the downfall of BRM.

a troublesome shop steward and you were on your way!

The downside of getting a job at Perkins was that I had to uproot my wife yet again after three years of living in Norfolk and return to Bourne. After two years at Perkins my wife became ill with tuberculosis and spent five weeks in Papworth Hospital in Cambridgeshire. A job vacancy became available in the inspection department of the Fiat-Allis factory, a company engaged in the manufacture of earth-moving equipment, at the nearby village of Essendine. Though reasonably content at Perkins, in view of my wife's illness I applied for the inspector's job and was successful, which meant I was finished with night shifts and could spend more time at home.

Fiat-Allis was a friendly and easygoing place to work. From inspection I graduated to the field service department, which included visits to dealers and operators in the UK and overseas. It was a job both interesting and enjoyable and which I would have been content with until retirement. Sadly, it was not to be: Fiat management in Italy decided that the plant at Essendine

Pictures: CHRIS LOWNDES

Farewell to great motors

8 Evening Telegraph, Friday, September 18, 1981
ANDREW MALKIN reports

BOURNE'S long associa-tion with the pride of Brit-ish motor racing comes to a sad end next month.

For it is then that famous cars from the golden age of grand-prix racing are to be moved from their home in the town for the last time.

The classic British Racing Motors' machines will be making their way to London and a Christ-ie's auction that will probably see most of them go abroad.

But, for now, the world-famous factory in Spalding Road is a hive of activity as the finishing touches are put to several cars by some of their original mechanics.

Tonight, enthusiasts in the town get a last chance to view two of the best known machines — the massive V16 and "The Bullet" which took Graham Hill into motor-racing history when he became world champion.

A night out for the enthusiast has been organised in honour of the late Raymond Mays. The Bourne man who took so many cars through the chequered flag.

The Raymond Mays Memorial Fund committee is running the event at Bourne Corn Exchange from 7.30 pm.

On show will be the V16, the V8 Bullet, the ex-Raymond Mays ERA R4D and a rare E-Type ERA.

The evening — called "Motor Rac-ing — the Bourne Connection" — will include a talk by motor-racing person-ality Mr A. F. Rivers-Fletcher, who will illustrate his talk from his large collection of films.

Memorial

Tickets are £2.50 each, including supper, and proceeds will go into the fund to provide a lasting memorial in the town to Raymond Mays.

The ERAs are in private owner-ship, the R4D belonging to J. C. Bamford, the JCB giant.

But the 10 BRMs housed at Bourne are to be sold by the Rubery Owen Holding Company at the auction on October 28.

Mr Stanley Hope has been in charge of restoration of the cars. He

BRM's for the racing circuit until production stopped as recently as three-and-a-half years ago.

He said: "I was moved from Coven-try to Bourne to work on a car for six weeks in 1949 and stayed on.

"I helped build the V16 in 1953. Even today, it would be one of the fastest grand-prix cars in a straight line. It is capable of speeds in excess of 200 mph.

"It was built as an ambassador for Britain and British engineering and was way ahead of its time."

Although of only 1500cc capacity, the sixteen cylinders drank a gallon of fuel every four-and-a-half miles and developed 600 brake horse power.

Mr Hope believes the car will fetch as much as £300,000 and will probably end up in America.

Three of the original team of skilled mechanics are left at Bourne and Mr Hope said he expects all the workers will be looking for new jobs once the renovation work is complete and the cars sold.

"It will be a sad, sad day for us and the end of an era for Bourne," he

Mechanic Alfred Pass puts a final shine on the 1.5 litre V16 BRM.

Dick Salmon works on a V16 supercharged BRM.

The badly damaged chassis of Jackie Stewart's car after his horrific accident at Spa. The big question being asked was: how did Jackie survive that wreck?

did not fit into its long-term plans and eventually the factory was closed.

What goes round comes around. Coinciding with my third redundancy, Stanley BRM eventually failed, and the Owen Organisation decided to put up the entire outfit for auction. Aubrey Woods, a design engineer who had returned to BRM, approached me to assist in rebuilding the racing cars. These, together with spares and all the assets, were to be auctioned by Christie's at Earls Court in London. It was bittersweet to be involved in the last moments of this once-great team which were immensely sad days for Bourne. The cars and equipment were

prepared and taken to London for auction on 22nd October, 1981. Gerry van der Weyden – also a former BRM mechanic – and I accompanied the cars on their final journey from Bourne to witness their departure to pastures new.

Following the sale of the BRMs, Gerry and I were approached to restore an early 1930s Triumph Tourer. Acquiring premises at the nearby village of Billingborough, we decided to go ahead with the task. From there we formed a partnership as SV Restorations and, though not richly rewarding financially, there was great pleasure in seeing what was once a complete wreck restored to good condition. We undertook the restoration of Rolls-Royce, Jaguar,

Sadness at Bourne as I, along with Gerry van der Weyden, Cyril Atkins, Aubrey Woods and Stan Hope, pose with the last BRM car to leave the Bourne works, fittingly a MkII V16, shortly before it was sold by Christie's at Earls Court.

Gerard and I with a 1932 Rolls Royce 20/25 saloon, recently restored for its Norfolk owner.

Humber, Alvis, and many other marques. Eventually, the business was sold to Richard Dyson-Harvey, whom Gerry and I continued to work for.

In 1990 Richard entered a 1952 Alvis TA21 saloon in the Monte Carlo Challenge. To be crewed by Richard, Gerry and myself, it was a fun rally from Glasgow to Monte Carlo for pre-1960 cars, and we drove to Glasgow for the start, celebrating Burns Night in traditional Scottish style on the eve of our departure. On Sunday morning 25th January we ventured south, a scheduled stop at the Angel Hotel in Bourne allowing a quick chat to friends and relations before we were off again. Unfortunately, our rally ended prematurely at Rochester in Kent when the cylinder head gasket failed.

I was now sixty five years of age and it seemed the right time to retire after a long and varied career.

Reflecting on my years at BRM, I recall one particular night working very late at Folkingham. Tired and hungry, having had nothing to eat since midday, we had a little moan to Peter Berthon. His response was that, far from moaning, we should appreciate how privileged we were to be working for BRM; years after, I realise how right his words were. I was fortunate indeed to have worked for some of the great drivers of the day, including World Champions Juan Fangio and Mike Hawthorn, but I consider

A partly restored Triumph Tourer; the first restoration project undertaken by Gerard van der Weyden and myself.

A Porsche 900 after restoration.

Almost ready to leave Glasgow in the 1952 Alvis TA 21 for the 1990 Monte Carlo Challenge. Unfortunately, the Alvis cried "enough!" at Rochester when the cylinder head gasket blew.

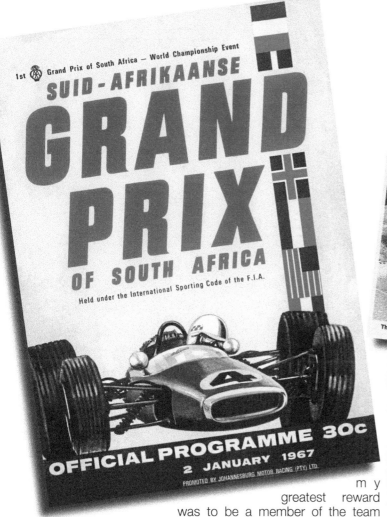

SUID - AFRIKAANSE

GRAND PRIX

OF SOUTH AFRICA

Held under the International Sporting Code of the F.I.A.

OFFICIAL PROGRAMME 30c

2 JANUARY 1967

PROMOTED BY JOHANNESBURG MOTOR RACING (PTY) LTD.

Ex-BRM men give Rolls a new look

TWO former BRM mechanics, who have set up together restoring cars of all ages, have given a new lease of life to a 1932 Royce 20/25 fitted with a Park Ward sports saloon body.

Dick Salmon and his partner Gerry Van der Weyden, estimate nearly a thousand man hours went into rebuilding the car, which was stripped down to the chassis and overhauled as necessary. New wood framing was fitted to the roof and the sunshine roof was unsealed and made to work again.

Another job tackled for the sake of originality was restoring and fitting the original steel wings which the Norfolk owner had acquired for the car.

Mr Salmon was made redundant from Fiat Allis in April 1981 and with little prospect of finding employment decided to set up his own firm, SV Restorations, at Billingborough, with Gerry Van der Weyden, a former mechanic for the BRM team.

Dick had formerly worked for BRM for 17 years and was Formula One motor racing mechanic with the late Graham Hill and other famous drivers.

SV Restorations are willing to tackle any job on vehicles ancient or modern and waiting in the wings or receiving attention at the moment, are an SP 250 Daimler, a 1939 Dodge, a 1940s Triumph Roadster, a Datsun 240Z and a Mini Cooper S.

SV Restorations can be contacted on Sleaford 240339.

The Rolls before work began.

Stripped down to the chassis which has been de-rusted and repainted.

The 1932 Rolls like new again with Mr Salmon (nearest car) and Mr Van der Weyden.

The body back on the chassis as re-assembly starts.

m y greatest reward was to be a member of the team that enabled Graham Hill and BRM to win both Driver's and Manufacturer's Championships. Though long working hours was the norm, the entire experience is best summed up by the title of Tony Rudd's book: *It Was Fun*.

BRM meant everything to me; good times and bad. I might have spent my working life at a garage in nearby Grantham or Peterborough, never leaving the remote, flat Fens. Instead, I had travelled the world. I had been involved in the challenging, hectic, stressful, sad, happy life of Grand Prix motor racing – the most glamorous of all sports. I started at BRM when the company was a national embarrassment, the butt of every joke, and yet went on to enjoy the good times when BRM was World Champion and a true giant. I had rubbed shoulders with some of the best drivers of the day and worked with the finest bunch of workmates one could wish for.

Today, other than Raymond Mays' old family home of Eastgate House, little remains that is recognisable as part

A far cry from the three-stopwatch clipboard. The modern timekeeper's box at Magny-Cours, with my son Michael, an official timekeeper, second from left.

of the BRM story. Fortunately, all has not been lost because, over the years, a remarkable collection of BRM photographs and memorabilia has been gathered and is proudly displayed on the second floor of Bourne's Old Mill Heritage Centre. In 2005 most of BRM's magnificent trophies were moved there

Here, I'm being interviewed by Doug Nye at Goodwood on the Tribute to Graham Hill day in September 2002.

Graham Hill Way, Bourne. Appropriately, Bourne's remaining connection with motor racing, Pilbeam Racing Designs, is located at the rear of the building.

from the board room of the Rubery Owen Group at Darlaston so that a wider audience can see them, and they are well worth a visit. In honour and remembrance of the most successful driver, a road on a small industrial estate was named Graham Hill Way.

Now, as an octogenarian – sadly, a widowed one – I experience a gentler pace of life enjoying bowls and snooker, meeting my pals over a pint at the Royal British Legion Club and moaning about Tony Blair and his gang of thieves. But most of all we enjoy reminiscing about BRM and the old days. Oh! I almost forgot; is senility creeping in? I've also been trying to write a book. Should you, by chance, be reading these words, then I must have succeeded …

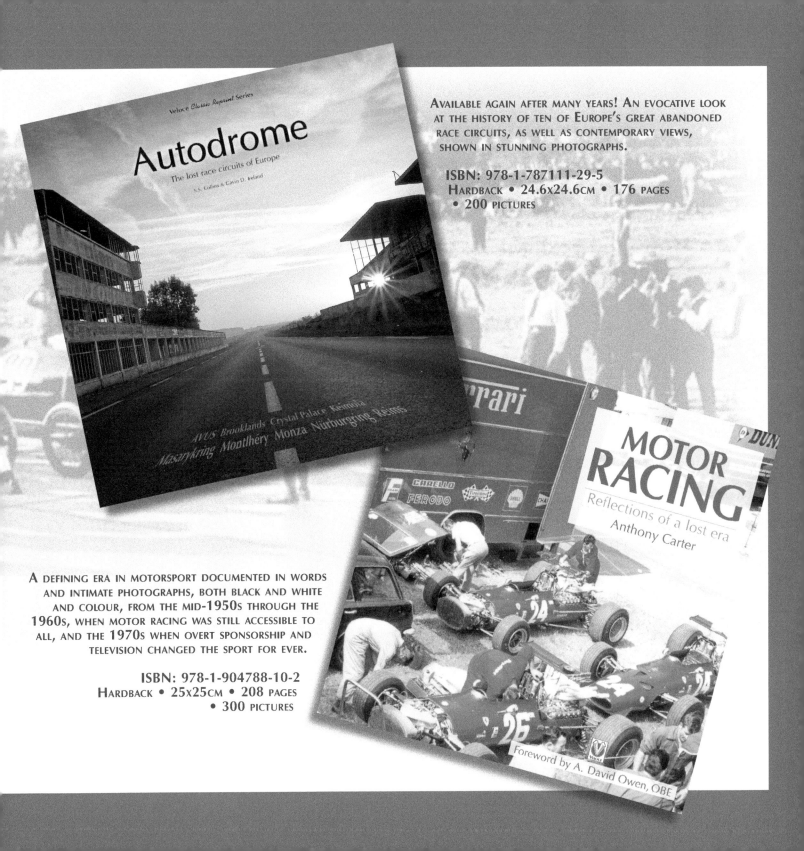

Autodrome

Veloce Classic Reprint Series

The lost race circuits of Europe

S.S. Collins & Gavin D. Ireland

AVUS · Brooklands · Crystal Palace · Keimola · Masarykring · Montlhéry · Monza · Nürburgring · Reims

AVAILABLE AGAIN AFTER MANY YEARS! AN EVOCATIVE LOOK AT THE HISTORY OF TEN OF EUROPE'S GREAT ABANDONED RACE CIRCUITS, AS WELL AS CONTEMPORARY VIEWS, SHOWN IN STUNNING PHOTOGRAPHS.

ISBN: 978-1-787111-29-5
HARDBACK • 24.6x24.6CM • 176 PAGES
• 200 PICTURES

MOTOR RACING

Reflections of a lost era

Anthony Carter

Foreword by A. David Owen, OBE

A DEFINING ERA IN MOTORSPORT DOCUMENTED IN WORDS AND INTIMATE PHOTOGRAPHS, BOTH BLACK AND WHITE AND COLOUR, FROM THE MID-1950S THROUGH THE 1960S, WHEN MOTOR RACING WAS STILL ACCESSIBLE TO ALL, AND THE 1970S WHEN OVERT SPONSORSHIP AND TELEVISION CHANGED THE SPORT FOR EVER.

ISBN: 978-1-904788-10-2
HARDBACK • 25x25CM • 208 PAGES
• 300 PICTURES

INDEX

222